IMAGES
of America

BARNETT BANK

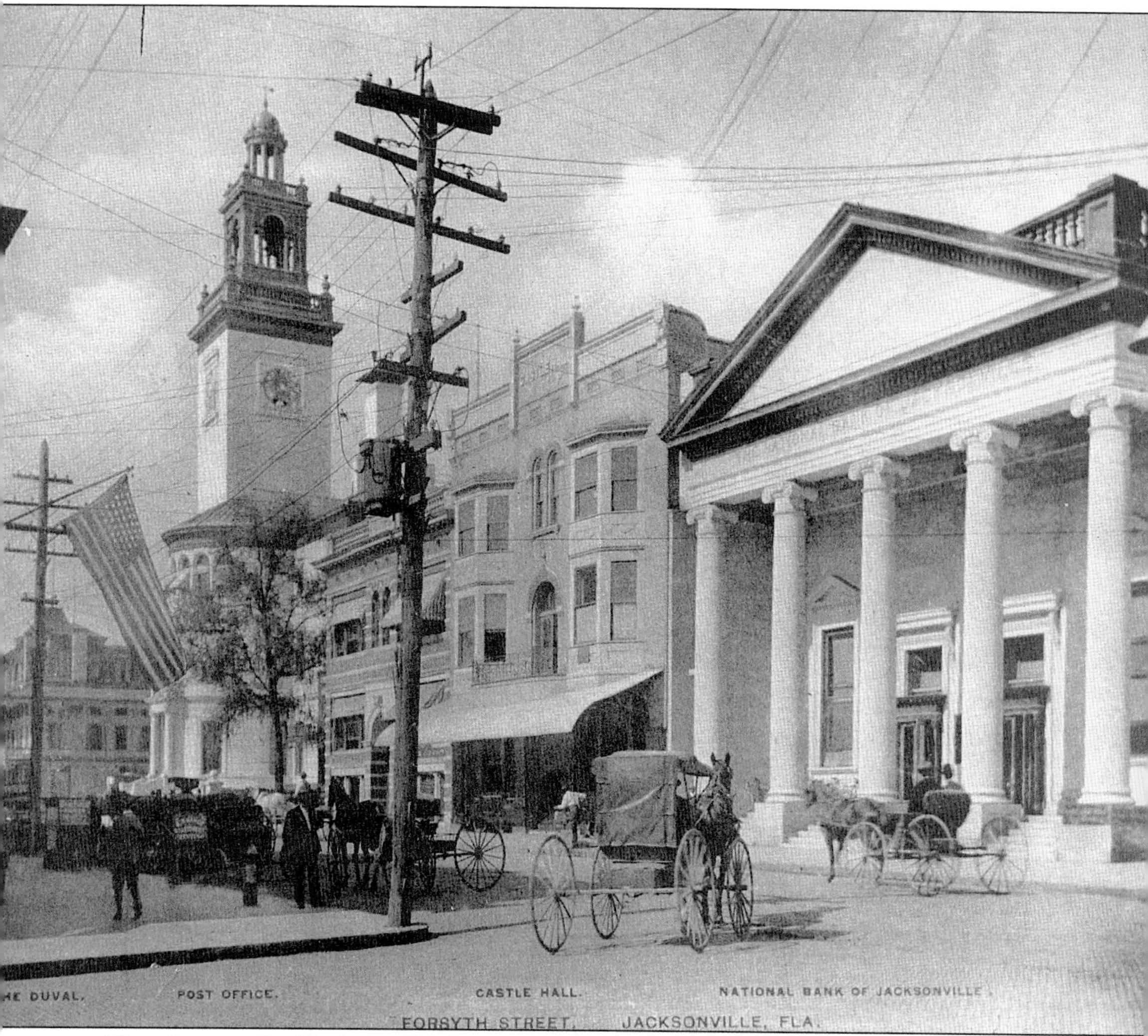

This photograph of Jacksonville shows Forsyth Street, between Laura and Hogan Streets, in the early 1900s. The National Bank of Jacksonville (the predecessor of the Barnett National Bank) is on the northwest corner of Forsyth and Laura. Castle Hall, an office building with rooms rented to attorneys, insurance agents, physicians, and others, is to its immediate west. The building with the tall tower on the corner of Forsyth and Hogan is the post office. (Courtesy of *Florida Times-Union*.)

IMAGES
of America

BARNETT BANK

David J. Ginzl

ARCADIA
PUBLISHING

ISBN 978-0-7385-0553-4

Published by Arcadia Publishing
Charleston, South Carolina

Printed in the United States of Amercia

Library of Congress Catalog Card Number: 99-068868

For all general information contact Arcadia Publishing at:
Telephone 843-853-2070
Fax 843-853-0044
Email: sales@arcadiapublishing.com
For customer service and orders:
Toll-Free 1-888-313-2665

Visit us on the Internet at www.arcadiapublishing.com

This book is dedicated to all of the Barnett Bank employees, from 1877 to 1998.

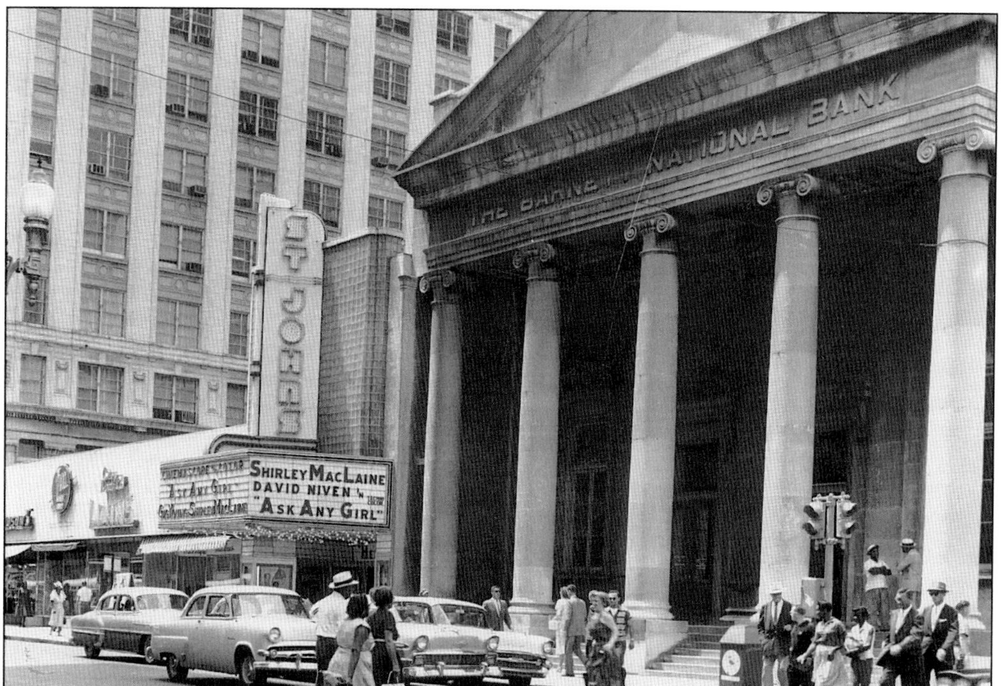

This photograph of Jacksonville shows Forsyth Street in 1959. Shortly afterwards, Barnett purchased the St. Johns Theatre and the retail shops to its west. In 1961, these buildings, together with the banking office, which had first opened in 1898, were razed to make way for Barnett's new ten-story headquarters building. (Courtesy of *Florida Times-Union*.)

Contents

ACKNOWLEDGMENTS

For most people who worked at Barnett, and for many of its customers, Barnett Bank was a special place—a caring employer, a respected financial services institution, and a generous supporter of its local communities. Many thanks go to all of those who have supported, financially and emotionally, the efforts to preserve the Barnett history. I wish to express my special appreciation to the directors of the Barnett Historic Preservation Foundation, Inc.—Allen Lastinger, Bill Barnett, Judy Beaubouef, John Cannon, Roseann Duran, and Roland Kennedy—for their support and encouragement.

This book is based principally upon the photographs that the bank assembled, as well as photos printed in its employee publications and annual reports. Many of the photographers who contributed their talents to this collection over the years remain anonymous; others have vanished. Of those that the author has found, I would like to thank Garry McElwee, Rita Smith (Berisford Photography), and J. Gordon Spottswood for their generous permission to use their photographs.

The Barnett photographic collection has been augmented by donations of photographs from the personal collections of Charles Rice, Allen Lastinger, and others. Thank you to all who have contributed. I also want to thank Gerard Clark of the Florida State Archives, Joan Pickett of the Jacksonville Historical Society, and Mary Ann Sterzel of the *Florida Times-Union* for their assistance in locating additional photographs for use in this book.

Two local Jacksonville photographers have been very helpful. Jerry Favorite Jr. photographed the presidential portraits in Barnett's board room so that the Foundation would have copies, and then the original paintings were given to the individuals or, if deceased, to family members. Oscar Sosa spent many hours photographing memorabilia, old ledgers, and brittle newspaper clippings. Thank you to both of these talented photographers.

Special recognition goes to Karen Clarke, a former Barnetter and my administrative assistant, who has contributed in so many ways to the completion of this project, as well as several others undertaken by the Foundation. I greatly appreciate all of her efforts.

Also, thanks to Teri Curry and Janice Fluegel, who proofread the narrative, and Eileen Brady and Linda Smith, who critiqued photo selections.

Finally, I want to thank Arcadia editor Christine Riley and other members of the Arcadia staff. Their professionalism and cooperation made the completion of this project not only possible but enjoyable.

INTRODUCTION

As the 20th century draws to a close, American businesses have been merging and restructuring at a dizzying pace in an effort to remain competitive in a rapidly changing world. Familiar companies, many with long and distinguished histories, are disappearing. Nowhere does this trend seem to be more prevalent than in the banking industry. Names of venerable institutions that dominated the banking scene just 20 years ago—Manufacturers Hanover, Continental Illinois, Citizens & Southern, Security Pacific—are gone and almost forgotten.

One of the casualties of this acquisition and merger frenzy is Barnett Banks, Inc. At the time of its sale to NationsBank, Barnett was the largest and oldest banking organization in Florida. When the familiar green-and-white Barnett logos were finally removed from more than 600 Florida banking offices in October 1998, it marked the end of an era. Over the course of its 120-year history, Barnett had been an important corporate contributor to the growth of Jacksonville, the city where it had been founded and maintained its headquarters, and had played significant roles in Florida's economic development and the evolution of the American banking industry.

Barnett Banks, Inc. traced its origins to 1877, when William Boyd Barnett, who had only recently moved to the city from Hiawatha, Kansas, opened a private bank, The Bank of Jacksonville. Banking in the sparsely settled, frontier Florida of the 19th century was not for the timid nor for those easily discouraged. The bank struggled in its first year of operation, with only minimal profits. But Barnett persevered, operating his bank on the following principles:

1] Follow the Golden Rule. You can't go wrong treating the other man as you would be treated.

2] Give a man 50¢ if you can make a dollar out of him. In other words, be liberal in your dealings but always have a net profit. Don't do business at a loss.

3] If a young man is of good habits, honest, capable, saving, giving close attention to his business, making progress but lacking in capital—help him. The young man of today is the businessman of tomorrow.

4] Never make a promise you can't and don't fulfill. Investigate carefully before granting a line of credit; once granted, there being no adverse change in your client's financial condition, fulfill your promise. Your word must be as good as your bond.

5] Watch your expense account and your losses; your profits will take care of themselves.

Following these five basic rules, Barnett and his two sons—Bion and William D.—built a successful business. By the early 1880s, The Bank of Jacksonville had become the depository for the state's banking accounts and the largest bank in Florida. During the next several decades, the bank played important roles in a number of historically significant events, from assisting with the financing of the Disston land purchase that solidified the state's finances in the 1880s to the rebuilding of Jacksonville after the 1901 fire destroyed the city. Meanwhile, the Barnetts had sold stock to local businessmen to raise additional capital and applied for a national bank charter. Renamed the National Bank of Jacksonville, it operated and prospered for 20 years before being re-chartered in 1908 as the Barnett National Bank, named in honor of its founder.

For the next 90 years, the Barnett name was synonymous with sound, conservative, well-managed banking. The Barnett National Bank became a major correspondent for smaller banks throughout the state. It did not expand outside of Jacksonville, however, until 1929, when it opened banks in DeLand and Cocoa, two cities left without any banking facilities following the collapse of the Florida real estate boom and the onset of the national Depression. Organizing the Barnett National Securities Corporation, an early form of a bank holding company, the Barnett National Bank helped to bring stability to the state's battered banking industry, although it too suffered serious problems during the economic collapse of the 1930s. With the outbreak of World War II and the transformation of Florida into a major center for military training and wartime construction, prosperity returned to the state and to Barnett. For the next two decades, first under the leadership of William R. McQuaid and, later, Frank W. Norris and William R. Barnett (great-grandson of the founder), the bank enjoyed steady growth.

By the early 1960s, Barnett was a profitable, well-respected financial institution. Nevertheless, in a period when Florida experienced enormous population growth and a booming economy, the Barnett National Bank and four affiliated banks, with combined assets of $225 million, remained concentrated in slower growing northeastern Florida. The election of Guy W. Botts as president in 1963 re-energized a conservative, even somewhat stodgy institution. Botts developed a strategic plan to make Barnett a leader in every major market in the state. He launched an aggressive acquisition program that by 1979 had transformed the company into a $3.6 billion multi-bank powerhouse with 120 offices in counties containing more than 85% of Florida's population. A visionary, Botts foresaw the advent of national banking and became a leading proponent of regional interstate banking as a means of developing larger, more competitive banking companies headquartered in the Southeast. Under the direction of Botts's successor, Charles E. Rice, Barnett continued its phenomenal growth in the 1980s and 1990s, becoming widely recognized as one of the most innovative and profitable banks in the United States.

Throughout its history, five generations of Barnetts worked for the bank. Perhaps the most significant, and certainly the most colorful, was Bion Hall Barnett. He had helped his father open the bank in 1877 and did not retire as chairman of the board until 1952, at the age of 94. Bion made major contributions to the development of banking in Florida and became a widely respected industry leader. He helped to found the Florida Bankers Association and served as one of its first presidents in the 1890s, the first in a long line of Barnett executives to head the state's banking organization. He objected to rules promulgated by the federal Office of the Comptroller of the Currency, the agency of the Treasury Department that regulates national banks, and in the 1890s successfully challenged them before the United States Supreme Court. He introduced a progressive, profit-sharing plan for all bank employees in 1920 and instituted other innovative business approaches. He became an ardent golfer, described by the local newspaper as "one of Florida's golfing pioneers" and even managed in his 80s to shoot scores lower than his age. Bion Barnett, with a somewhat scandalous lifestyle, was larger than life.

Barnett Bank had numerous prominent executives, from the founding Barnett family to Charlie Rice. The story of the bank, however, is more than just a series of strong leaders, or the annual recap of asset growth and profitability. Barnett developed over the years a corporate culture that encouraged strong employee dedication and loyalty. During the bleak years of the Depression, the Barnett National Bank did not fire any employees. Instead, all employees, from the top executives to the custodial staff, took a series of pay cuts so that all could keep their jobs. In 1940, longtime bank director Joshua Chase wrote to Bion Barnett, commenting on the "close cooperation between all those associated with you in the Barnett banks. There is more of a family feeling than is to be found among other similar institutions."

This "family feeling" continued, even after Barnett began its rapid statewide expansion in the late 1960s. With the addition of new affiliates through the purchase of existing banks or the organization of new bank charters, Barnett operated as a "confederation" of largely autonomous affiliates, with locally based decision-making on matters that affected customers and communities and centralized support in technology, accounting, audit, and other control functions. The company fostered a "Team Barnett" atmosphere throughout the various banking and non-banking subsidiaries. While reflecting on what it was like to work for Barnett, Marsha Cantrell, who headed the company's political action committee office in Tallahassee, ended her oral history interview with tears in her eyes: "There will never again be a company like Barnett . . . It was like Camelot. It was a beautiful time and place."

To many of its employees and its loyal customers, the Barnett story should not be forgotten. Consequently, shortly after the sale of the bank, a group of senior officers, under the leadership of Barnett president Allen Lastinger, established the Barnett Historic Preservation Foundation, Inc. The purpose of this not-for-profit foundation is to preserve and publicize the historical legacy of Barnett Bank. A board of directors composed of former Barnett executives and bank presidents oversees the Foundation's activities. The Foundation has organized the historical documentation that the parent company maintained over the years, while augmenting these records by gathering additional materials from former employees throughout the state. These records, which include annual reports, employee publications, investor presentations, press releases, scrapbooks, news clippings, marketing materials, videos, correspondence, and miscellaneous ledgers and account books, have been donated to the Florida State Archives in Tallahassee, where they are being processed and catalogued for use by future researchers interested in Florida banking history and related business subjects. Memorabilia is being given to the Museum of Florida History, closely associated with the State Archives, to be used in the development of a traveling museum exhibit about Florida banking.

In addition, the Foundation is sponsoring an oral history project to interview former Barnett executives, directors, and others who have insights about the company. To date, more than 60 interviews have been completed and transcribed, and these too will be given to the State Archives when this project is completed.

Finally, the Foundation is sponsoring the publication of two books on the history of Barnett Bank. This volume in Arcadia Publishing's *Images of America* series is the first and is based principally on the photographs in the Barnett collection. It is hoped that former Barnett employees and customers, and all who are interested in Florida history, will enjoy this volume. The second volume, a more detailed and lengthy account of the bank's history, will be completed soon.

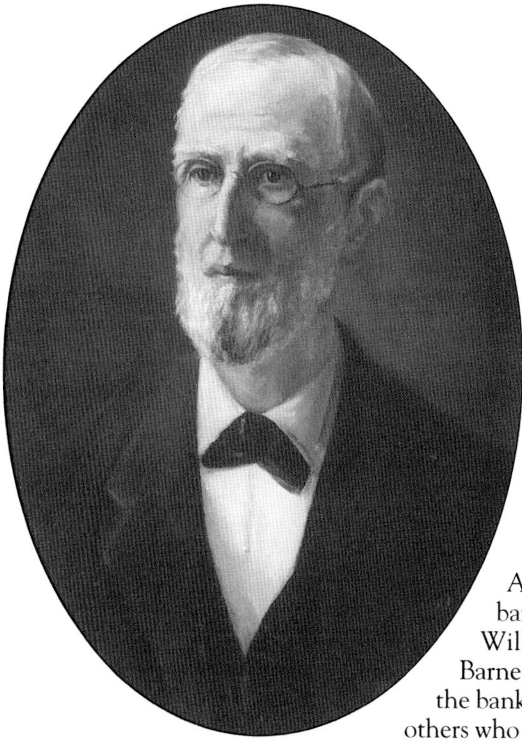

A portrait of William Boyd Barnett (left), the bank's founder, and portraits of his two sons, William D. Barnett (below left) and Bion Hall Barnett (below right), hung in the board room of the bank and, later, the holding company. Portraits of others who became president of the Barnett organization were added to the board room wall.

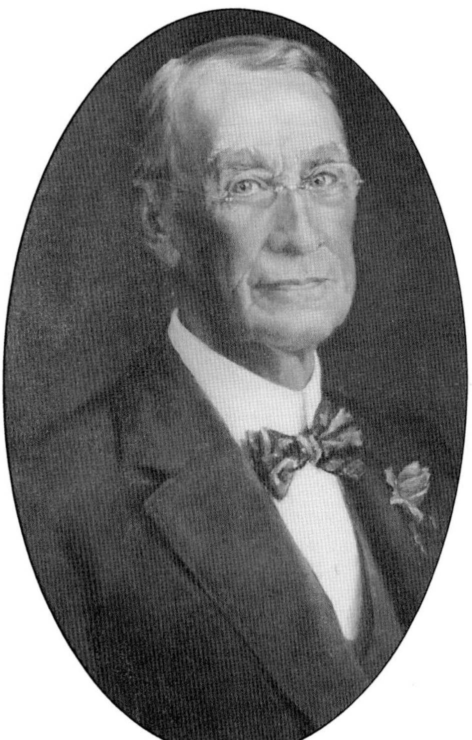

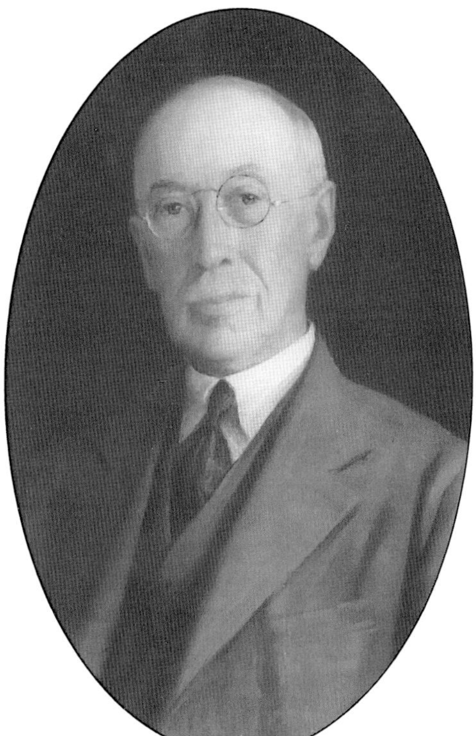

One

The Barnetts

It would be impossible to tell the story of Barnett Bank without also telling the story of the remarkable family that founded the bank and the five generations of Barnetts who worked there.

The bank's founder was William Boyd Barnett, who at the age of 52 had already succeeded at several careers by the time he opened The Bank of Jacksonville in May 1877. Born in Nicholas County, Virginia (now West Virginia), Barnett was one of twelve children, only six of whom survived infancy. He was raised in Greenfield, Ohio, where he learned to be a saddle and harness maker. After completing his apprenticeship, he traveled throughout Ohio, working odd jobs in his trade. Having saved $100, the 20-year-old Barnett settled in Leesburg, Indiana, where he opened a saddle and harness shop and later became a partner in a country store. He married and began raising a family.

Although now a successful merchant, Barnett began to grow restless in Leesburg. Drawn by the glowing descriptions of the western prairies, Barnett visited the Kansas Territory in the fall of 1857. He purchased large tracts of land in northeast Kansas, as well as the country store in the village of Hiawatha. The following year, he moved to the Kansas frontier with his wife, Sarah, and their two young sons—Will, age six, and Bion, less than six months old. He tried farming, but soon discovered that he was a better merchant than farmer. In addition to running the store, Barnett became involved in local government, serving on the board of the county commissioners and as county treasurer. He also became a railroad investor and, in 1871, one of the organizers of a private bank, Barnett, Morrill and Company. The bank, now known as the Morrill & Janes Bank and Trust Company, is still in existence.

In 1874, Barnett's older son, William D., who had been operating a dry goods business in Hiawatha, moved to Jacksonville, Florida. Why Will Barnett chose Jacksonville as his new home is unclear. Nevertheless, the following year, his parents made the arduous journey from Kansas to visit. During their stay, William B. Barnett noticed that his wife, who suffered from migraine headaches, enjoyed improved health in the Florida climate. In addition, the elder Barnett thought that north Florida offered some promising business prospects. Returning to Hiawatha, Barnett sold his interests in the bank and other business ventures. Joined by their younger son Bion, then a student at the University of Kansas, the Barnetts moved to Jacksonville, arriving on St. Patrick's Day, 1877.

Six weeks later, William B. Barnett opened The Bank of Jacksonville, assisted by the 19-year-old Bion and one other clerk. The elder Barnett would remain in charge of the bank for the next 26 years. A good judge of character, with an intuitive business sense, he followed a cautious operating philosophy. For example, when the phosphate boom of the early 1890s set off a speculation frenzy, Barnett refused to do business with the mining companies being organized, neither accepting their deposits nor making them loans. He warned, "There is too much wild speculation. We will keep out of it; all these companies cannot succeed; we will wait until it becomes a settled industry. Some of these companies will survive and be solvent;

we will then do business with them." This proved an excellent course of action when the boom collapsed after two years and the bank remained unscathed.

In 1880, Barnett's older son, William D., sold his furniture business and joined the family banking firm. William D. left the bank in 1888, the same year that the bank received a national charter and was renamed the National Bank of Jacksonville, moving his family to North Carolina for health reasons. He returned in 1897 and remained an officer until his death, including serving as chairman of the board from 1911 to 1920. His only son, Harlow, also worked for the bank. When William B. died in 1903, Harlow replaced his grandfather on the board of directors. Harlow's banking career, however, was cut short by the death of his young wife in 1912. Devastated, he left both the bank and Jacksonville, thereafter to live a largely reclusive life.

Bion Hall Barnett succeeded his father as president of the National Bank of Jacksonville in 1903. He had been his father's principal lieutenant in operating the bank for years. In addition to being a savvy businessman, he took an active role in local government and was a noted philanthropist. With the exception of the years 1911 to 1917, Bion remained as president or chairman of the board until he retired in 1952. Bion had four children, but only the youngest, Don, expressed any interest in banking. After attending the Wharton School of Business at the University of Pennsylvania, Donald Murray Barnett joined the bank in 1913 and, during his father's lengthy absences in the 1920s and 1930s, watched over the family's interests. Don played a key role in Barnett's expansion during the Depression and was president or chairman of the affiliated banks established in Cocoa, Avon Park, and Fort Lauderdale. At the time of his death in 1948, he was vice chairman of the board of the Barnett National Bank of Jacksonville.

Don Barnett's only son had died in a childhood swimming pool accident, and his sister and brothers had contributed mostly nieces to the family tree. To ensure that the family had representation among bank management, he convinced his younger cousin, William Randle (Bill) Barnett, to join the bank. Bill, Harlow's oldest son, had wanted to be an engineer, but joined the bank full time in 1932 following graduation from Emory University. Like all the Barnett family members, he started at the bottom, learning the banking business first as a "runner" collecting bad checks, and then in the Transit Department and on the teller line. By 1948, with the death of Don Barnett and Bion's advancing age, Bill Barnett had become the key family representative, both in management and in civic involvement in Jacksonville. In 1958, he became president of the Barnett National Bank of Jacksonville. In 1964, he moved to chairman of the board and served on the board of the holding company, Barnett Banks, Inc., as an active director and, after turning 70, as an advisory director until his death in 1991.

In 1958, the year that Bill Barnett became president, his son, William Bion Barnett, started his career as a management trainee. Over the next 40 years, Billy—or young Bill—worked in the commercial lending and asset management areas of both the Jacksonville bank and the holding company. The last of the family members to work for the bank, he retired shortly after the sale to NationsBank.

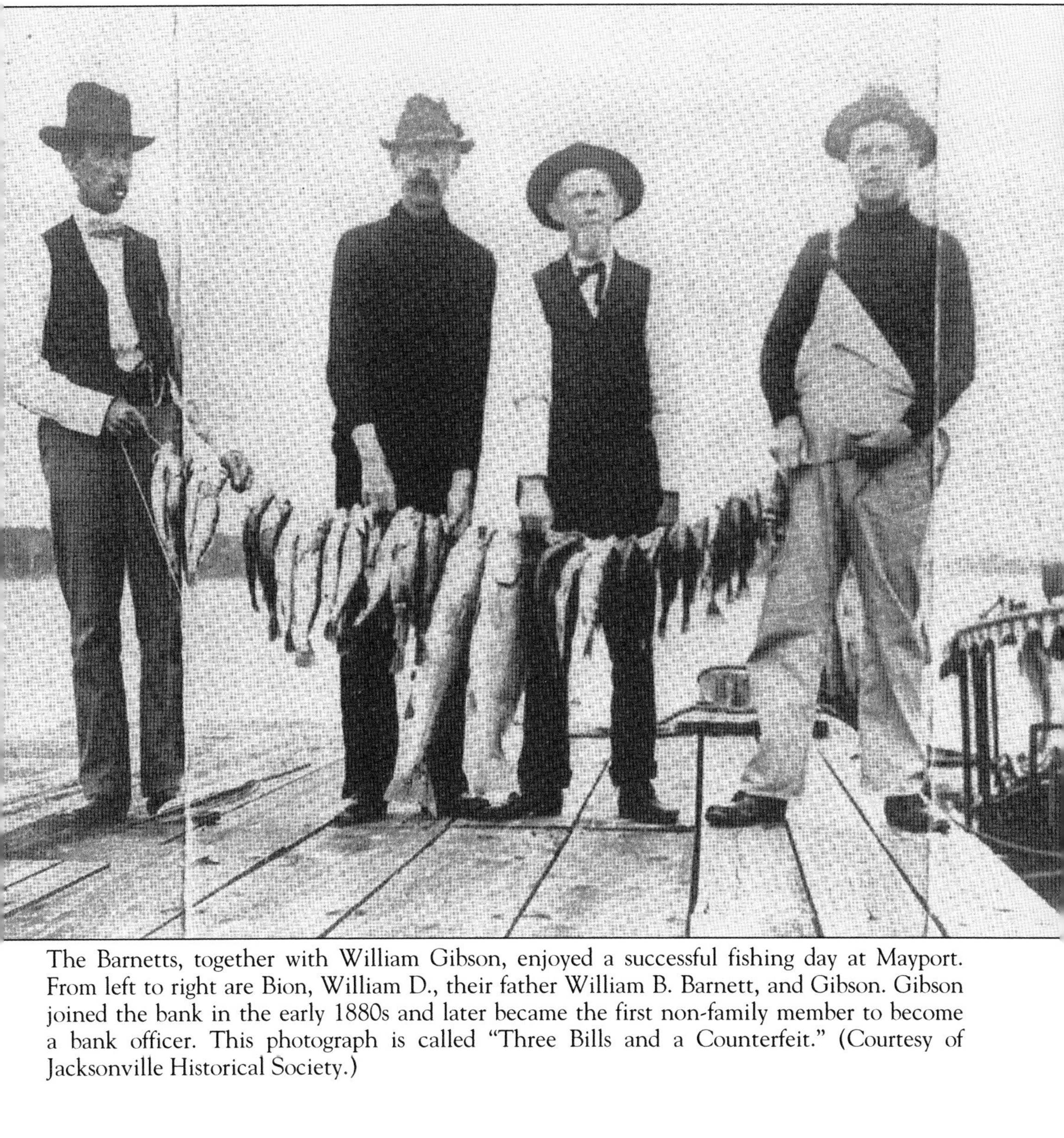

The Barnetts, together with William Gibson, enjoyed a successful fishing day at Mayport. From left to right are Bion, William D., their father William B. Barnett, and Gibson. Gibson joined the bank in the early 1880s and later became the first non-family member to become a bank officer. This photograph is called "Three Bills and a Counterfeit." (Courtesy of Jacksonville Historical Society.)

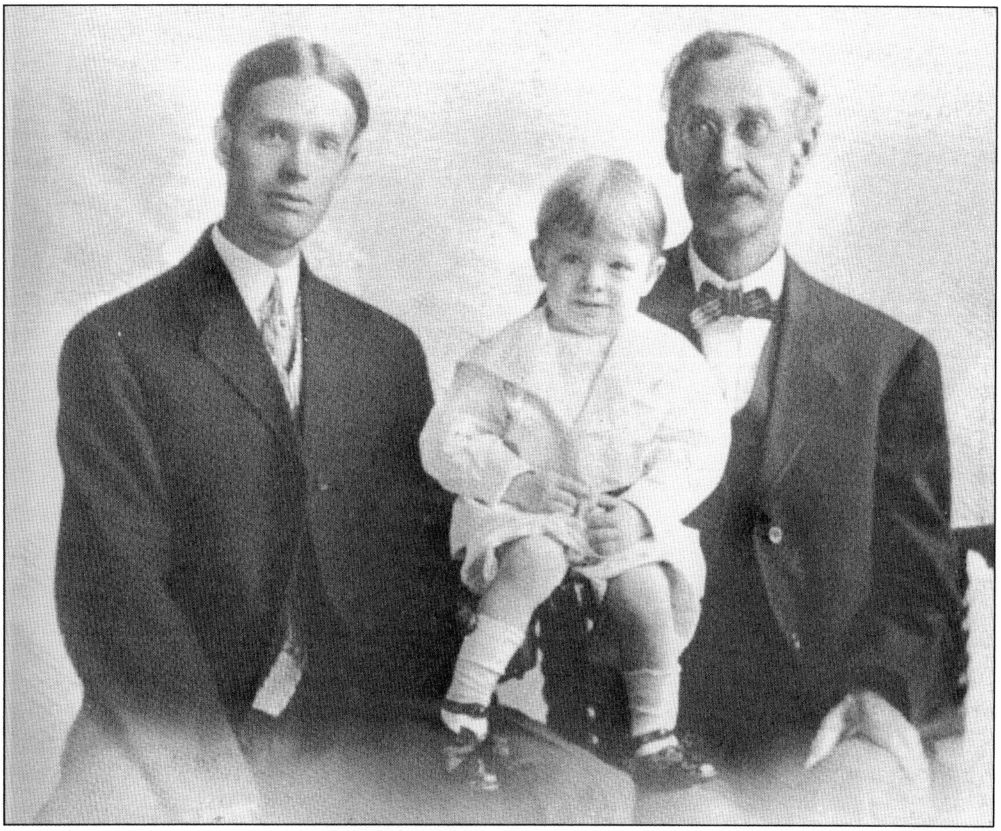

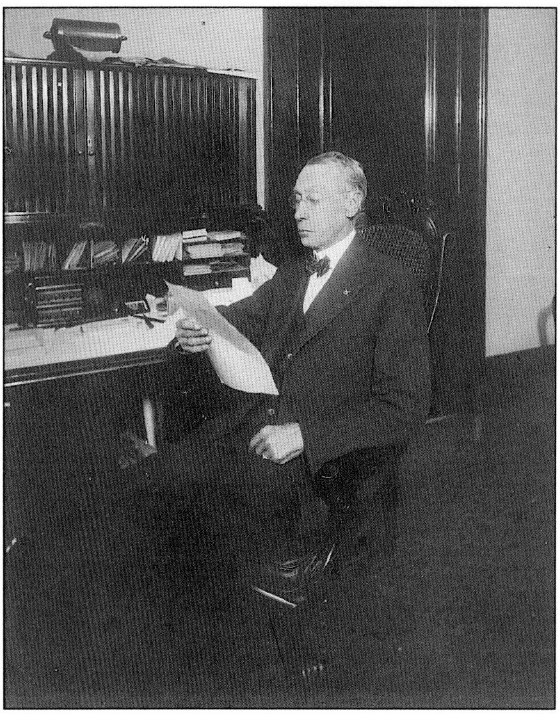

This 1911 photograph shows William D. Barnett (right) with his son Harlow and three-year-old grandson William R. Harlow Barnett had only a brief banking career. William R. had a long tenure with the bank, serving as president and, later, chairman of the board.

William D. Barnett is seated at his desk at the bank for this 1919 photograph. At the time, he was chairman of the board.

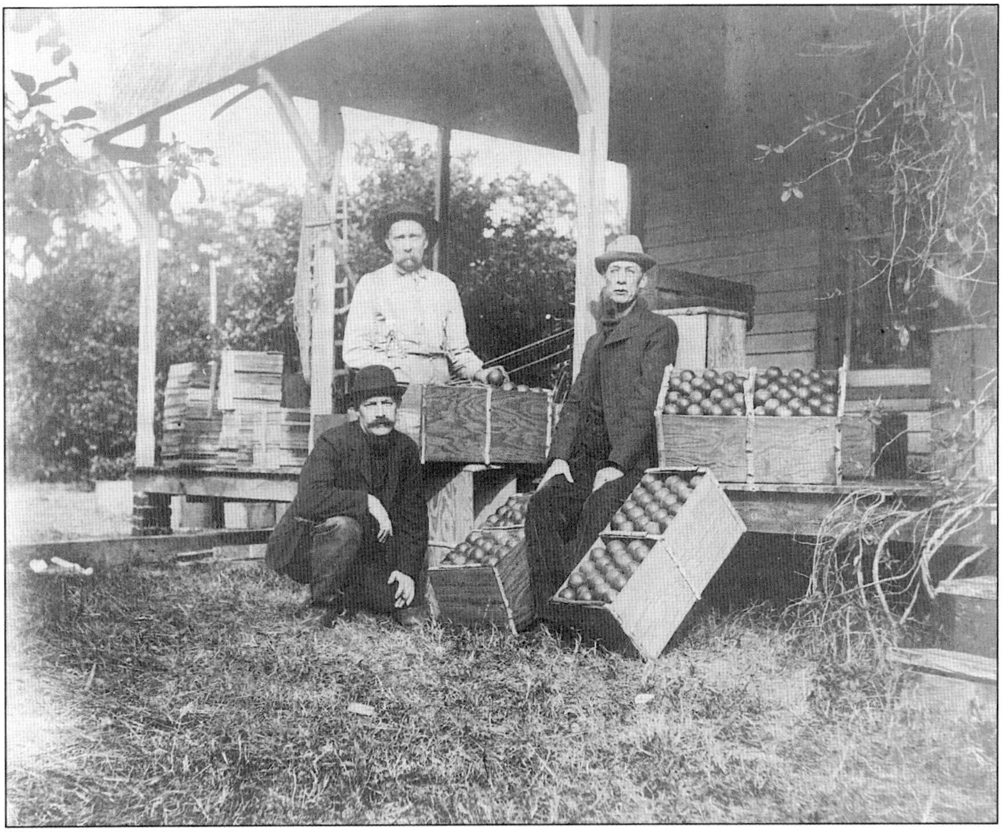

William D. Barnett had many business interests outside of the family bank. Above, he is shown with several of his workers at his orange grove in Tangerine (north of Orlando), from which he shipped fruit to both domestic and overseas markets. (Courtesy of Jacksonville Historical Society.)

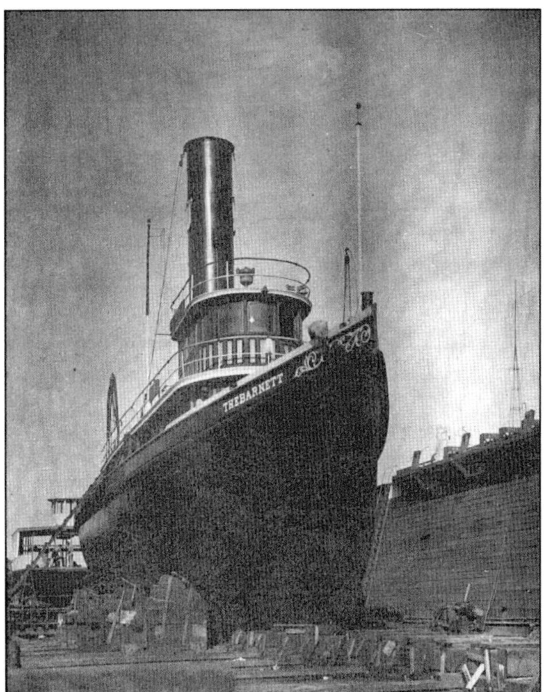

On the right is the tugboat, *The Barnett*, that William D. purchased in 1911 to work in the increasingly busy port of Jacksonville. (Courtesy of Florida State Archives.)

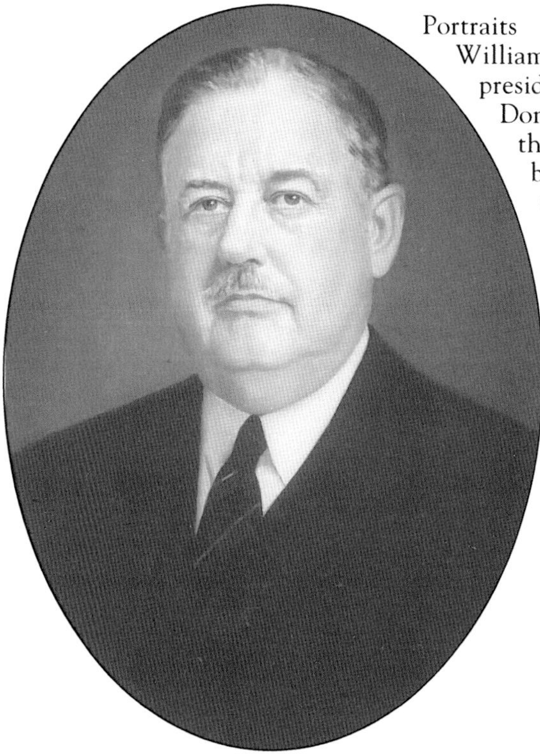

Portraits of Donald Murray Barnett and William Randle Barnett hung among the presidential portraits in the bank's board room. Don Barnett never served as president of the Barnett National Bank of Jacksonville but played a key role as the senior family member during Bion's lengthy absences abroad. Don was a critical figure during the bank's Depression-era expansion outside of Jacksonville.

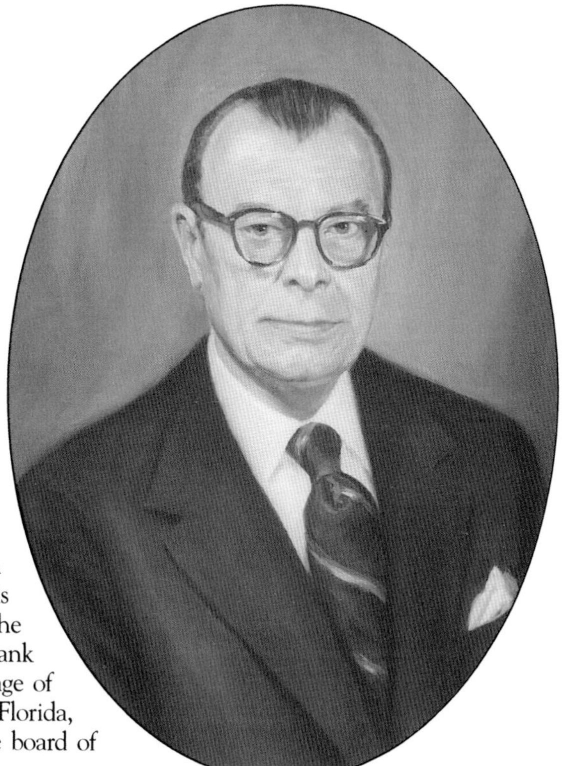

William R. (Bill) Barnett became president of the Barnett National Bank of Jacksonville in 1958, when William McQuaid retired and Frank Norris moved to chairman. Beginning in 1964, he served as chairman of the Jacksonville bank until reaching the mandatory retirement age of 65 in 1973. He also was Barnett Banks of Florida, Inc. (BBFI) treasurer and chairman of the board of the Avon Park and DeLand affiliates.

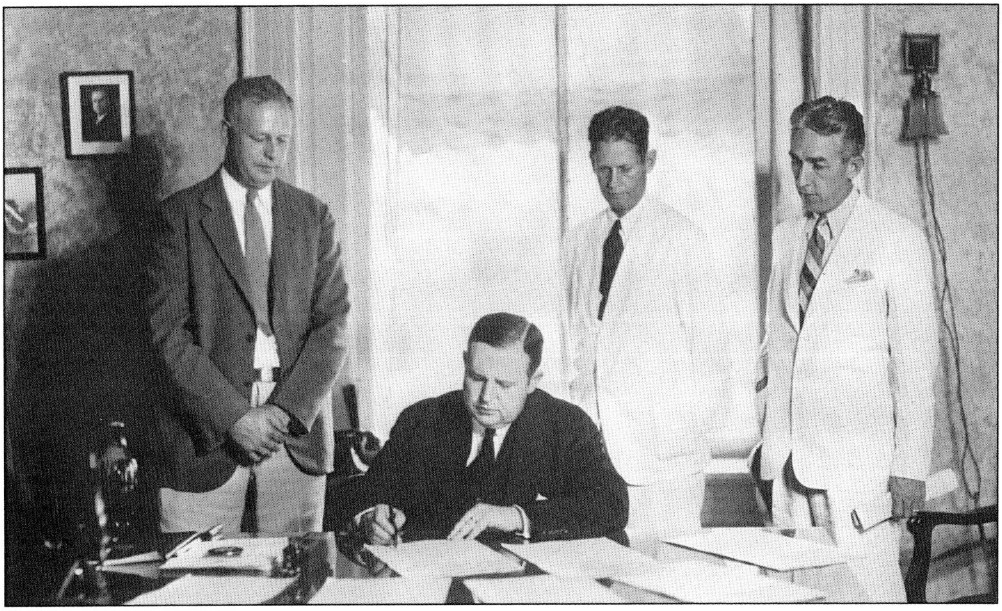

Neither of Bion Barnett's twin sons, Bion Hall Jr. or William L'Engle, had any interest in banking. Bion Jr. lived in France during the 1920s and 1930s and became a noted landscape artist. William L. was one of the founders of the Florida Forestry Association and its first president. W.L. Barnett is standing secdon from the right, watching as Florida governor David Scholtz signs several forestry bills in 1935. (Courtesy of Florida State Archives.)

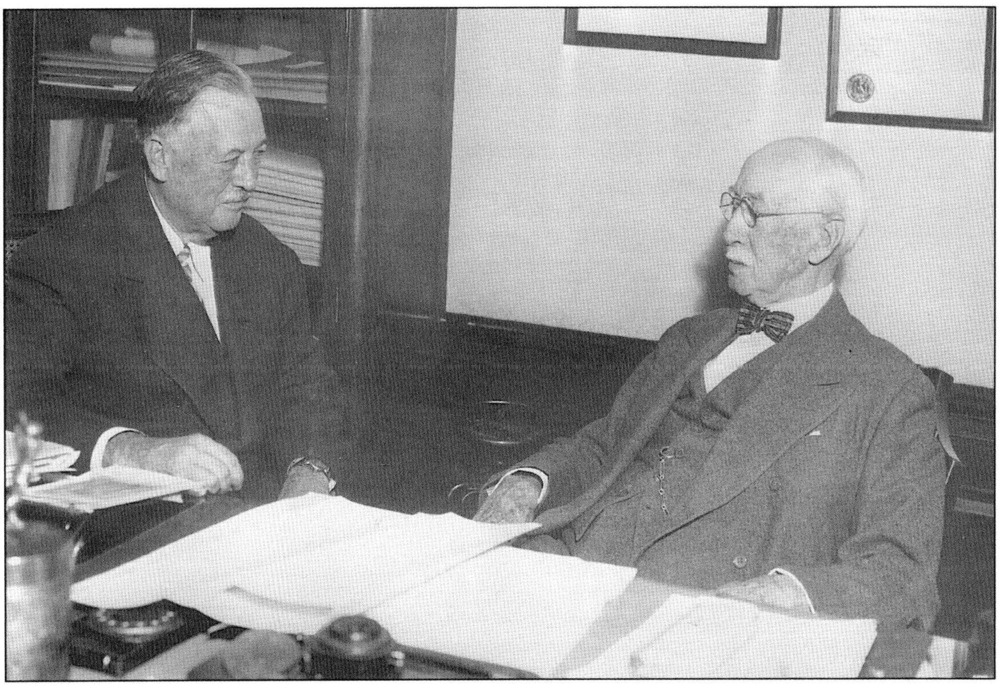

Don Barnett visits with his father at Bion's office at the Barnett National Bank during the 1940s. In poor health, Don died in 1948 at the age of 56. His father outlived him by ten years. (Courtesy of Florida State Archives.)

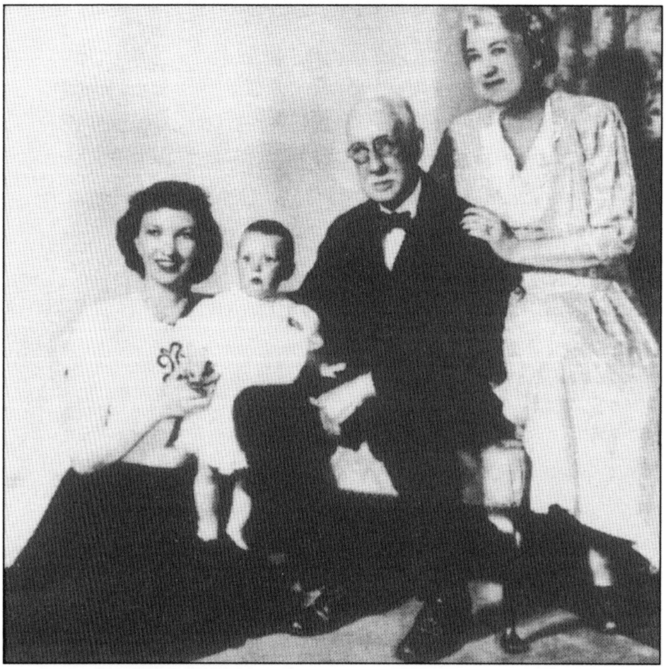

Four generations of Barnetts are featured in this photograph—Bion is surrounded by his daughter Madeleine Camp, who cared for him during his last years; granddaughter Madeleine Camp Franklin (subsequently an award-winning author, writing under the name Madeleine L'Engle); and great-granddaughter Josephine Franklin. This photo appeared in a Barnett Bank of Tampa newsletter, compliments of mortgage loan processor Amy Prue. Her grandfather, James Shortland, worked as Bion's personal secretary from 1922 to 1946.

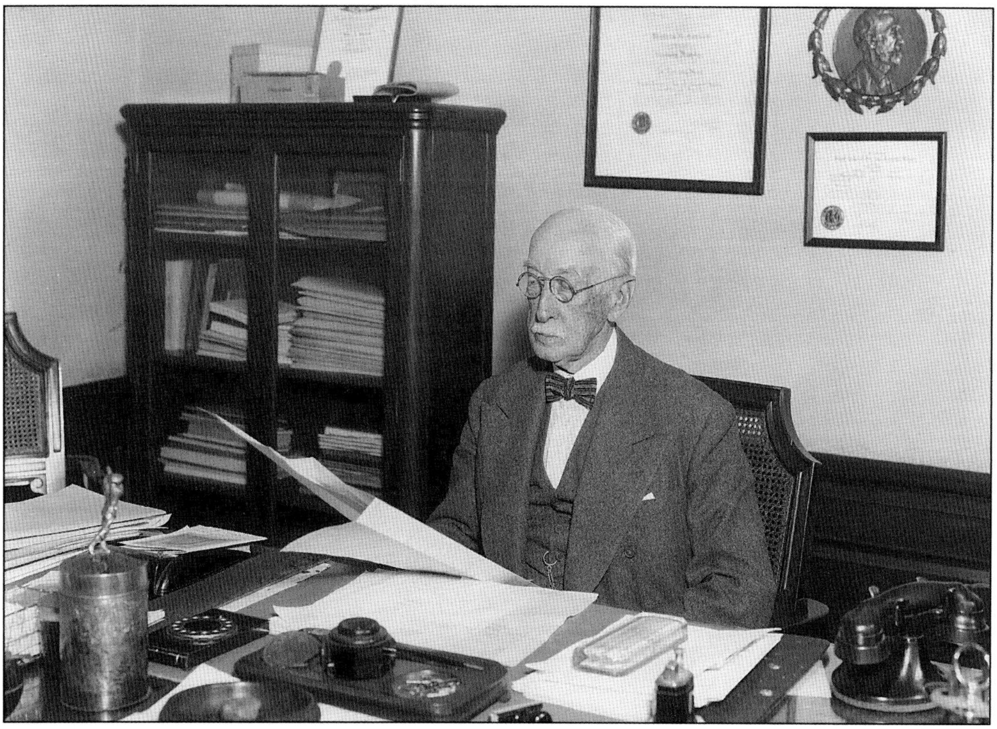

Bion Barnett continued to come to his office at the bank into his early 90s. On reaching his 90th birthday in 1947, he announced, "I have decided to establish a rule of the bank to the effect that no officer or employee who reaches the age of 89 need return to work after the noon lunch hour." He remained as chairman of the board until 1952, and then honorary chairman until his death in 1958, at the age of 101. (Photo by J. Gordon Spottswood.)

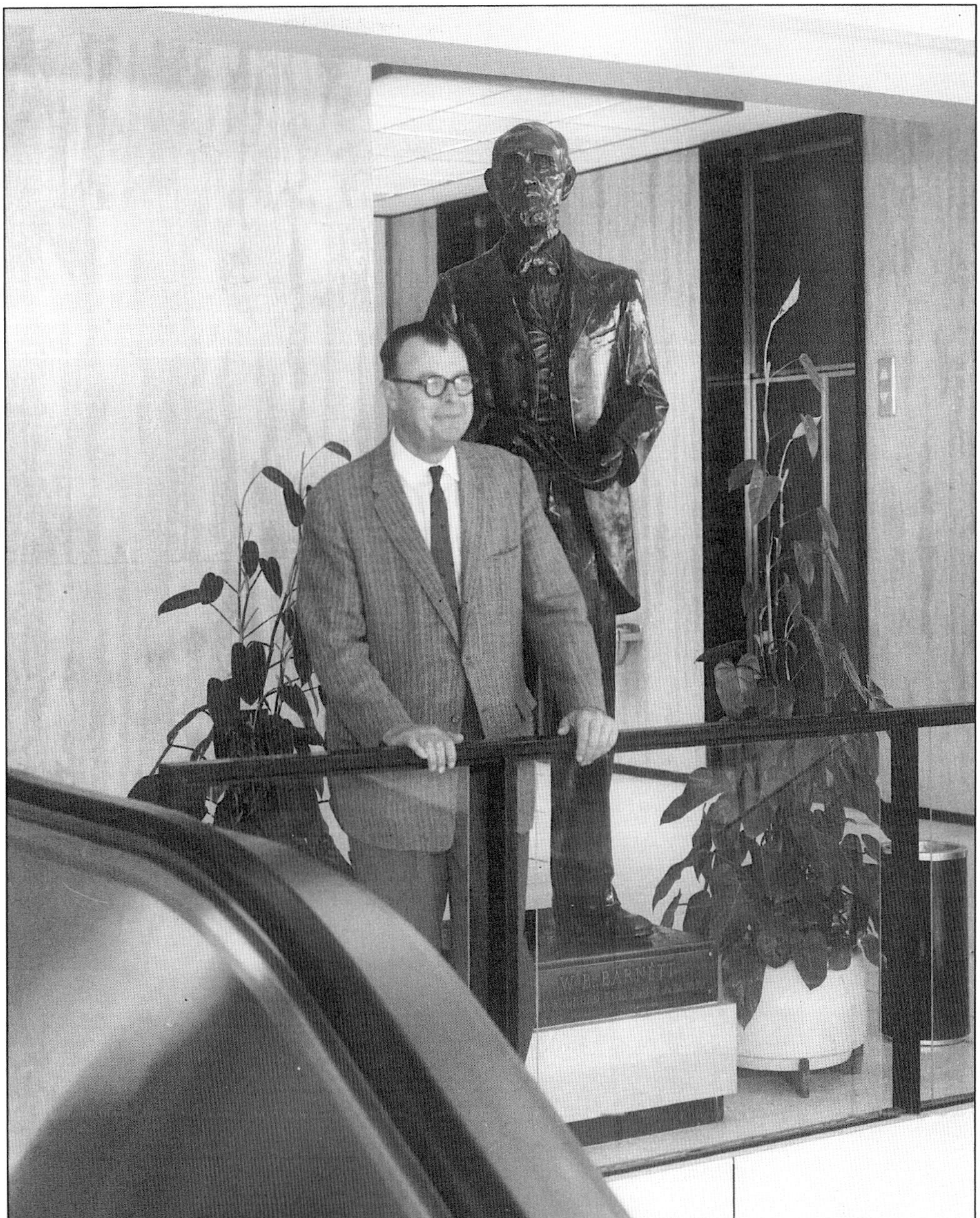

William R. Barnett, president of the Barnett National Bank, stands at the top of the escalator leading to the main banking lobby on the second floor of the downtown Jacksonville office in April 1963. Behind him is the bronze statue of his great grandfather, William Boyd Barnett. The bank commissioned the statue as part of its 50th anniversary celebration. St. Augustine sculptor Charles Adrian Pillars had previously completed the two Florida statues—John Gorrie, the inventor of mechanical refrigeration machines, and Confederate general Kirby Smith—for the Capitol in Washington, D.C. Pillars took nearly two years to complete the Barnett statue, which was placed in the main lobby of the bank on New Years Day 1931. (Courtesy of *Florida Times-Union.*)

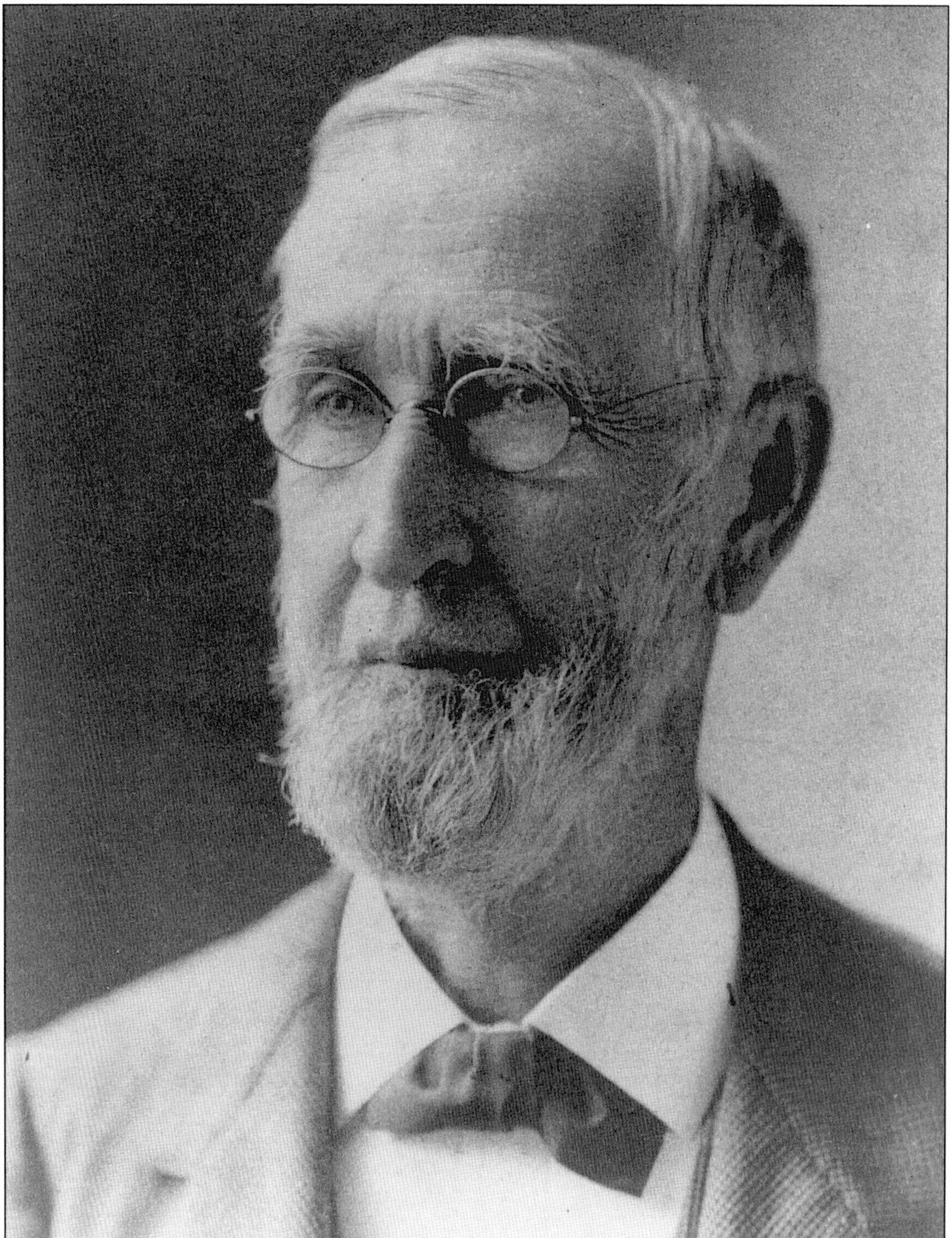

William Boyd Barnett founded The Bank of Jacksonville. He was president of the bank (later renamed the National Bank of Jacksonville) from 1877 until his death in 1903.

Two

THE EARLY YEARS: 1877 TO 1908

Florida in the 1870s was a poor, sparsely settled wilderness. Although Jacksonville was the largest city in the state, it was still very much a frontier town. It had no paved roads. There were no sewers nor city water, and the poor sanitary conditions led to periodic outbreaks of yellow fever. Nevertheless, Jacksonville was a commercial center for the shipment of lumber, naval stores, cotton, and other products harvested in the interior, as well as a winter destination for Northern tourists seeking a more temperate climate.

Jacksonville already had three banks in 1877, a sufficient number to service a population of less than ten thousand. Undeterred, William B. Barnett rented a room in the Freedmen's Bank Building at the corner of Pine (now Main) and Forsyth Streets, close to the city's principal business district along Bay Street. Only six weeks after arriving from Kansas, on May 7, 1877, he opened for business as The Bank of Jacksonville, with a capital investment of $43,000.

The Bank of Jacksonville was a private bank, with no legal or regulatory requirements to be met. All that Barnett needed to operate was a safe, some large leather-bound ledgers for the manual recording of transactions, and the ability to inspire sufficient trust and confidence that his new neighbors would entrust their cash to him for safekeeping. Initially, business was slow, compounded by the outbreak of a yellow fever epidemic later in the year and then a major robbery that resulted in the loss of more than one-sixth of the bank's capital.

The bank struggled until 1880. That year, Henry L'Engle, the tax collector for Duval County, complained to Bion Barnett about the fees charged by one of the other Jacksonville banks where he kept the county's funds. The bank charged one-quarter of one percent to transfer funds to a New York bank, where the state treasurer required tax receipts to be sent. The fee had totaled $6.25 the preceding month, which L'Engle had to personally pay. Bion knew L'Engle from the First Florida Light Artillery, a local militia organization to which they both belonged. L'Engle also happened to be a cousin of Bion's new wife. Bion agreed to waive the charge, provided that L'Engle transfer the county's business to The Bank of Jacksonville.

The following year, L'Engle became state treasurer. He moved all of the state's depository accounts to The Bank of Jacksonville, which then became Florida's largest bank. Gaining the state's banking business coincided with the Disston land purchase, one of the most significant events in the history of the state. The sale of 4 million acres of unimproved land, for 25¢ per acre, to Philadelphia industrialist Hamilton Disston helped the debt-ridden state government avoid insolvency. As the state depository, The Bank of Jacksonville benefited from Florida's improved finances. The bank even played a role in the land sale, providing a loan to Sir Edward Reed, an English shipbuilder who had bought a half interest in the land claim and then had difficulty getting the cash to complete the deal.

With the Disston land purchase, Florida's economic prospects, which had been hampered in the 1870s by a national depression and the state's weak financial condition, improved dramatically. An era of prosperity began, with Northern capital and settlers flowing into the state. The Bank of Jacksonville shared in the state's growth and prosperity, with its deposits increasing to $358,873 by the end of 1887. William B. Barnett decided to raise additional capital by selling stock to prominent Jacksonville citizens, such as government official Joseph H. Durkee, wholesale grocer John G. Christopher, and dry goods merchant Leopold Furchgott. With capital of $150,000, he obtained a national charter and, in May of 1888, opened the National Bank of Jacksonville.

Later in 1888, yellow fever again struck the city of Jacksonville. Nearly five thousand people were stricken, including William B. Barnett. Panic engulfed the city, with thousands fleeing and a strict quarantine imposed on those left behind. Even though business activity nearly came to a halt during the crisis, the Barnetts kept their bank open. William B. recovered, but three of the bank's clerks died during the epidemic. Over the next decade, the bank faced even more crises—the widespread business failures that followed the collapse of the phosphate speculation frenzy of the early 1890s; the depositor runs caused by the financial panic of 1893; and the widespread damage to agricultural interests following devastating freezes during the winter of 1894–1895.

The National Bank of Jacksonville not only survived but prospered. By 1890, it had outgrown its original quarters and rented offices at a new location at the southeast corner of Bay and Laura Streets. By the mid-1890s, deposits had increased to more than $1 million, and the Barnetts employed a staff of ten men—William L. Gibson was an assistant cashier, and there were two tellers, three bookkeepers, two collection clerks, a utility clerk, and a porter. These new quarters soon proved inadequate for the expanding volume of business. In 1897, the Barnetts purchased a lot at the northwest corner of Forsyth and Laura Streets, where they constructed a massive stone building with Greek columns, quadrupling the size of the banking facility.

The new banking offices opened in 1898. Three years later—on May 3, 1901—a massive fire devastated Jacksonville. It destroyed more than 450 acres in the oldest and most populated part of the city and left nearly ten thousand people—including William B. and both his sons—homeless. The National Bank of Jacksonville was the only bank building not destroyed by the fire. The Barnetts offered to allow the other banks in town to store cash and valuables in their safe until they could find new quarters.

The decade following the 1901 fire was a period of booming prosperity as the citizens of Jacksonville rebuilt their city. The Barnetts—both personally and through the financing provided by the National Bank of Jacksonville—played an active role in the business expansion. In 1908, Bion Barnett, who had become president of the bank after the 1903 death of his father, proposed to again reorganize the bank. With the 20-year charter of the National Bank of Jacksonville about to expire, he found additional investors to increase the bank's capitalization and sought a new charter, renaming the bank in honor of its founder. On August 15, 1908, the Barnett National Bank opened. To the general public—which for years had referred to it as "the Barnett's bank"—there was no change. Same building, same employees, same services. But the Barnett National Bank, with $4.3 million in deposits and capital of $750,000, had come a long way from its humble beginnings in 1877.

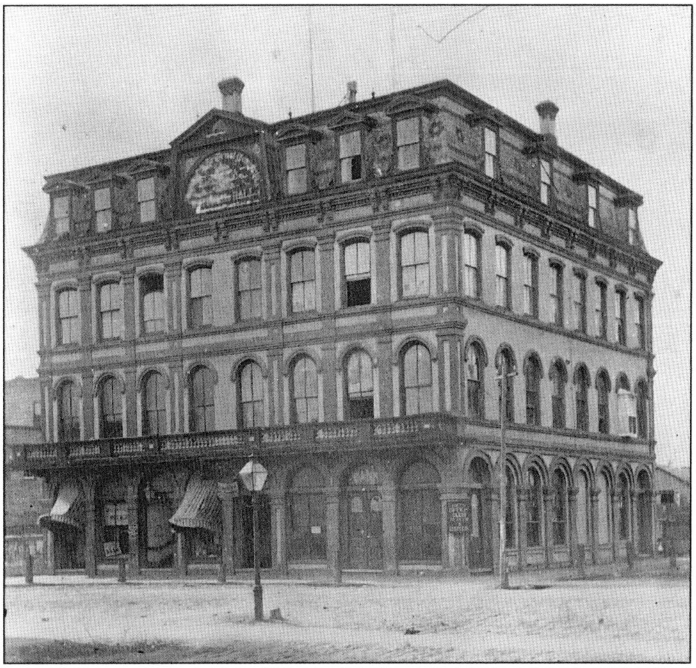

The Bank of Jacksonville opened in a rented room at the Freedmen's Bank Building, at the southwest corner of Pine (now Main) and Forsyth Streets. This building had housed the Freedmen's Savings Bank, which had operated from 1866 to 1874 to accept the savings of newly emancipated slaves. The Barnetts operated their bank at this location from 1877 to 1890. The following year, fire destroyed the building. (Courtesy of Jacksonville Historical Society.)

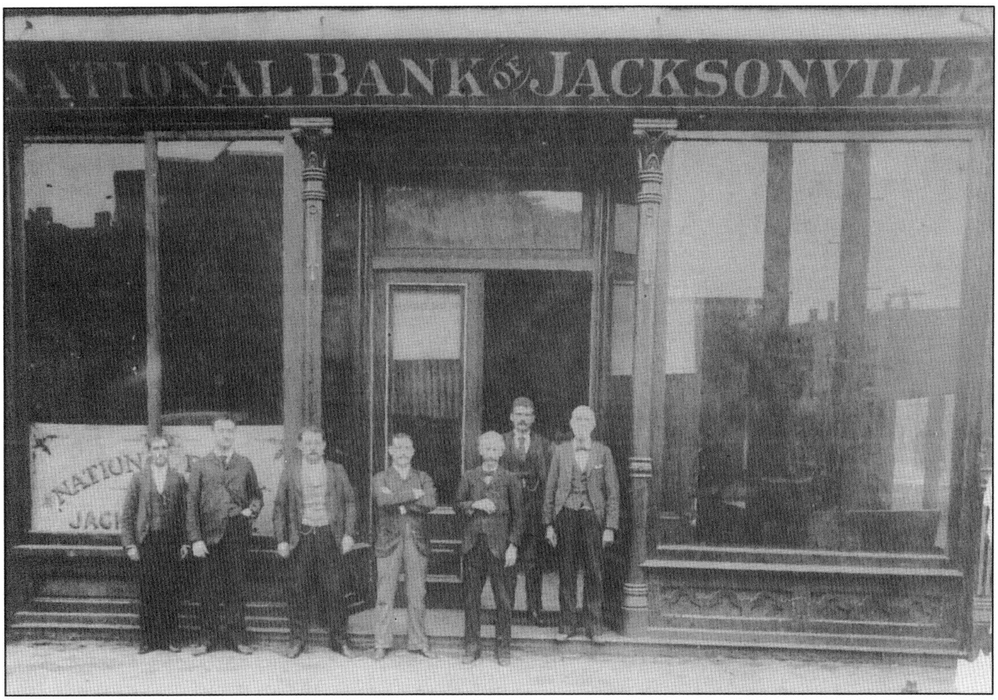

The staff of the National Bank of Jacksonville pose outside of the bank's second office at the southeast corner of Bay and Laura Streets, where the bank operated from 1890 to 1898. From left to right are B.A. Leite (assistant collection clerk), W.H. Treadwell (collection clerk), Tom Hutchinson (general bookkeeper), R.E. Wheeler (teller), S.H. Kooker (bookkeeper), L.C. Emery (bookkeeper), and W.B. Barnett.

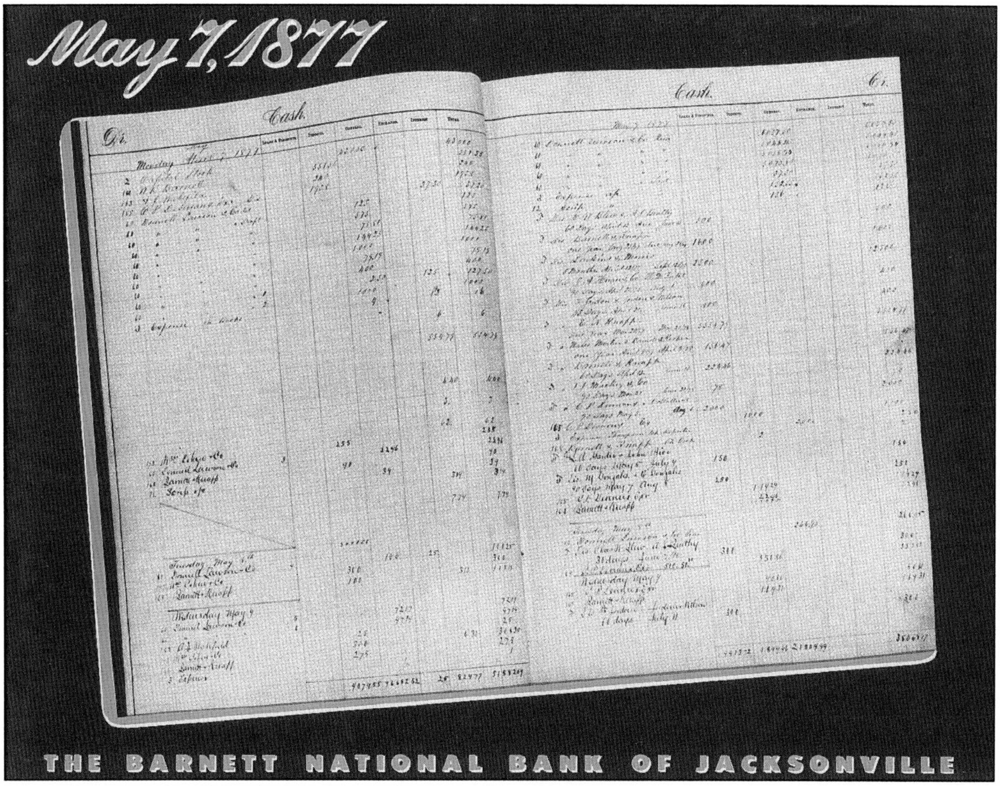

This photograph of the ledger from the first day of business, Monday, May 7, 1877, appeared on the cover of the 1956 Annual Report, as the bank prepared for its 80th anniversary. This original ledger is part of the historical records collection that has been donated to the Florida State Archives.

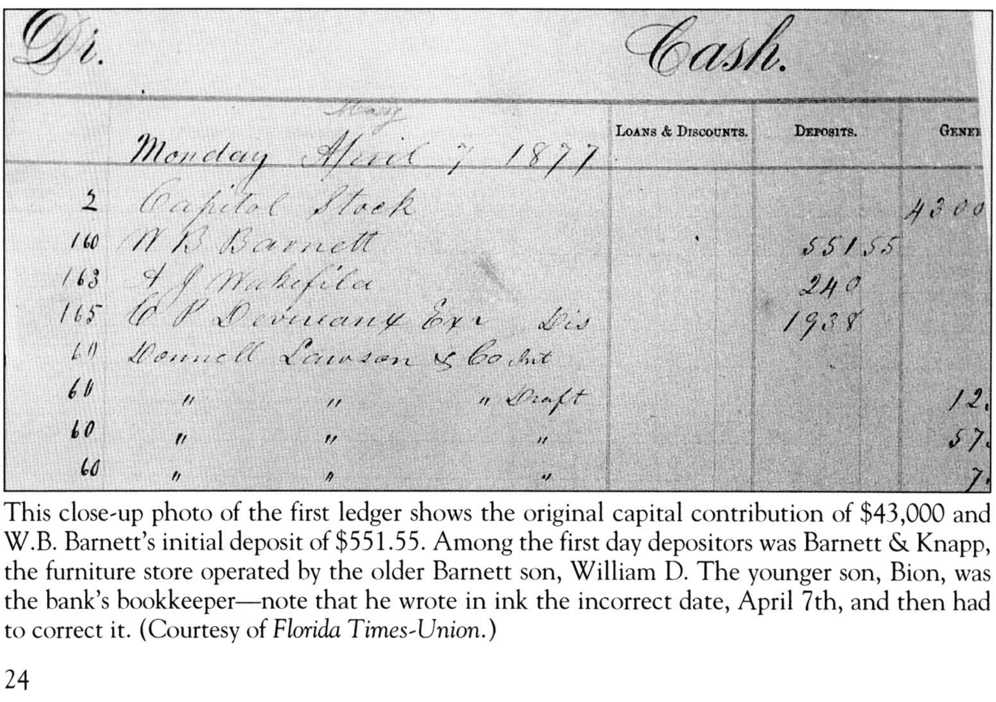

This close-up photo of the first ledger shows the original capital contribution of $43,000 and W.B. Barnett's initial deposit of $551.55. Among the first day depositors was Barnett & Knapp, the furniture store operated by the older Barnett son, William D. The younger son, Bion, was the bank's bookkeeper—note that he wrote in ink the incorrect date, April 7th, and then had to correct it. (Courtesy of *Florida Times-Union*.)

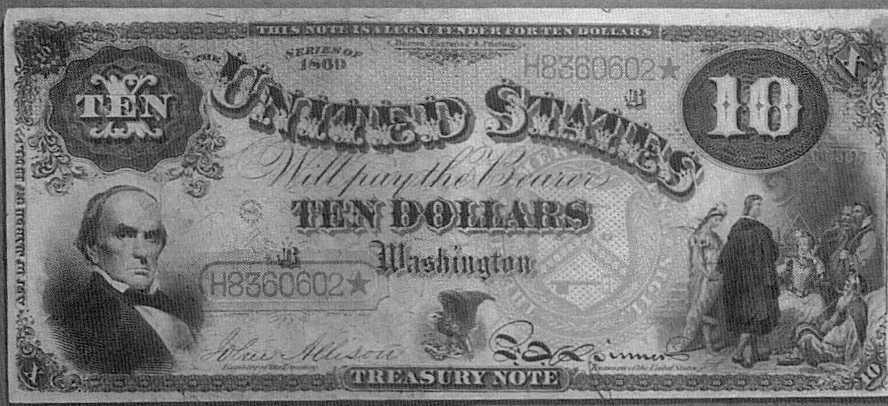

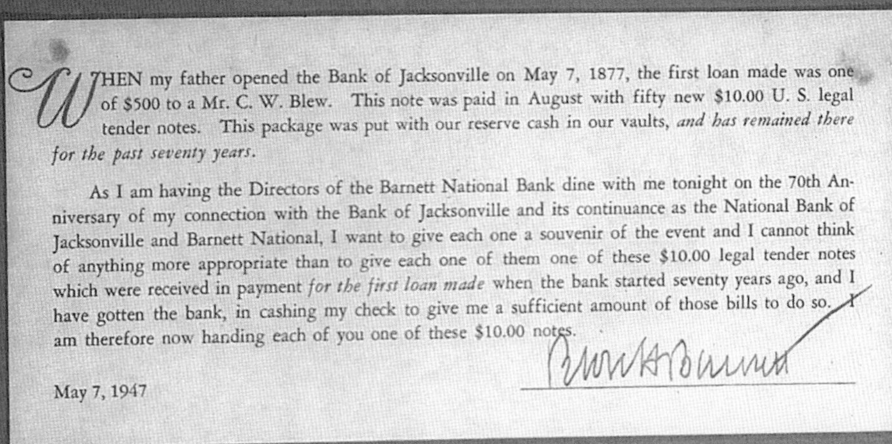

WHEN my father opened the Bank of Jacksonville on May 7, 1877, the first loan made was one of $500 to a Mr. C. W. Blew. This note was paid in August with fifty new $10.00 U. S. legal tender notes. This package was put with our reserve cash in our vaults, *and has remained there for the past seventy years.*

As I am having the Directors of the Barnett National Bank dine with me tonight on the 70th Anniversary of my connection with the Bank of Jacksonville and its continuance as the National Bank of Jacksonville and Barnett National, I want to give each one a souvenir of the event and I cannot think of anything more appropriate than to give each one of them one of these $10.00 legal tender notes which were received in payment *for the first loan made* when the bank started seventy years ago, and I have gotten the bank, in cashing my check to give me a sufficient amount of those bills to do so. I am therefore now handing each of you one of these $10.00 notes.

May 7, 1947

On the bank's first day of operation, W.B. Barnett loaned $500 to C.W. Blew. In 1947, Bion Barnett presented to each bank director a framed $10 Treasury Note used to repay this first loan, together with an explanation that the bank had kept these bills in its cash reserves for 70 years.

1877 1937

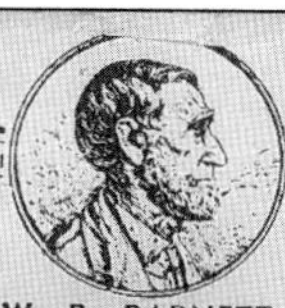

W. B. BARNETT
Founder the Barnett National Bank

Sixty Years Ago . . . . and Today

In 1877, when this bank was founded, little was known about the peninsula of Florida south of Orlando. Jacksonville was a tourist resort, though more people came South in the Winter for their health than came for pleasure. The leading physicians of the city were Doctors Sable, Daniel and Mitchell. The climate was considered then, as it should be now, particularly good for pulmonary troubles. However, we are sorry to relate, many waited too long before coming and were sent back in coffins.

There was a tale told about Mr. Calvin Oak, the undertaker, whose establishment was on the site now occupied by the Atlantic National Bank. We tell this story with the permission of Mr. Oak's grandson, Calvin H., a local resident and perhaps the oldest living customer of our first depositors.

It is said that Mr. Oak used to stand on the dock when Charleston steamers came in and with a tall rod gauge the height of the passengers as they left the steamboat. He would estimate the sized coffin needs for any he thought would not survive the Winter, then return to his shop to get them ready so there would be no delay when the time came.

Other interesting stories about the early life of Jacksonville that reveal the human side of its citizens will be told in this space during the series of weekly advertisements celebrating our Sixtieth Anniversary.

Jacksonville was a frontier town with few modern amenities when the Barnetts settled there. In 1937, to celebrate its 60th anniversary, The Barnett National Bank ran a series of advertisements "Sixty Years Ago . . . and Today." The story of Calvin Oak offers an interesting glimpse of life in the late 1870s.

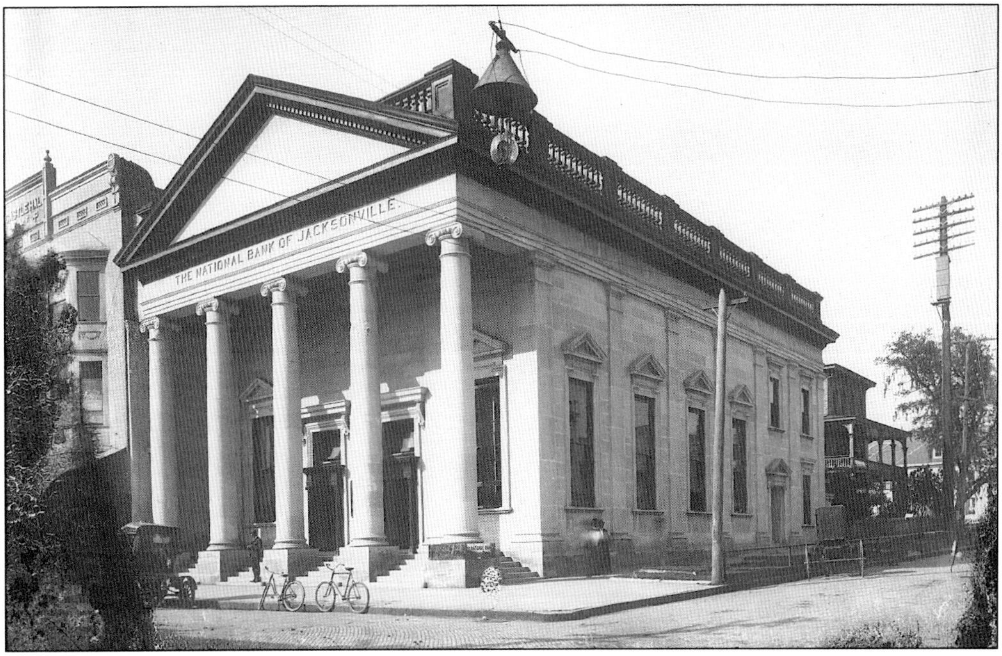

The bank's third office, a massive stone building with Greek columns, first opened in 1898. It was the only bank building in the city not destroyed by the 1901 fire. Located at the northwest corner of Laura and Forsyth Streets, it continued in operation, with several significant renovations, until 1961.

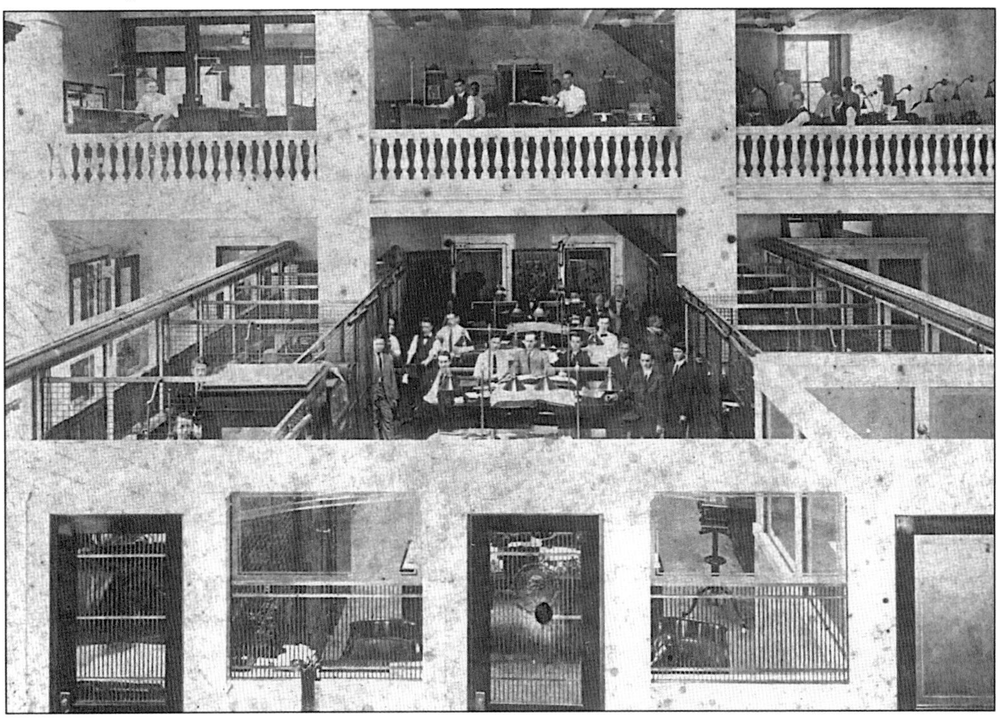

This photograph of the interior working space of the 1898 bank building shows the teller cages and mezzanine.

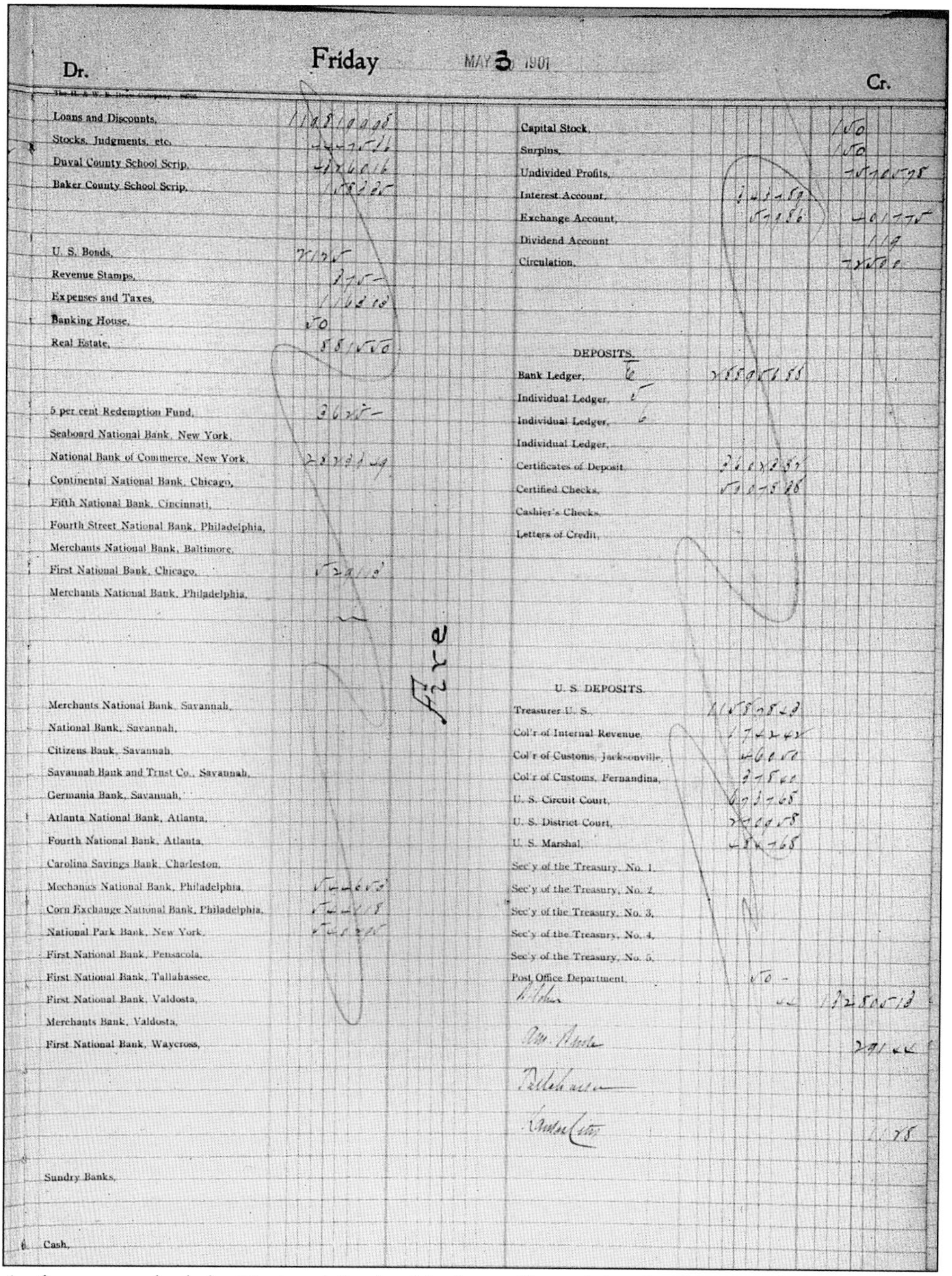

Dr. Friday MAY 3 1901 Cr.

Loans and Discounts,
Stocks, Judgments, etc.
Duval County School Scrip,
Baker County School Scrip,
U. S. Bonds,
Revenue Stamps,
Expenses and Taxes,
Banking House,
Real Estate,
5 per cent Redemption Fund,
Seaboard National Bank, New York,
National Bank of Commerce, New York,
Continental National Bank, Chicago,
Fifth National Bank, Cincinnati,
Fourth Street National Bank, Philadelphia,
Merchants National Bank, Baltimore,
First National Bank, Chicago,
Merchants National Bank, Philadelphia,
Merchants National Bank, Savannah,
National Bank, Savannah,
Citizens Bank, Savannah,
Savannah Bank and Trust Co., Savannah,
Germania Bank, Savannah,
Atlanta National Bank, Atlanta,
Fourth National Bank, Atlanta,
Carolina Savings Bank, Charleston,
Mechanics National Bank, Philadelphia,
Corn Exchange National Bank, Philadelphia,
National Park Bank, New York,
First National Bank, Pensacola,
First National Bank, Tallahassee,
First National Bank, Valdosta,
Merchants Bank, Valdosta,
First National Bank, Waycross,
Sundry Banks,
Cash,

Capital Stock,
Surplus,
Undivided Profits,
Interest Account,
Exchange Account,
Dividend Account,
Circulation,

DEPOSITS.
Bank Ledger,
Individual Ledger,
Individual Ledger,
Individual Ledger,
Certificates of Deposit,
Certified Checks,
Cashier's Checks,
Letters of Credit,

U. S. DEPOSITS.
Treasurer U. S.,
Col'r of Internal Revenue,
Col'r of Customs, Jacksonville,
Col'r of Customs, Fernandina,
U. S. Circuit Court,
U. S. District Court,
U. S. Marshal,
Sec'y of the Treasury, No. 1,
Sec'y of the Treasury, No. 2,
Sec'y of the Treasury, No. 3,
Sec'y of the Treasury, No. 4,
Sec'y of the Treasury, No. 5,
Post Office Department,

Fire

As fire approached the National Bank of Jacksonville on May 3, 1901, terrified clerks wrote "Fire" across the page of the Daily Balance Book and fled the building, without balancing and reconciling the day's accounts. The fire spared only a narrow fringe of the downtown business district—those blocks west of Laura Street and south of Adams Street to the St. Johns River. Fortunately, the National Bank of Jacksonville was located in this area. The following day, the bank reopened and the clerks reconciled the bank's books for both May 3rd and May 4th. This Daily Balance book is part of the bank's records now housed at the Florida State Archives.

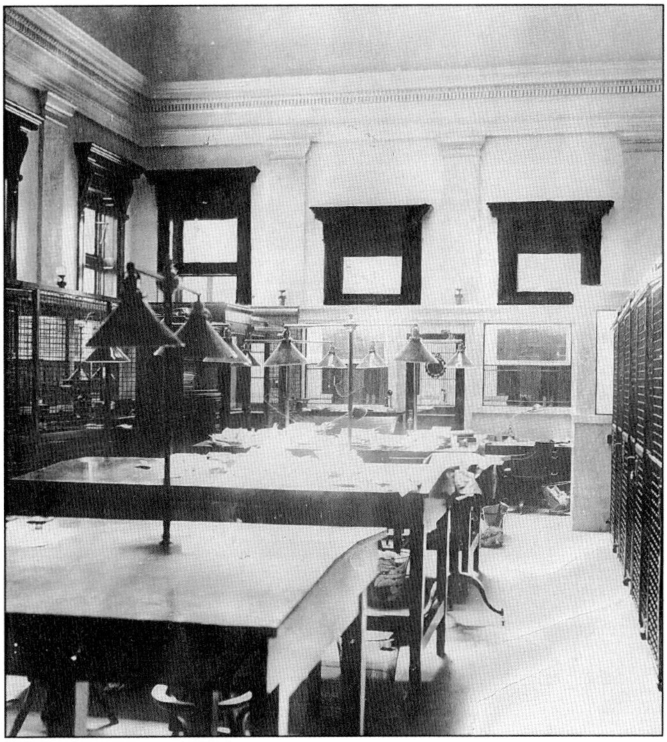

Two photographs show the interior of the 1898 bank building. The upper photo is taken from inside the working space on the main floor, looking south. Note the locked teller cages and the work tables (and wastebaskets filled with papers). The lower photo is of the eastern side of the lobby (along Laura Street), looking north.

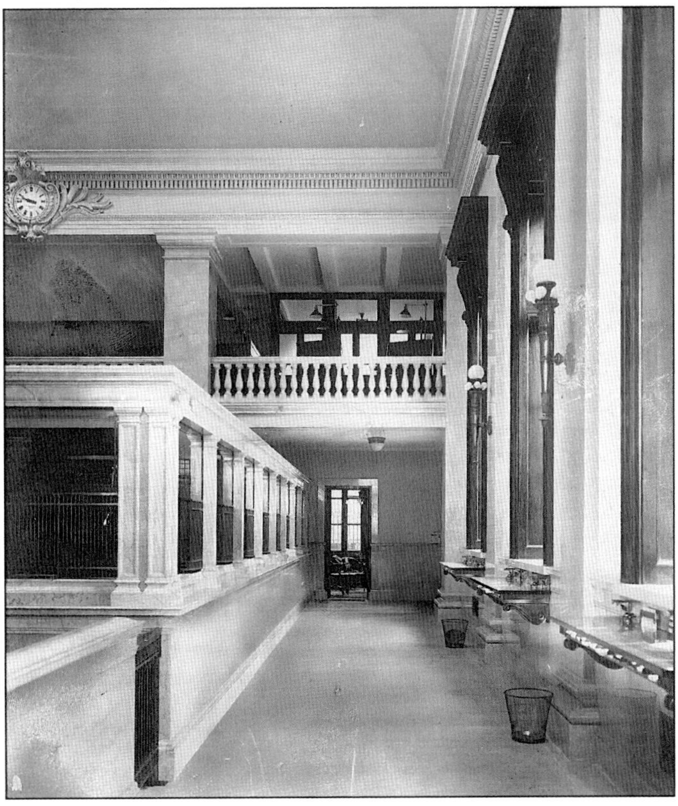

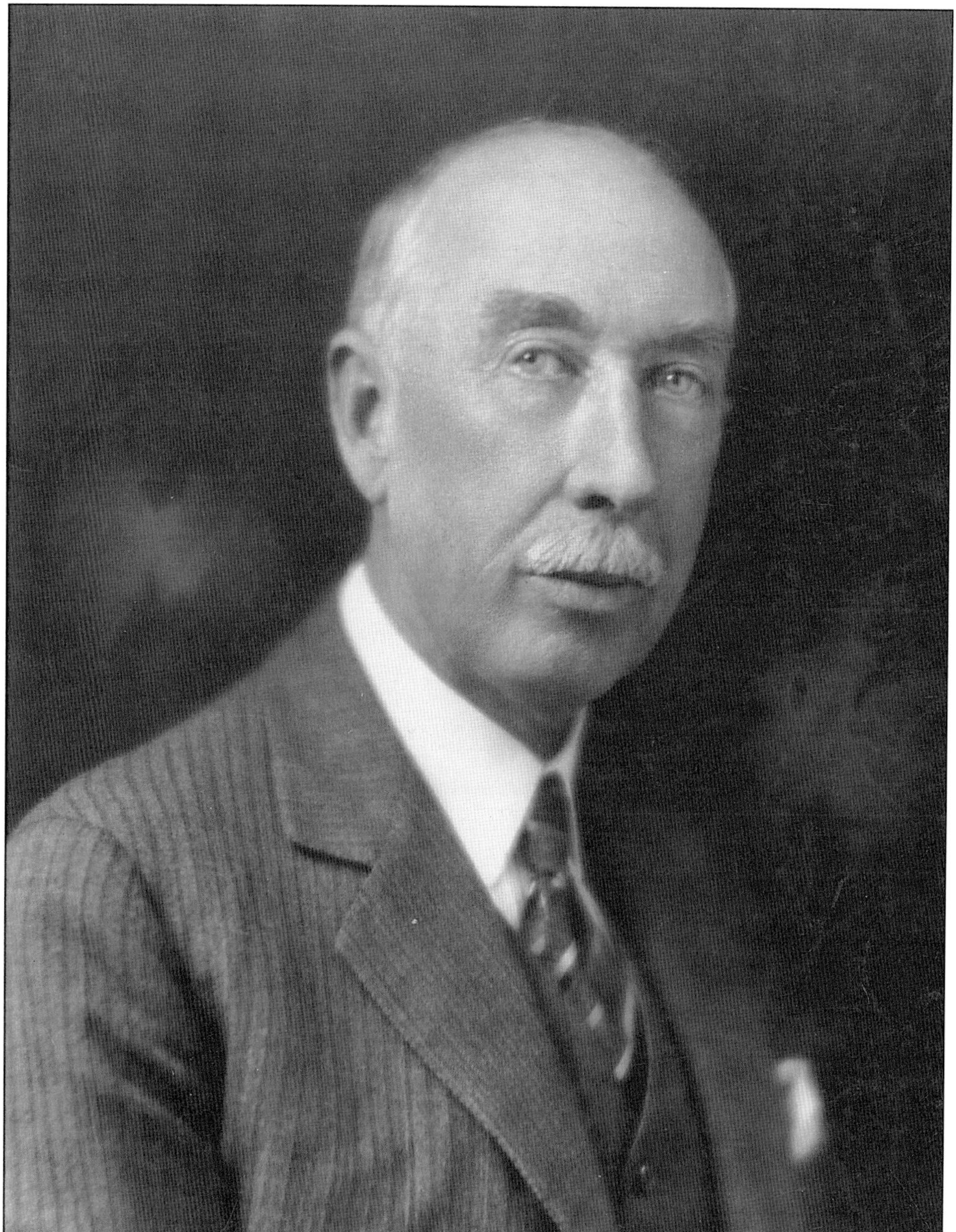

Bion Hall Barnett, son of the bank's founder, served as either president or chairman of the board for 43 years. (Photo by Woodward Studio.)

Three

Prosperity and Depression: 1908 to 1940

In January 1910, less than two years after the re-chartering of the Barnett National Bank, Bion Barnett became chairman of the board, a newly created position, and Frank Adams became president. Adams, a businessman and politician from the small rural community of Jasper, had purchased 1,000 shares (out of 7,500) to become the largest shareholder after the two Barnett brothers. The following year, Bion declined reelection to the board of directors. His older brother, William D., replaced him as chairman to oversee the family's interests.

Thus began the first of Bion's disappearances from Jacksonville, about which there are only fragmentary clues. In later years, Bion promoted the misconception of his continuous service to the Barnett National Bank, when actually he had no official connection with the bank (other than being a shareholder) from 1911 to 1917. Health reasons may have played a factor in the timing of his departure, since he contracted Bright's disease, a potentially fatal kidney ailment, at about this time. Marital problems certainly played a role. For several years, the city directories listed Bion as vice president of the New York Laundry Company. He disappeared from the city directories altogether in 1914 and began spending considerable time abroad, especially playing golf in Scotland.

Adams's tenure as president was not a successful one. By 1913, with the city fully rebuilt from the 1901 fire, a slowdown in the construction business began. When the First World War erupted in Europe the following year, the real estate slowdown turned into a widespread recession that lasted until the United States entered the war in 1917. The Barnett National Bank struggled with stagnant revenues and rising expenses, many related to slow paying or defaulted loans to naval stores, lumber, and other businesses impacted by the war. The bank lost ground to its competitors, and rival Atlantic National Bank passed it to become the largest bank in the state. Beset by earnings problems and criticisms of the bank's loan portfolio by the national bank regulators, an exhausted Adams suffered health problems.

In January 1918, amidst rumors that Barnett would merge with another local bank, Bion returned to seize control of the bank. Reelected president, he reorganized management. He charged off large numbers of defaulted loans and then established a separate company (not subject to the scrutiny of bank regulators) to which he sold the remaining problem loans, together with real estate properties and company stocks taken from delinquent borrowers. He returned the bank to profitability and increased its quarterly dividends. He instituted an innovative profit-sharing plan that allocated 30% of the bank's annual profits to be paid to all officers and clerks. Then, suddenly, in early 1920, he again left Jacksonville and the bank.

For the next two decades, Bion Barnett remained a largely absent chief executive. He traveled extensively with his new female companion and spent considerable time in London, or Scotland, or at his villa, "La Biondella," in Monte Carlo. Bion, who had kept the title of president, would return to Jacksonville once or twice each year, generally during the winter months, to confer with friends and business associates. From Europe, he kept in close touch by letters and wires with his two principal vice presidents, Courts P. Kendall and William R. McQuaid, as well as his son Don.

In 1925, Bion again became chairman and named McQuaid as president. They soon began planning for the construction of a new 18-story headquarters building to be opened in 1927 as part of the bank's 50th anniversary celebration. The Barnett National Bank was enjoying record profitability, and its deposits had nearly tripled since the end of the First World War, totaling more than $25 million. But by 1927, the Florida real estate boom had just collapsed. Throughout the state, widespread bank failures, municipal bond defaults, and plummeting real estate values signaled that hard times lay ahead.

During the next two years, the bank's deposits declined by 24%, and the bank struggled to remain profitable amidst widespread economic decline. Bion sought to solidify the bank's condition by initiating secret negotiations with Florida National president and longtime friend, Arthur F. Perry. On April 17, 1929, the two banks, with their offices in downtown Jacksonville separated only by the width of Laura Street, signed a merger agreement to form the Florida-Barnett National Bank of Jacksonville. The *Florida Times-Union* enthusiastically declared, "Florida's financial growth, ability and soundness could not be more convincingly illustrated than by this bank merger. Nor could faith in the future of Jacksonville and in the future of the state be more emphatically or practically declared than by the combining of these two leading banks of the South." Within the next two weeks, however, the merger unraveled, as wealthy industrialist Alfred I. duPont successfully stirred up opposition to the merger among Florida National shareholders. DuPont then gained control of Florida National for himself.

During the merger negotiations, Bion had two important allies—William J. Kelly, president of Jacksonville-based Consolidated Naval Stores and a Barnett director, and Calvin Fentress, a Chicago financier whose investment company owned a majority interest in Consolidated. With the collapse of the Florida National deal, Bion and Fentress negotiated the sale of a significant portion of the Barnett family's stock to Baker, Fentress & Company as the first step in a major reorganization of the bank. By January 1930, the Barnett National Bank had raised an additional $1 million in capital through a stock offering and had organized the Barnett National Securities Corporation. The Securities Corporation, a subsidiary of the bank (and similar to a bank holding company), became the vehicle for Barnett to expand outside of Jacksonville, opening new banks in DeLand, Cocoa, and Avon Park and purchasing a controlling interest in the St. Augustine National Bank.

With this reorganization, the Barnett family ceded full control of the bank, although a close working relationship with the Consolidated/Baker, Fentress group allowed the Barnett management team to operate with little interference. Controlling the ownership of more than one-third of the bank's stock, Calvin Fentress was elected to Barnett's board, thus beginning a long succession of Consolidated/Baker, Fentress directors over the next 60 years, including the very influential Elgin Bayless and Fentress's two sons, Paul and James. Most importantly, the stock sale and subsequent recapitalization of the bank gave Barnett the financial strength to weather the Depression years.

The 1930s was the most dire period in the bank's history, especially during the financial panic immediately preceding the "bank holiday" declared by President Franklin Roosevelt in March 1933. The bank suffered from shrinking deposits and loans, while simultaneously experiencing increased expenses related to loan defaults and depreciating values in its bond portfolio. The bank suffered operating losses and had to reduce its dividend payments, although it never failed to pay a quarterly dividend. Not until 1937, the 60th anniversary of the bank's founding, did the Barnett National Bank fully recover from these difficult times.

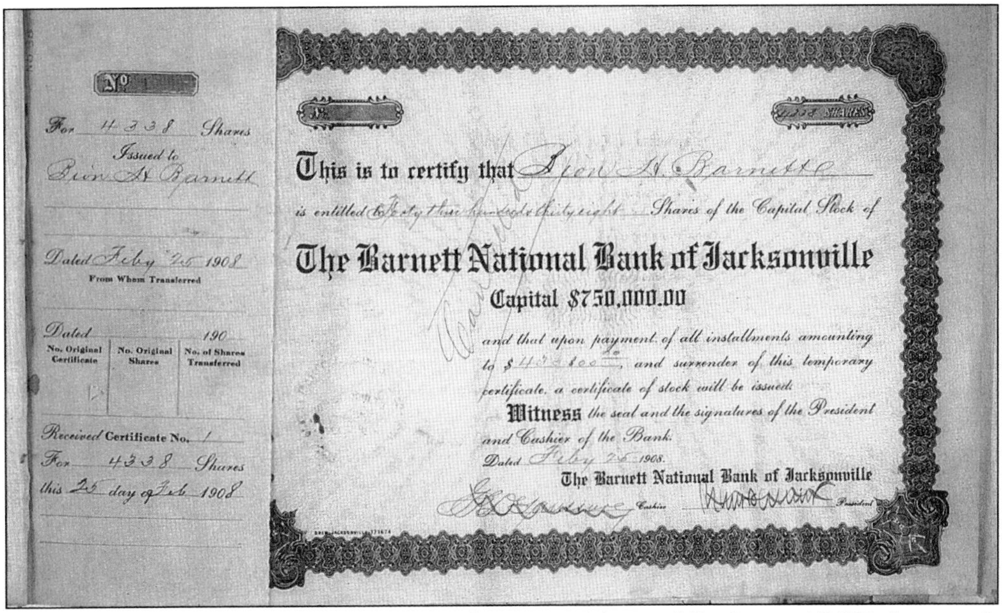
No 1

For 4338 Shares
Issued to
Bion H Barnett

Dated Feby 25 1908
From Whom Transferred

Dated 190

No. Original Certificate	No. Original Shares	No. of Shares Transferred

Received Certificate No. 1
For 4338 Shares
this 25 day of Feb 1908

This is to certify that Bion H. Barnett
is entitled to ... Shares of the Capital Stock of
The Barnett National Bank of Jacksonville
Capital $750,000.00
and that upon payment of all installments amounting to $..., and surrender of this temporary certificate, a certificate of stock will be issued.
Witness the seal and the signatures of the President and Cashier of the Bank.
Dated Feby 25 1908.
The Barnett National Bank of Jacksonville
Cashier President

With the rechartering of the bank in 1908, the Barnett National Bank issued 7,500 shares with a par value of $100. Bion Barnett received certificate number 1 for 4,338 shares. His brother, William D., received certificate number 2 for 2,657 shares.

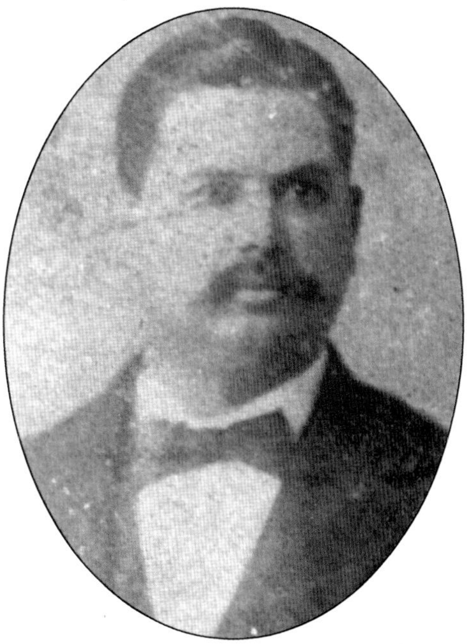

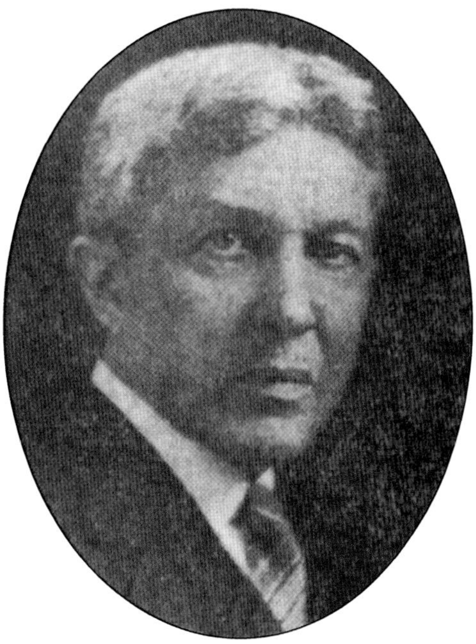

Two forgotten figures from Barnett's history are Frank Adams and Courts P. Kendall. Adams (left) was president of the bank from 1910 to 1918. After Bion Barnett returned to power in 1918, company records never mentioned his name again. Kendall (right) was the bank's principal vice president throughout the early 1920s, when Bion spent most of his time abroad. After Bion selected William R. McQuaid rather than Kendall as president in 1925, he headed the newly created Trust Department. Kendall finally left the bank in 1929. (Adams photo courtesy of Florida State Archives.)

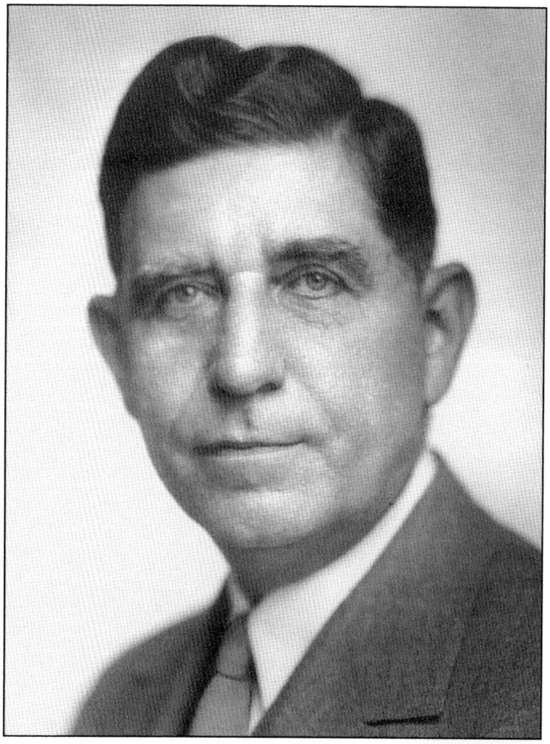

Camillus Saunders L'Engle was a nephew of Lina Barnett, Bion's first wife. He joined the National Bank of Jacksonville in 1902 as a "runner," collecting payments on bad checks. He advanced to become one of its most influential vice presidents. He served on the bank's board of directors from 1918 until his death in 1946. He also was president of the Barnett National Securities Corporation and president of the St. Augustine National Bank. (Photo by Dishinger-Woodward.)

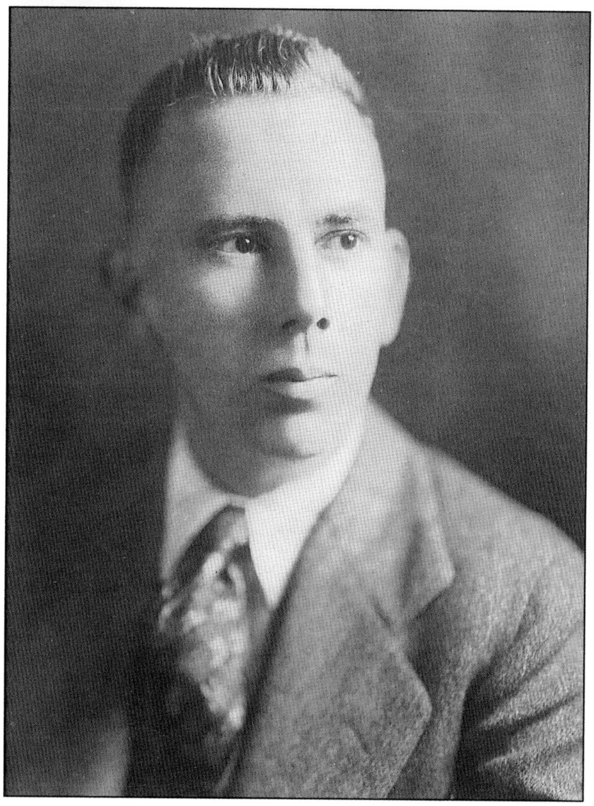

Frank Wisconsin Norris earned both a bachelors and a law degree at the University of North Carolina. Stationed in Jacksonville during World War I, he joined Barnett as a credit clerk in 1918 following his discharge from the Army. Norris organized the bank's first credit department, establishing requirements for obtaining financial statements from borrowing customers and analyzing loan requests. Named an assistant cashier in 1923, he soon became one of the bank's most senior officers.

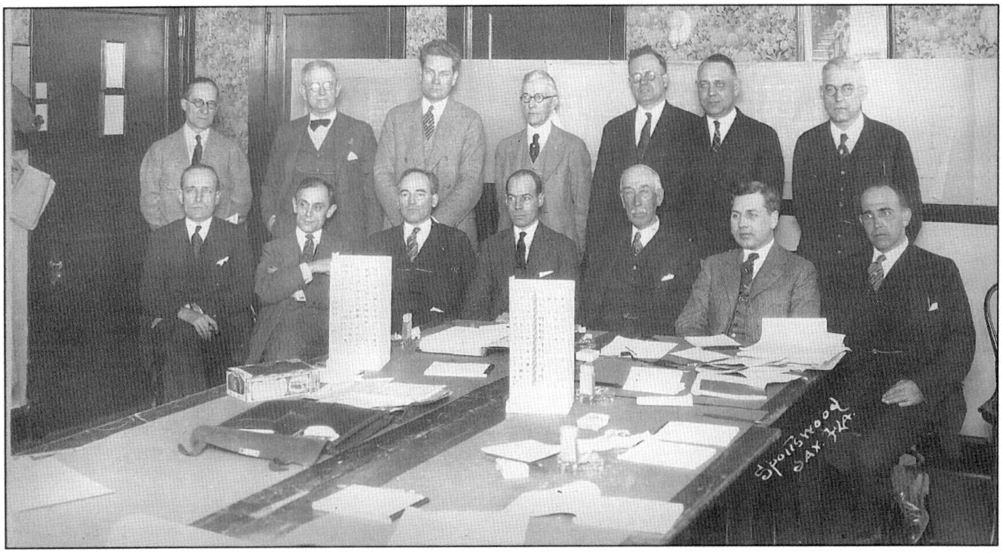

Planning for the construction of a new headquarters building for the Barnett National Bank began in the early 1920s. The bank hired the New York architectural firm of Mowbray and Uffinger, Inc. to design the building. In February 1925, William R. McQuaid (seated far left) and Bion Barnett (seated third from right) hosted a two-day conference at the Hotel Seminole with building managers from a number of major cities to review and critique the architectural plan. (Photo by Jack Spottswood.)

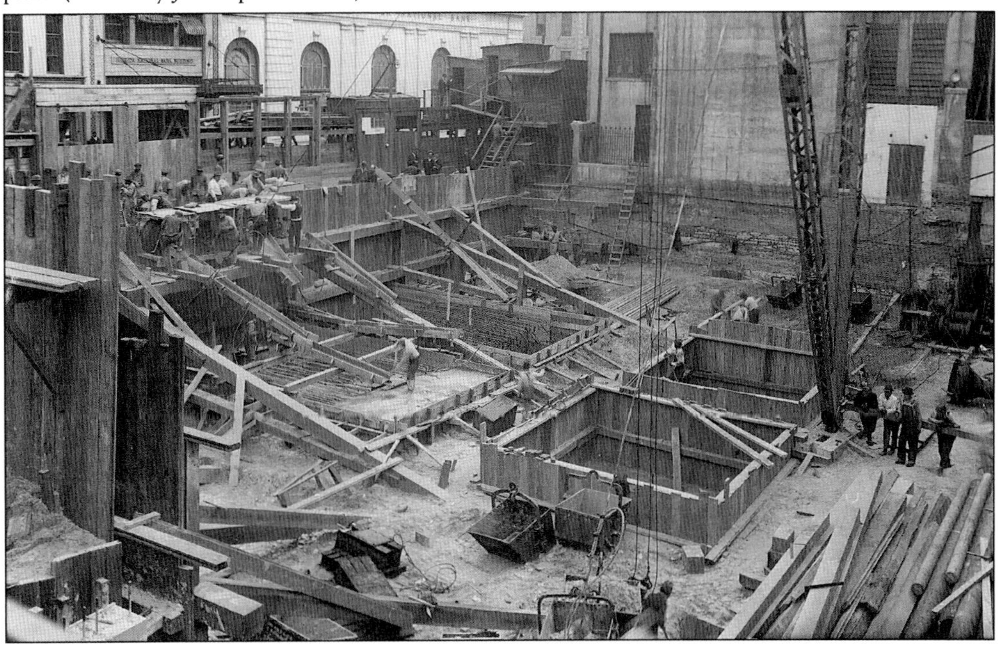

Site work for the construction of the new 18-story headquarters building got underway in November 1925. The Atlantic National Bank Building Annex was located on the adjacent lot to the west on Adams Street. The contractors soon discovered that the foundation of the Atlantic building protruded onto the Barnett property. As the foundations were sunk, the Atlantic building started to list, and there were fears that it might collapse. Delays and litigation ensued. (Photo by O'Brien & Russell.)

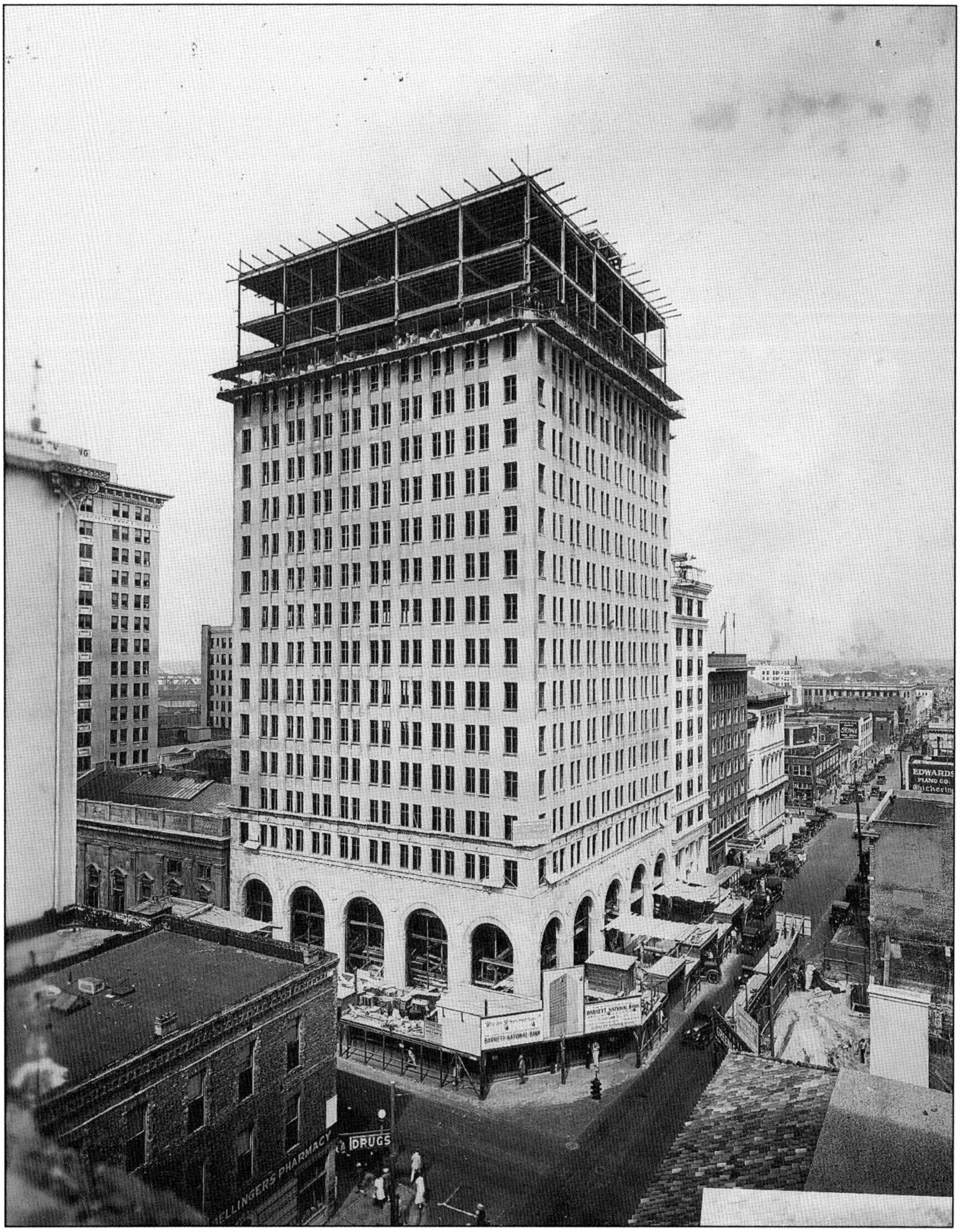

Construction on the new headquarters building at the southwest corner of Adams and Laura Streets began in late February 1926. By May 17th, the 18-story steel frame had been completed after only 76 days, which included many rainy days, holidays, and Sundays. This photo shows the construction in progress, looking west along Adams Street. (Photo by Jack Spottswood.)

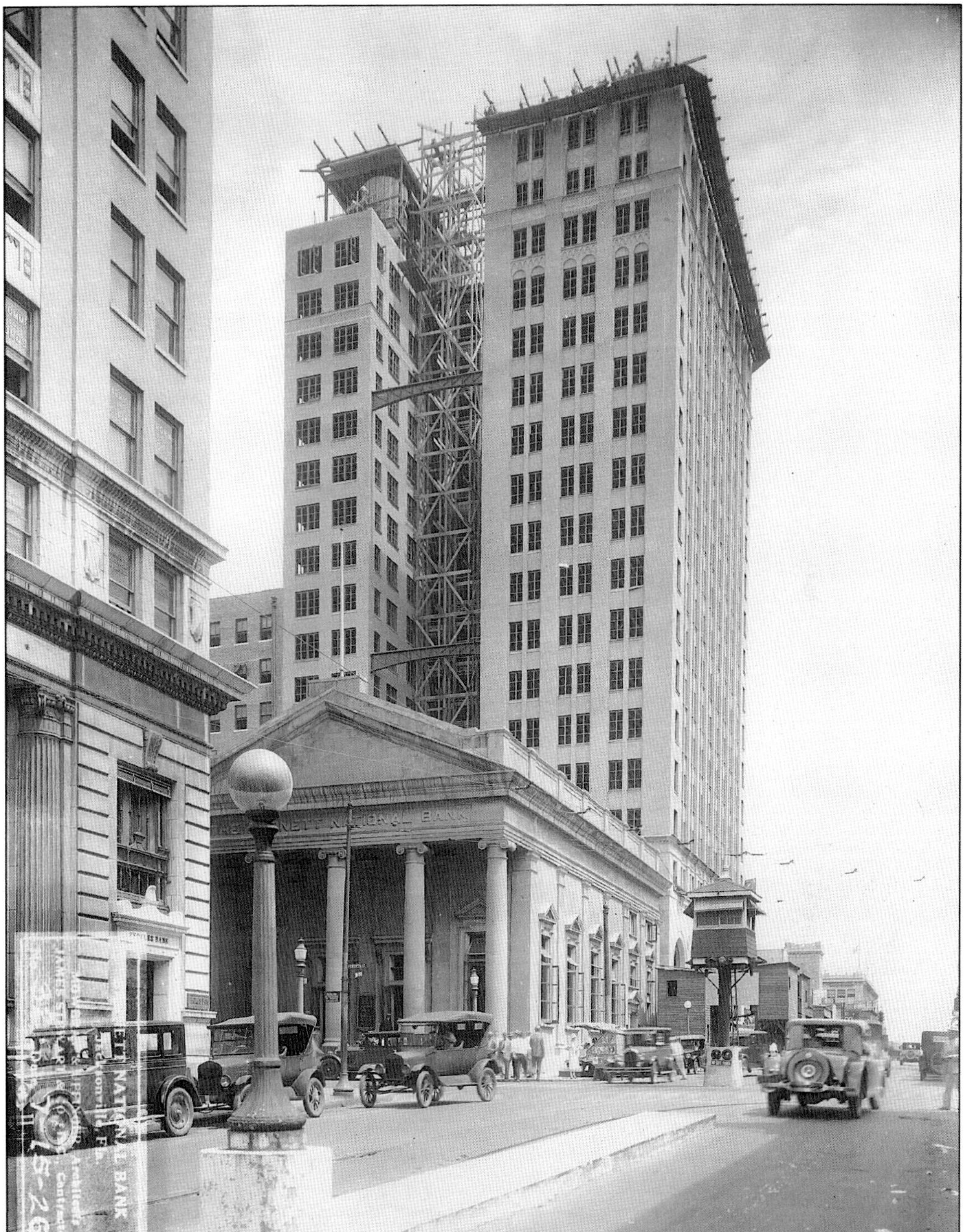

This photo shows the construction, looking north along Laura Street, with the 1898 bank building in the front. The contractor, James Stewart & Company of New York (a prominent firm that had previously built New York City's Madison Square Garden), completed construction on December 1, 1926. Tenants began moving into the offices on the 16 floors above the main banking lobby, and by the bank's grand opening in February 1927, 85% of the available rental space had been occupied. (Photo by O'Brien & Russell.)

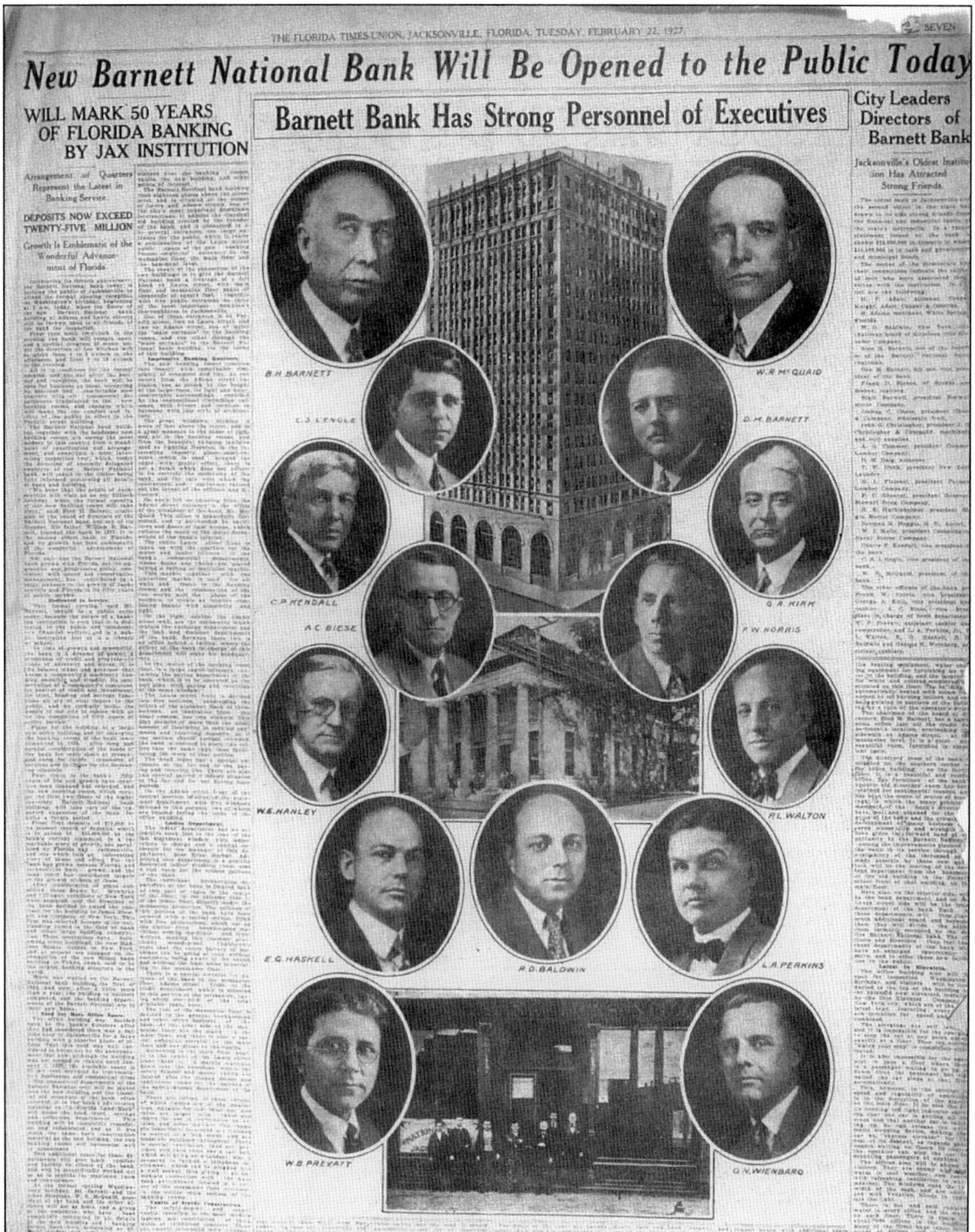

THE FLORIDA TIMES-UNION, JACKSONVILLE, FLORIDA, TUESDAY, FEBRUARY 22, 1927 SEVEN

New Barnett National Bank Will Be Opened to the Public Today

WILL MARK 50 YEARS OF FLORIDA BANKING BY JAX INSTITUTION

Arrangement of Quarters Represent the Latest in Banking Service

DEPOSITS NOW EXCEED TWENTY-FIVE MILLION

Growth Is Emblematic of the Wonderful Advancement of Florida

Barnett Bank Has Strong Personnel of Executives

B.H. BARNETT
W.R. McQUAID
C.S. L'ENGLE
D.M. BARNETT
C.P. KENDALL
G.A. KIRK
A.C. BIESE
F.W. NORRIS
W.E. HANLEY
P.L. WALTON
E.G. HASKELL
R.D. BALDWIN
L.A. PERKINS
W.B. PREVATT
G.N. WIENBARG

City Leaders Directors of Barnett Bank

Jacksonville's Oldest Institution Has Attracted Strong Friends.

The full-page article in the *Florida Times-Union* on February 22, 1927 announced the formal grand opening of the new banking offices, with a reception beginning at 2 p.m. Under the direction of Don Barnett, who headed the Entertainment Committee, the bank spent nearly $10,000 for music, souvenirs, invitations, and other expenses associated with the festivities. Bion Barnett invited the citizens of Jacksonville to visit the bank's new home—"The formal opening should be a public ceremony because the nature of a banking institution is such that it is dedicated to the public and community's financial welfare, and is a public institution just as is a library or school." Specially trained employees acted as guides for visitors, who came in large numbers to view the city's most modern office building.

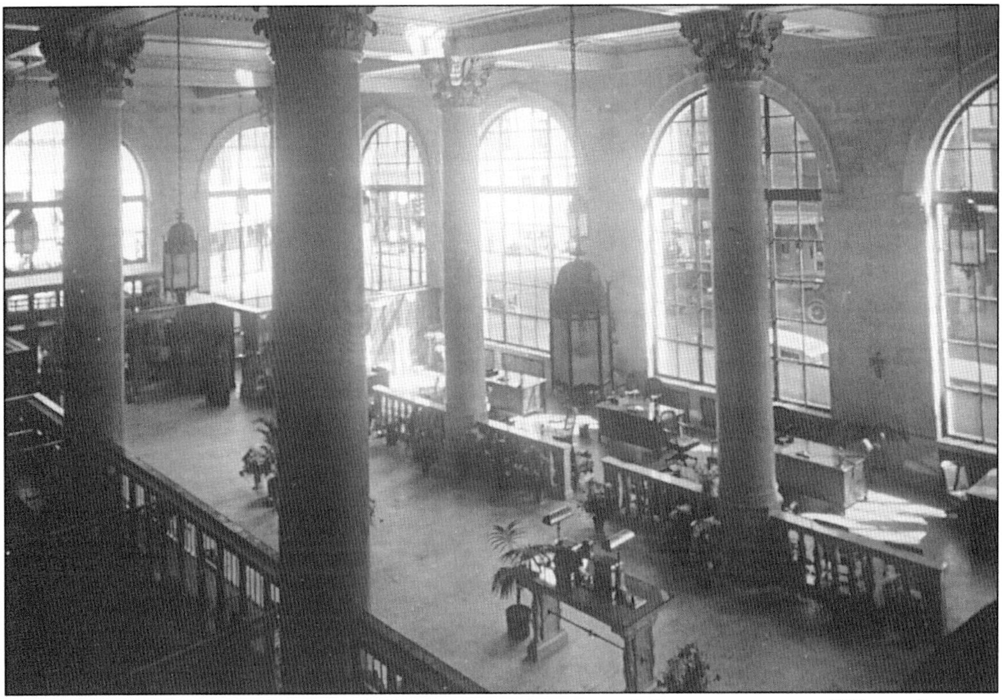

This view of the main banking lobby is from the second-floor mezzanine. When the new banking offices opened, the credit and general bookkeeping departments were located on the mezzanine, together with Bion Barnett's private office.

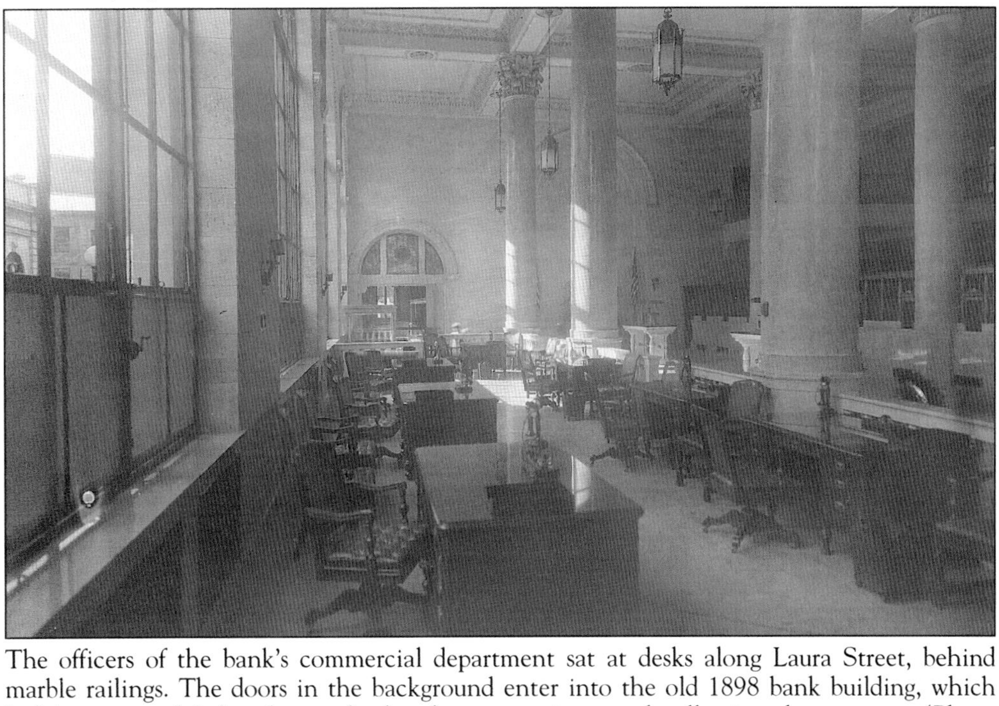

The officers of the bank's commercial department sat at desks along Laura Street, behind marble railings. The doors in the background enter into the old 1898 bank building, which had been remodeled to house the bond, trust, savings, and collection departments. (Photo by Woodward Studio.)

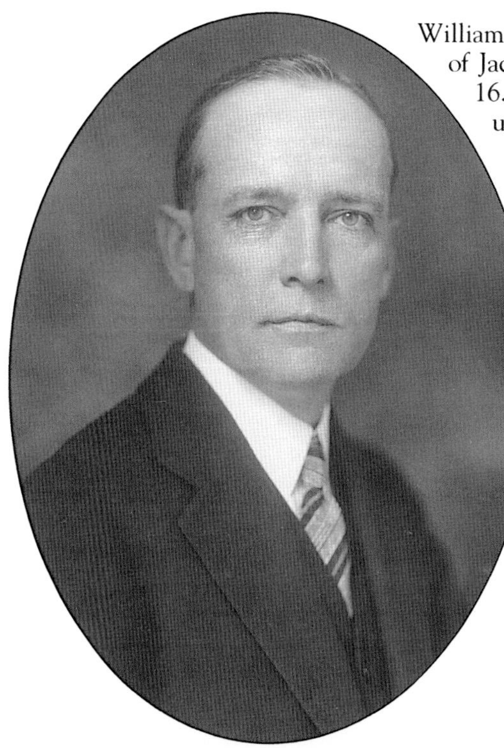

William Ravenel McQuaid joined the National Bank of Jacksonville as a "runner" in 1897 at the age of 16. He worked in increasingly important positions until 1917 when, with the U.S. entry into the First World War, he resigned to enter the Army. Volunteering as a private, he rose to the rank of major. Returning to the bank, Major McQuaid was elected vice president and put on the board of directors. In 1925, he became president, a position he held for the next 27 years. (Courtesy of Woodward Studio.)

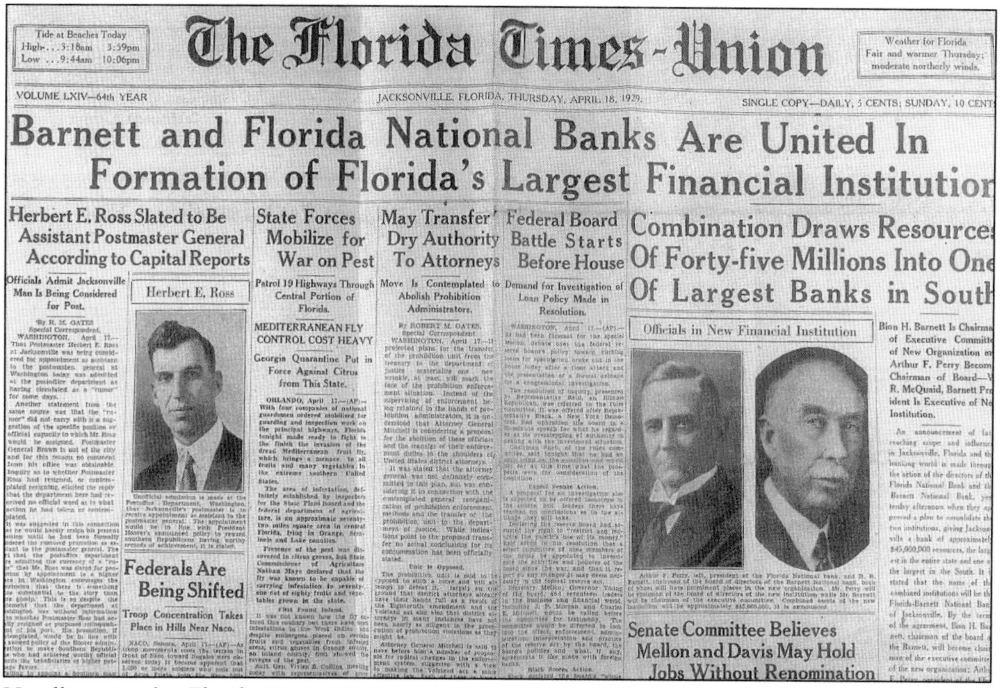

Tide at Beaches Today
High-...3:18am 3:59pm
Low ...9:44am 10:06pm

The Florida Times-Union

Weather for Florida
Fair and warmer Thursday; moderate northerly winds.

VOLUME LXIV—64th YEAR | JACKSONVILLE, FLORIDA, THURSDAY, APRIL 18, 1929. | SINGLE COPY—DAILY, 5 CENTS; SUNDAY, 10 CENT

Barnett and Florida National Banks Are United In Formation of Florida's Largest Financial Institutio

Herbert E. Ross Slated to Be Assistant Postmaster General According to Capital Reports

Officials Admit Jacksonville Man Is Being Considered for Post.

Herbert E. Ross

State Forces Mobilize for War on Pest

Patrol 19 Highways Through Central Portion of Florida.

MEDITERRANEAN FLY CONTROL COST HEAVY

Georgia Quarantine Put in Force Against Citrus from This State.

Federals Are Being Shifted

Troop Concentration Takes Place in Hills Near Naco.

May Transfer Dry Authority To Attorneys

Move Is Contemplated to Abolish Prohibition Administrators.

Federal Board Battle Starts Before House

Demand for Investigation of Loan Policy Made in Resolution.

Combination Draws Resource Of Forty-five Millions Into One Of Largest Banks in South

Officials in New Financial Institution

Bion H. Barnett Is Chairman of Executive Committee of New Organization and Arthur F. Perry Becomes Chairman of Board—W. R. McQuaid, Barnett President Is Executive of New Institution.

Senate Committee Believes Mellon and Davis May Hold Jobs Without Renomination

Headlines in the *Florida Times-Union* announced the proposed merger of Barnett and Florida National Bank. Under the merger agreement, Bion Barnett would become chairman of the Executive Committee of the new institution and "the ranking Officer of the bank." Florida National president Arthur F. Perry would be chairman of the board and McQuaid president.

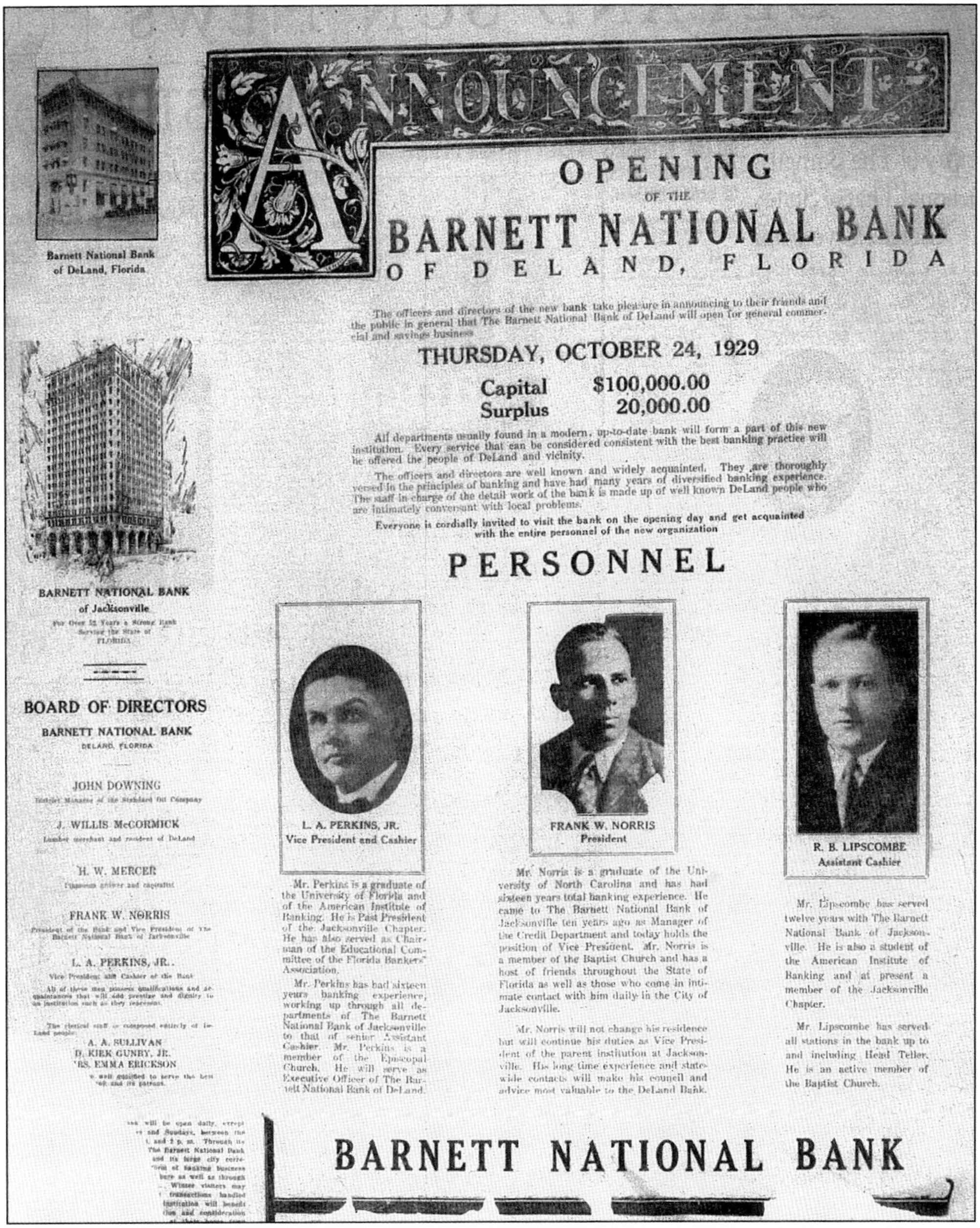

Full-page advertisement in the *DeLand Sun News* announced the opening of the Barnett National Bank of DeLand, the first Barnett affiliate outside of Jacksonville. Frank Norris was named president of the new bank, but he remained in Jacksonville and continued his responsibilities there. Loren A. Perkins Jr., who had worked for Barnett since 1913, moved to DeLand as vice president and cashier to manage the day-to-day operations of the bank. Another Barnett veteran, R. Boone Lipscombe, transferred to the DeLand bank as assistant cashier.

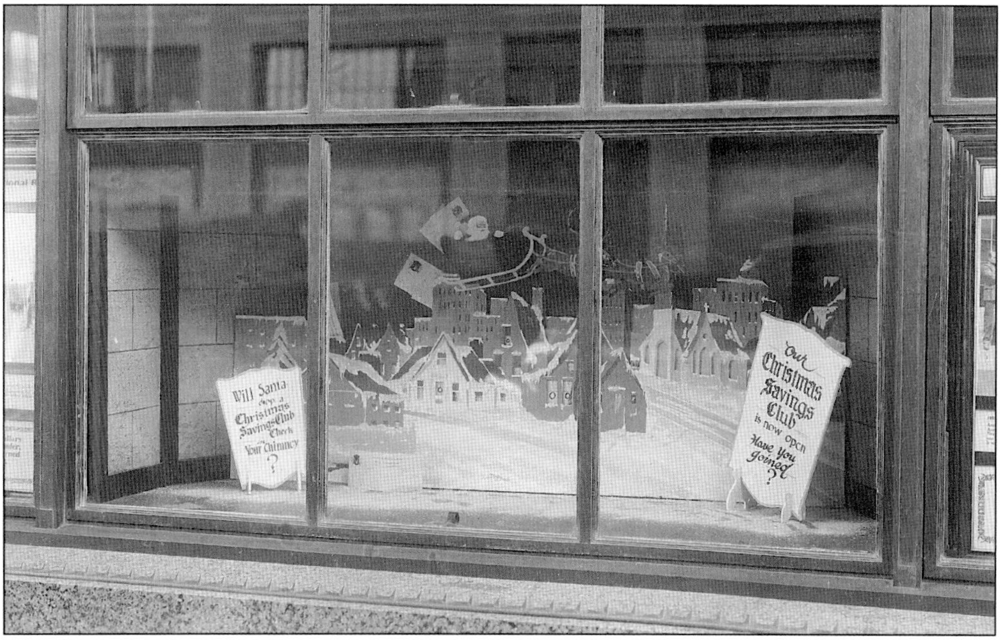

This display in the "Bank Business window" encouraged customers to open a Christmas Savings Club. According to the bank's public relations department, "The snow scene was especially attractive to our Southern citizens."

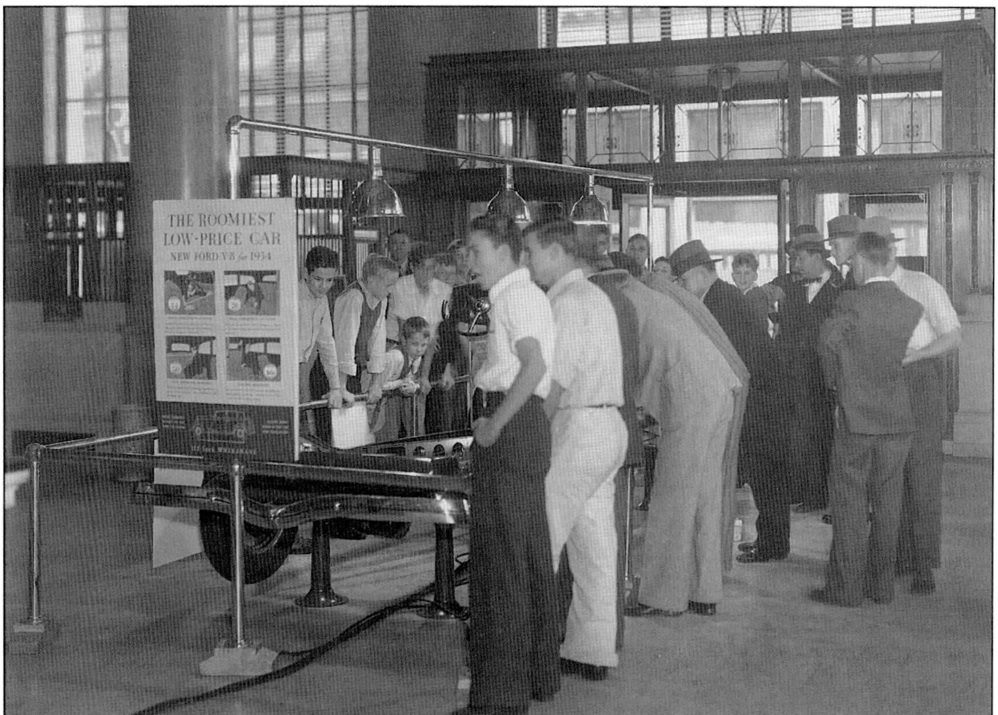

This exhibit of a new 1934 model Ford in the bank lobby attracted considerable interest from both young and old. (Photo by Jack Spottswood.)

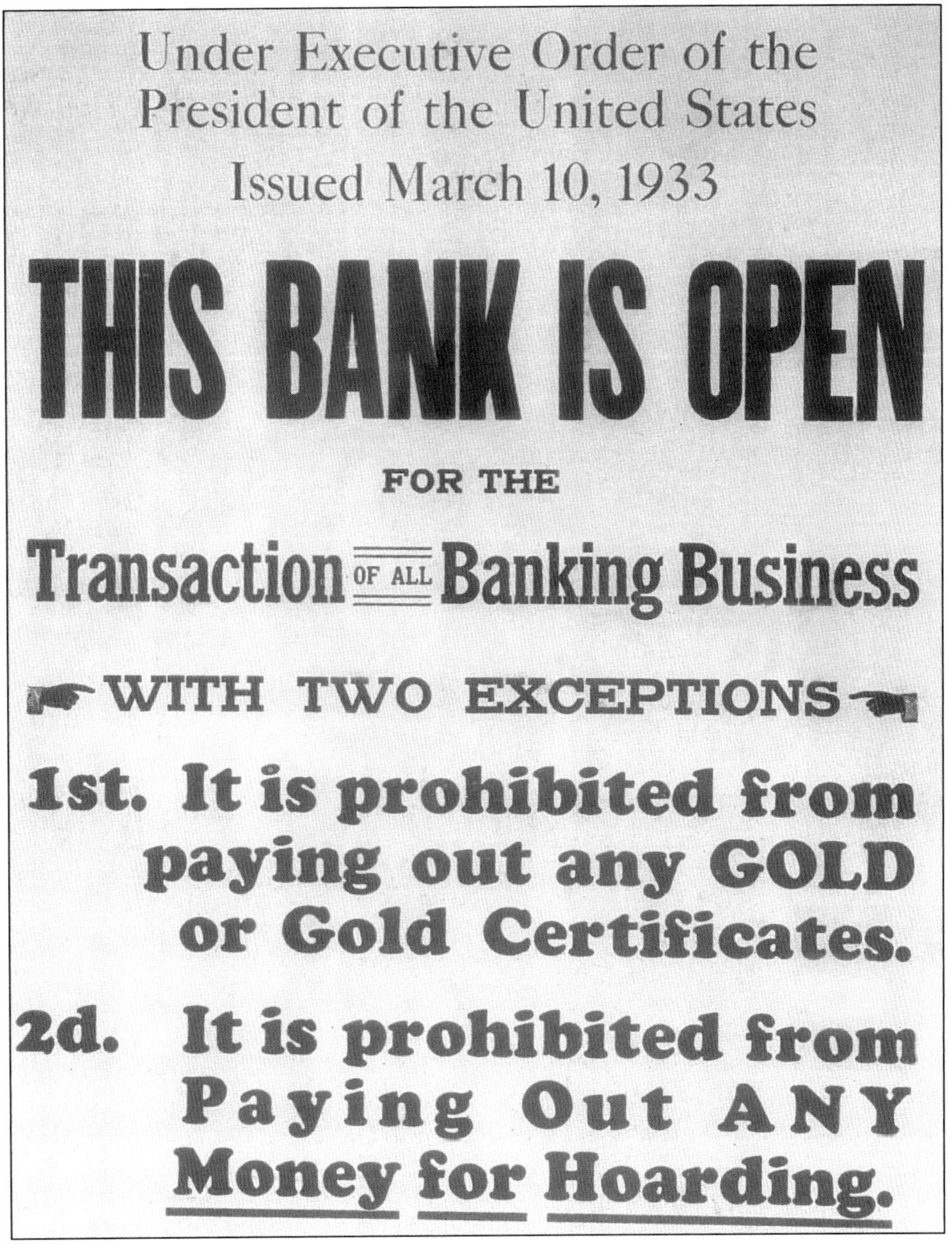

This sign announced the reopening of the Barnett National Bank of Jacksonville following the national "bank holiday" declared by President Franklin Roosevelt on March 6th. Following congressional passage of the Emergency Banking Act of 1933, Roosevelt authorized the secretary of the treasury to reopen banks that belonged to the Federal Reserve System, provided that the District Reserve banks endorsed their soundness. On March 13th, the Federal Reserve Bank of Atlanta announced that it had issued licenses to 56 Southern banks to resume normal operations. The following day, Barnett and other banks in the city reopened. The headline in the *Florida Times-Union* read, "Era of Fear is Ended As Deposits Mount In Sound Banks of Nation."

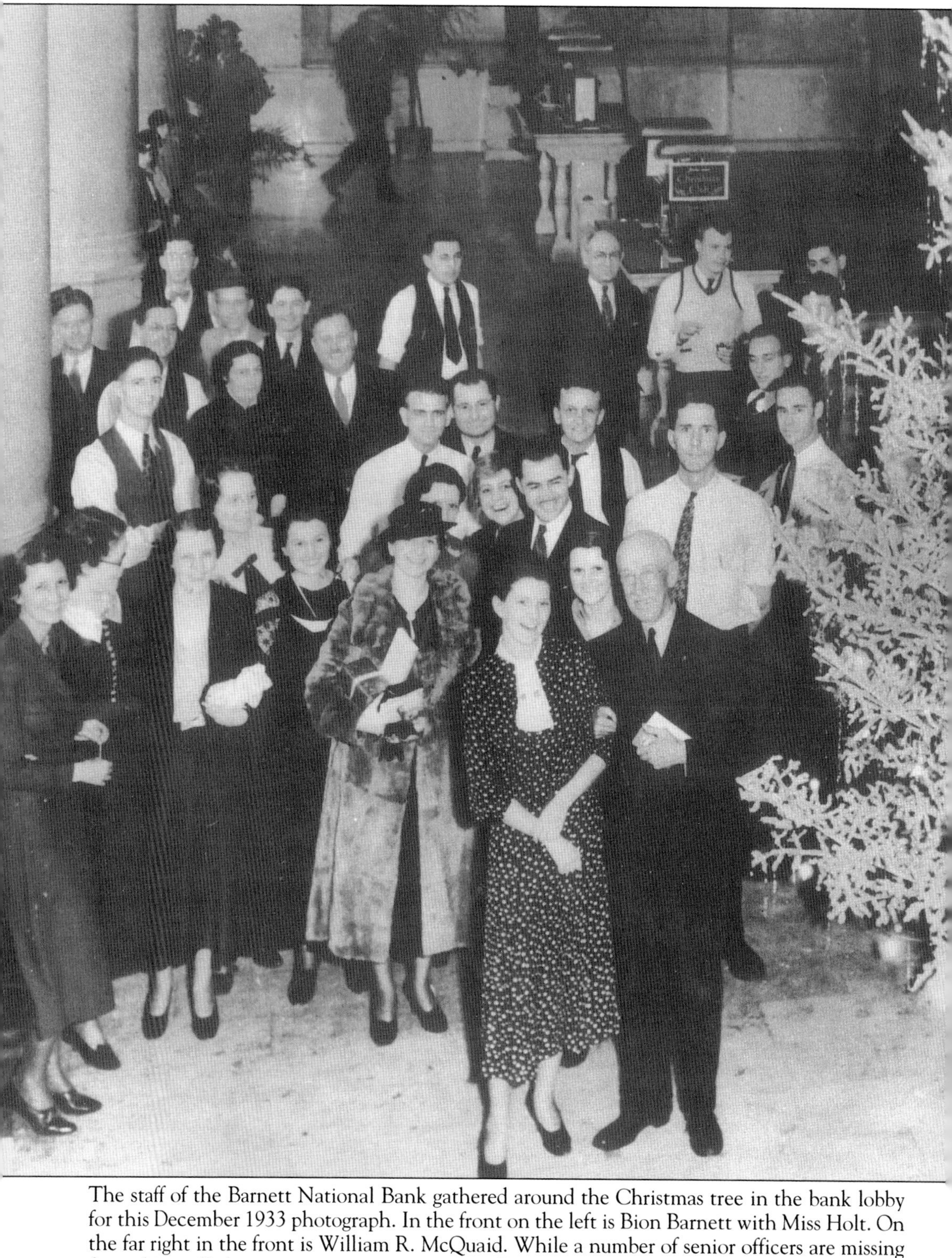

The staff of the Barnett National Bank gathered around the Christmas tree in the bank lobby for this December 1933 photograph. In the front on the left is Bion Barnett with Miss Holt. On the far right in the front is William R. McQuaid. While a number of senior officers are missing from this staff photo, executive vice president Don Barnett, vice president Camillus L'Engle,

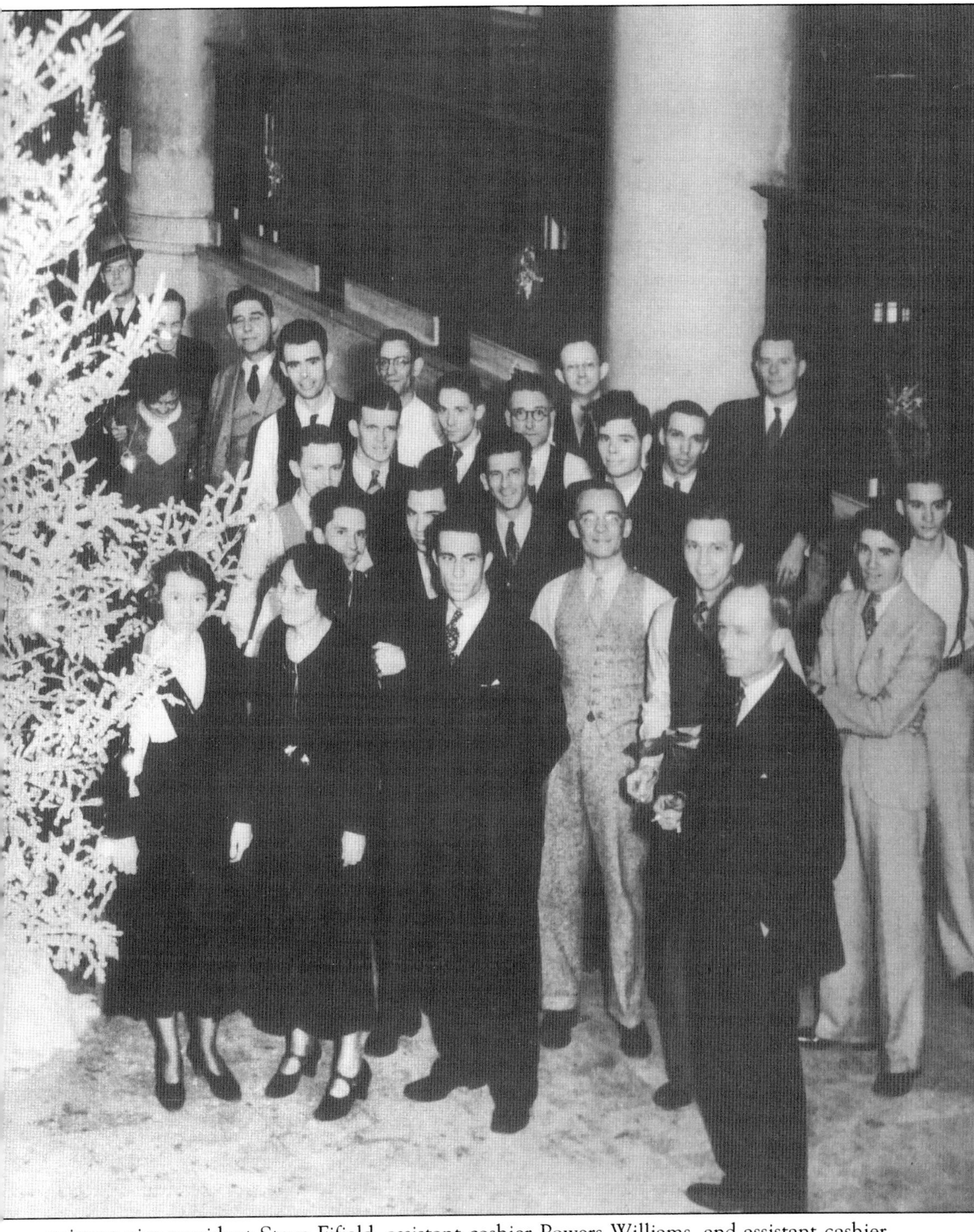

assistant vice president Steve Fifield, assistant cashier Powers Williams, and assistant cashier George Wienbarg are present. Among the clerical staff, several destined for distinguished Barnett careers are pictured, including Bill Barnett, Ed Clements, Jim Condra, LeRoy Gardner, Herb Hart, Bert Haynes, and Charlie Robinson.

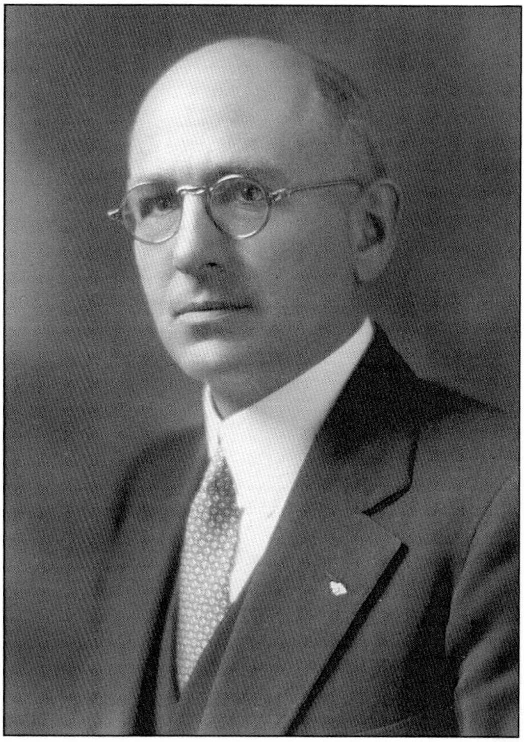

Stephen H. Fifield, an Iowa native, began his banking career in 1904 as an office boy with the Schenectady (New York) Savings Bank. He spent 20 years with the bank before joining the First National Bank of Bradenton as the assistant to the president in charge of advertising and new business. He joined Barnett in 1929 and directed the bank's public relations and business development efforts for the next 25 years. (Photo by Woodward Studio.)

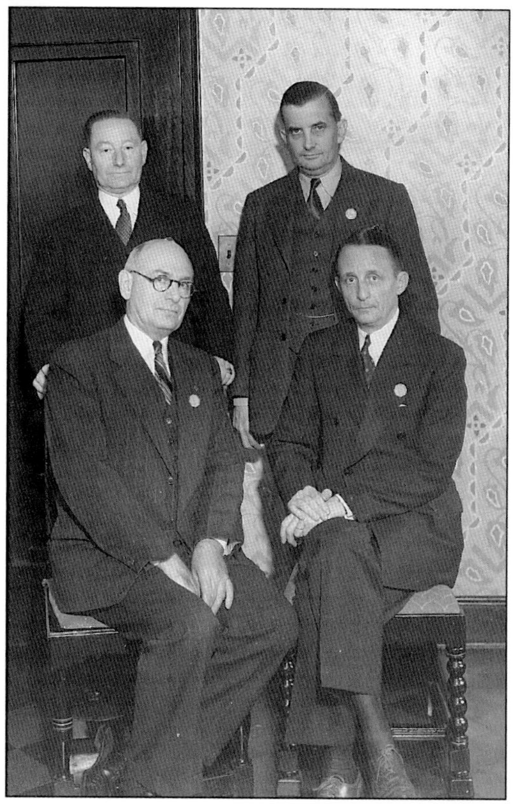

Fifield gained a national reputation through his activities with the Financial Advertisers Association (FAA). At its annual convention in Toronto in September 1939, the FAA elected Fifield president. He is pictured with the other newly elected officers. Seated next to him is incoming first vice president Robert J. Isant (Central National Bank, Cleveland). Standing on the left is third vice president L.E. Townsend (Bank of America, San Francisco), and on the right is second vice president Victor Cullen (Mississippi Valley Trust Company, St. Louis). (Photo by E. Mackintosh.)

After serving in World War I, Sam S. Conoly became a court reporter and was admitted to the Georgia bar. He moved to Jacksonville in 1925 to become secretary of the Consolidated Land Company. With the encouragement of Consolidated president William J. Kelly (a Barnett director), Conoly joined the Barnett National Bank in 1928.

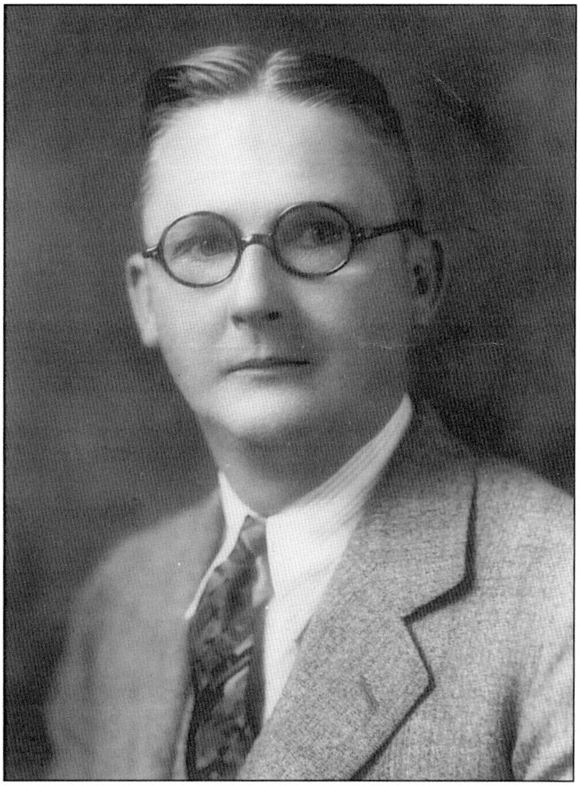

After joining Barnett, Conoly spent his first year training at Chemical Bank in New York and several other Eastern banks, learning about trust operations. In 1929, he replaced C.P. Kendall as head of Barnett's Trust Department. He remained as the bank's senior trust officer for the next 37 years. During the last three years of his Barnett career (1963–1965), Conoly was a member of the bank's board of directors. (Photo by J. Gordon Spottswood.)

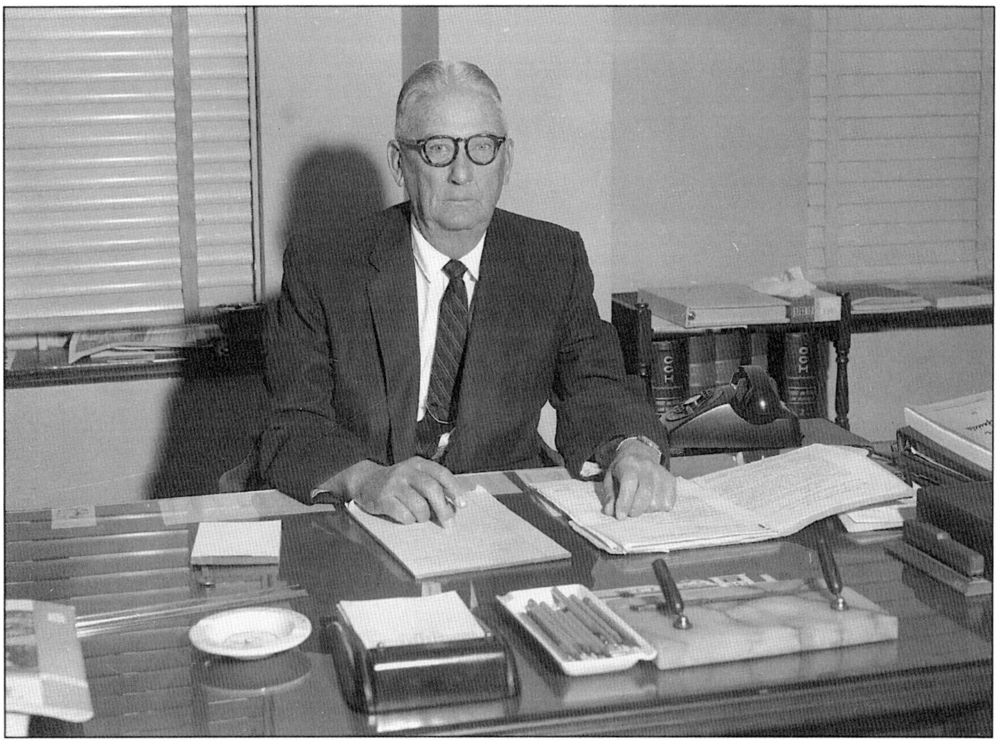

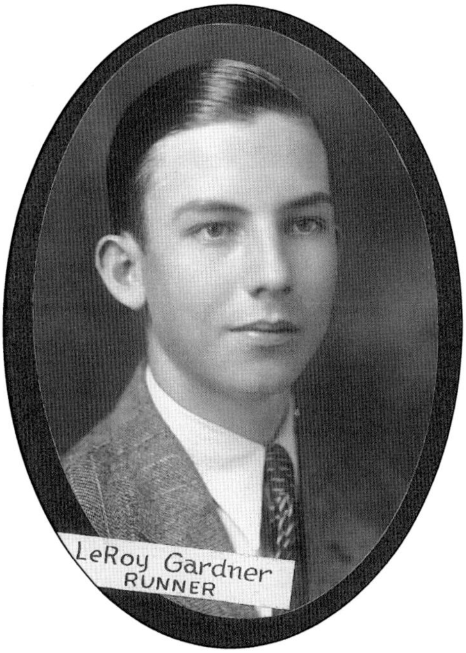

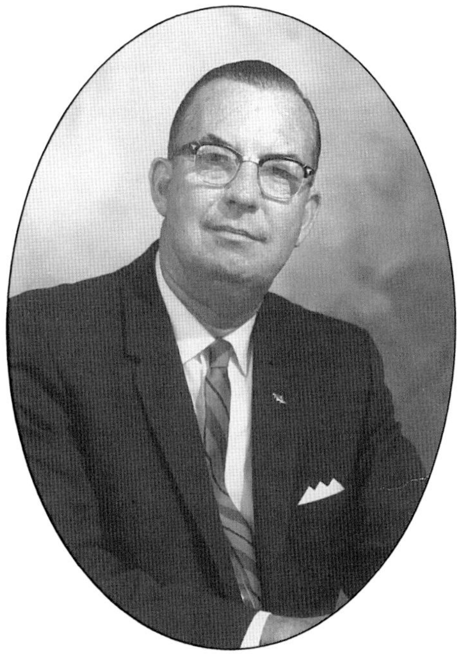

LeRoy Gardner had a 40-year career with Barnett. Starting as an office boy in 1928, he rose to be chairman of the San Jose Barnett Bank and a director of the Barnett National Securities Corporation. He headed Barnett's Installment Loan Department from 1954 to 1968. Expressing regret at Gardner's sudden death, the 1968 Annual Report concluded, "It was under his guidance that we became a leader in consumer lending." (Photo by Charles Smith Studio.)

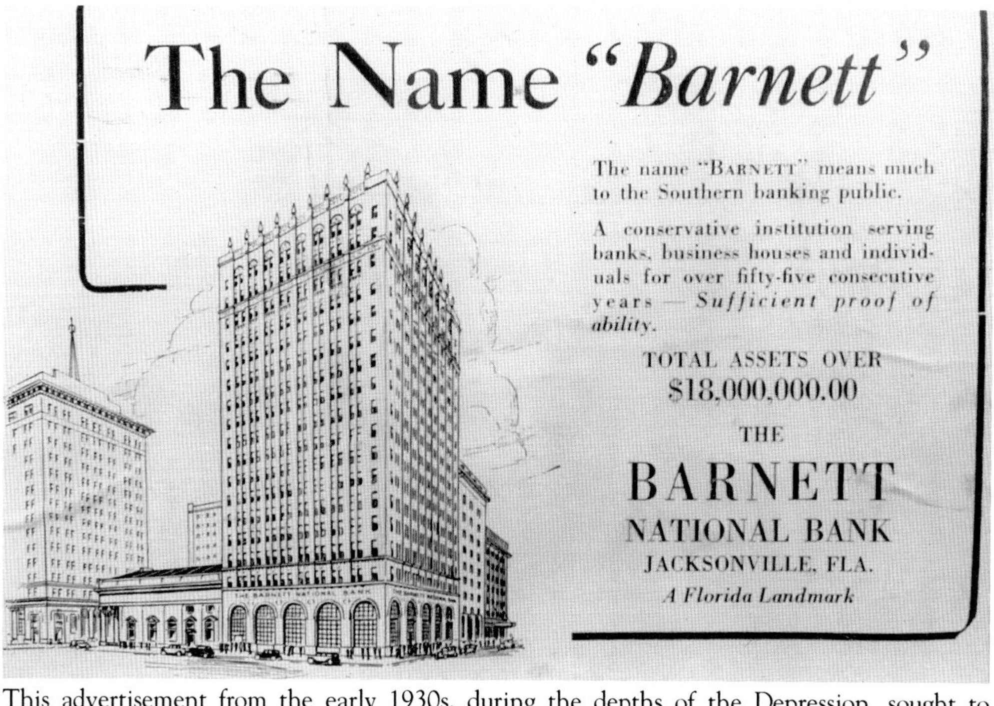

This advertisement from the early 1930s, during the depths of the Depression, sought to emphasize the bank's financial strength.

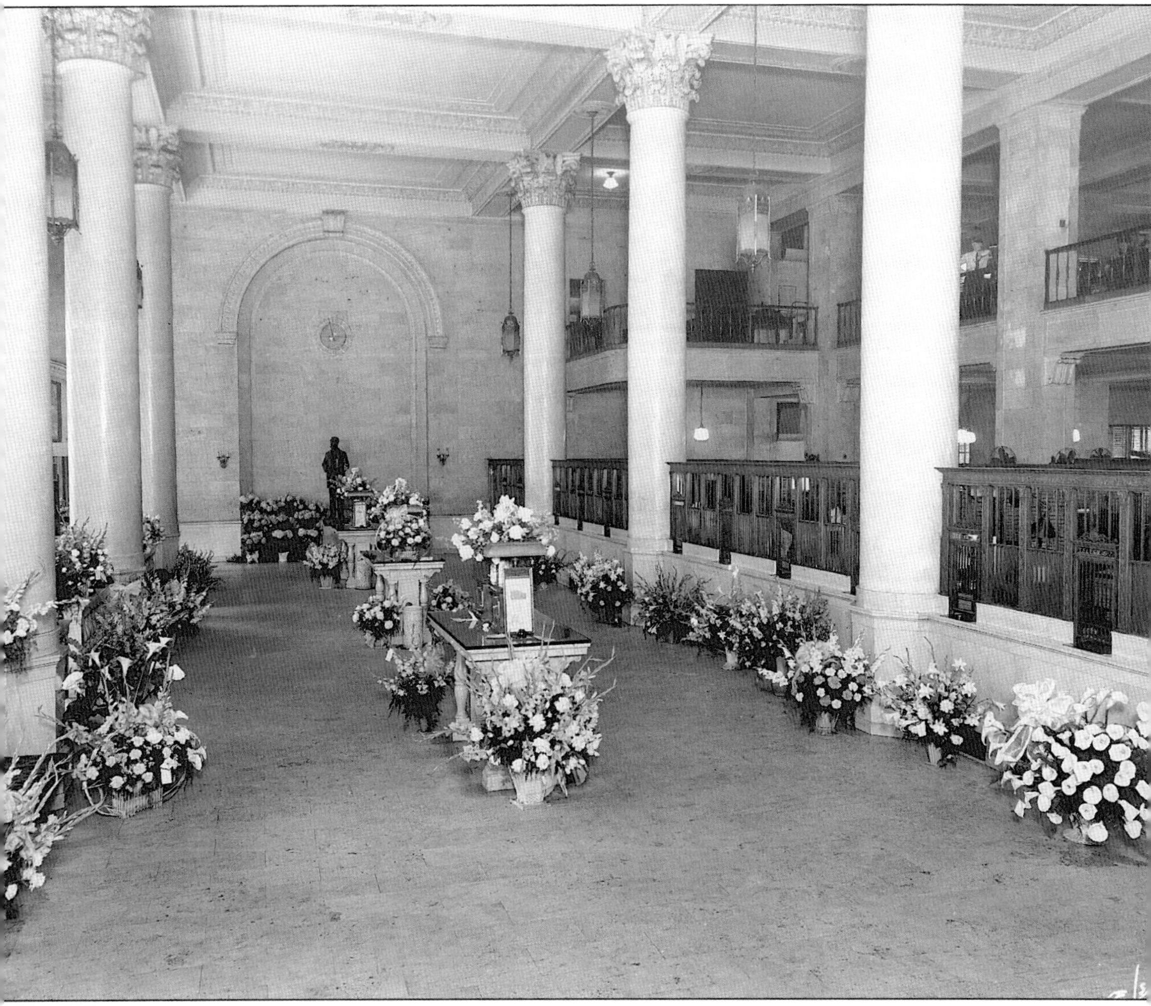

Flowers decorate the main lobby of the Barnett National Bank, May 7, 1937, on the bank's 60th anniversary. The caged enclosures on the right are for the paying and receiving tellers. Note that the teller cages are subdivided by the alphabet. The teller window on the far right is for customers whose last names begin with the letters S through Z. (Photo by Eisner.)

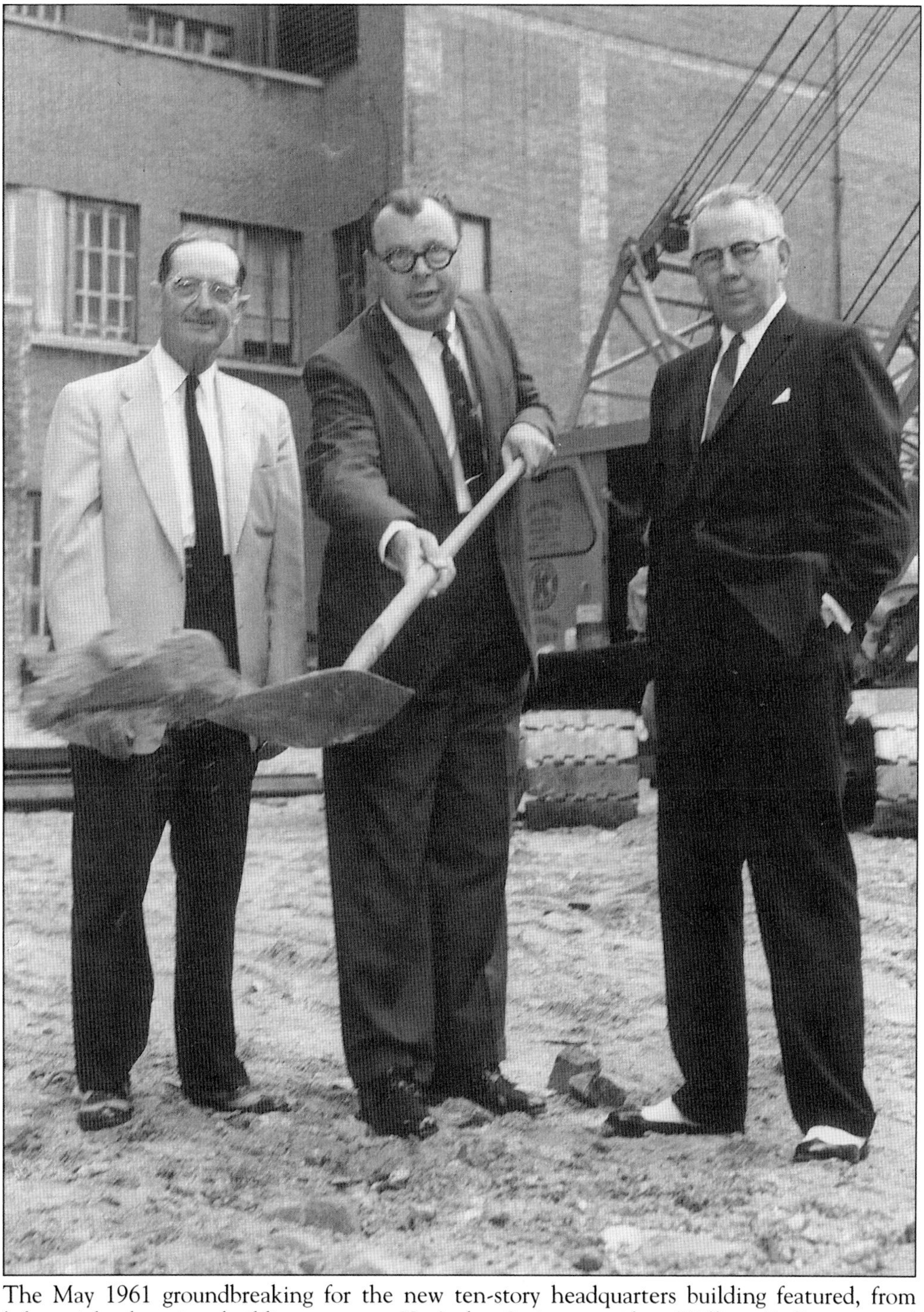

The May 1961 groundbreaking for the new ten-story headquarters building featured, from left to right, longtime building manager H. Arthur Irving, president William R. Barnett, and chairman Frank W. Norris. (Courtesy of *Florida Times-Union*.)

Four

The War Years and Beyond: 1940 to 1963

In October 1940, the United States Navy commissioned the Jacksonville Naval Air Station (NAS), and construction of this military installation stimulated local business and employment. With the subsequent establishment of the Mayport Naval Station and Cecil Field (together with the Army training facility at nearby Camp Blanding), Jacksonville became a major military center. At the height of the Second World War, the military stationed more than 42,000 servicemen at Jacksonville NAS, and the base employed 11,000 civilian workers. Shipbuilding and other wartime industrial production attracted thousands of job seekers to Jacksonville. Similar wartime expansion took place throughout Florida, which became home to numerous military training sites and defense-related industrial plants.

The military buildup converted widespread Depression-era joblessness to a full-employment economy. The Barnett National Bank and its subsidiary banks shared in the wartime prosperity, although new challenges arose. While the Jacksonville bank's deposits more than tripled during the war years to $87 million, the increase in deposit transactions and other banking services (including the sale of war bonds) was accompanied by severe clerical problems. Many employees joined the military, and others left for better-paying defense and manufacturing jobs. Staff turnover exceeded 100% in both 1942 and 1943. It became increasingly difficult to find competent staff, with government-ordered wage controls preventing salary levels from keeping pace with rising living costs. During the war years, the bank found itself struggling to conform with government regulations and increased paperwork, from wage and hour laws that governed overtime pay to the introduction of the withholding system for collecting income taxes on wages and salaries.

The end of the war in the summer of 1945 brought an abrupt end to wartime spending. The subsequent dislocation caused by efforts to convert back to a peacetime economy led to sluggish activity and declining deposits for several years at Barnett and other banks throughout Florida. Beginning in 1949, however, the Barnett National Bank of Jacksonville began a steady growth that by 1960 had reached $142 million in assets and $129 million in deposits. Throughout these years, the bank reported consistent profitability, and in 1959, for the first time, exceeded $1 million in operating profits.

The operating results of the Barnett National Bank of Jacksonville and its four affiliated banks during the 1950s were solid but not exceptional. In fact, if one placed the bank's performance in the context of the phenomenal growth and dramatic demographic changes taking place in Florida, one might consider it a decade of missed opportunities. During the 1950s, the large-scale migration to Florida that had begun in the 1940s accelerated—the state's population grew by 79%, from 2.8 million in 1950 to 5 million residents in 1960. Yet Barnett made no effort to open new banks in high-growth areas. Its only expansion occurred with the 1956 opening of a newly chartered bank on the west side of Jacksonville, the Barnett Bank of Murray Hill.

The post-war years, however, did see a number of far-ranging changes at Barnett. Women had come to dominate the employee ranks during the war, as men, unless too old or infirm, went into the armed services. Prior to the war, 27% of the clerical staff were women; by the end of 1943, 75% percent were women. But there were no women officers until 1947 when the bank elected Miss O. Kathryn "Kitty" Bell as assistant cashier. Bell specialized in commercial lending and, in 1956, became a vice president. She paved the way for other women at Barnett and, by 1960, six out of the Jacksonville bank's 52 officers were women.

Prior to the war, Barnett, like most banks, had focused its operations on commercial activity and meeting the needs of businesses and their owners. It had largely avoided consumer lending. As early as 1936, Don Barnett had suggested establishing a Small Personal Loan Department, but his father disapproved of the idea. Not until 1946 did Barnett establish an automobile finance department. While initially focusing on providing credit services to automobile dealerships, the department's activities soon expanded to include a wide variety of monthly installment payment loans for appliances, automobiles, boats, motors, heavy equipment, and home improvements. Later renamed the Installment Loan Department, it grew from two employees in 1946 to 25 employees and approximately 13,000 accounts by 1960.

During these years, Barnett began to address the most important invention to affect the entire state of Florida—air conditioning. In 1950, the bank installed air conditioning for the main banking areas of the Barnett National Bank Building and, three years later, for the top 15 stories so as not to lose tenants to newer office buildings being constructed downtown. In 1957, the bank introduced its first computers, installing a primitive punch card system to track stock transfers and other record keeping functions for the Trust Department. Soon, high-speed electronic equipment to scan and sort the magnetic ink character recognition (MICR) encoded on the bottom of checks was added, a major advance over the cumbersome manual, alphabetical sorting of checks by the names of the account holders.

While the emerging technology, still somewhat primitive, promised to dramatically transform the banking industry, perhaps the most significant events of the post-war years centered around management changes. Many long-term senior officers with 30, 40, or more years of service retired. Bion Barnett finally retired in 1952, after 68 years with the bank, and six years later his successor as chairman, William R. McQuaid, stepped down after 60 years. Frank W. Norris was then elevated to chairman and chief executive officer in 1958, and William R. (Bill) Barnett, Bion's great nephew, to president.

Over the next five years, two major events dominated management's attention. First, a new banking facility was needed, with drive-ins, additional space for computers and other back room functions, and modern office conveniences. In 1961, the old bank building, first opened in 1898, was razed along with several adjoining buildings that had been purchased. A new ten-story headquarters building was constructed on the site and opened in November 1962. Meanwhile, Norris and Bill Barnett had been engaged in secret negotiations with three other Florida banks—the First National Bank of Miami (later Southeast), First National Bank at Orlando (later Sun), and Exchange Bank of Tampa. In November 1961, the four banks announced that they had agreed to join together to form a new bank holding company, First Bancorporation of Florida, Inc. Headquartered in Orlando, the banking group would have combined deposits of $600 million, making it the eighth-largest bank holding company in the nation. The following July, however, the Federal Reserve Board rejected the proposed merger, allegedly because of its adverse effect on competition. One can only speculate about what would have happened to Florida banking if the merger had been approved.

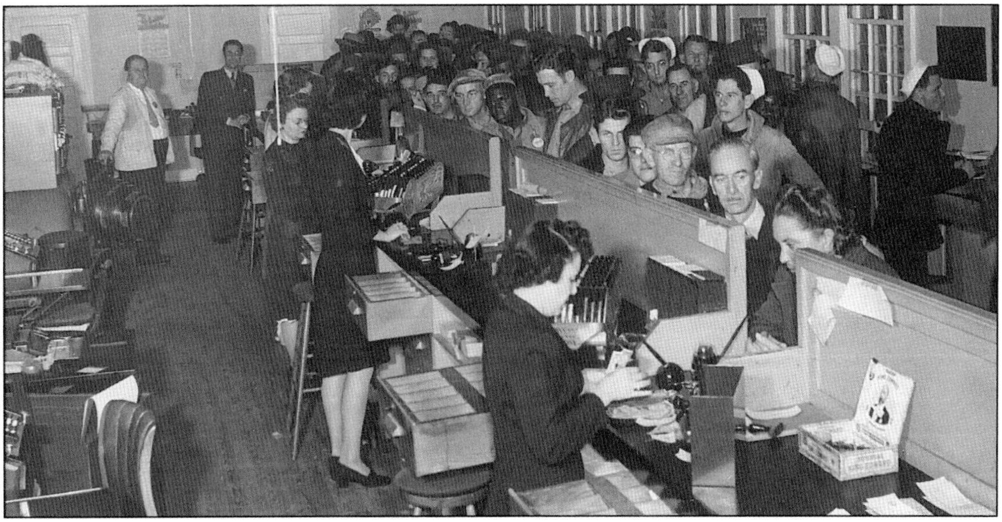

In July 1943, Barnett opened a satellite facility at the Jacksonville Naval Air Station. Although Florida law prohibited branch banking, limited service offices restricted to cashing checks, accepting deposits, and performing other routine bank services were permitted on military installations. During the war years, the NAS office cashed an estimated 50,000 to 60,000 checks each month. This photograph shows an inside view of the office on a January 1946 payday. (Courtesy of U.S. Navy.)

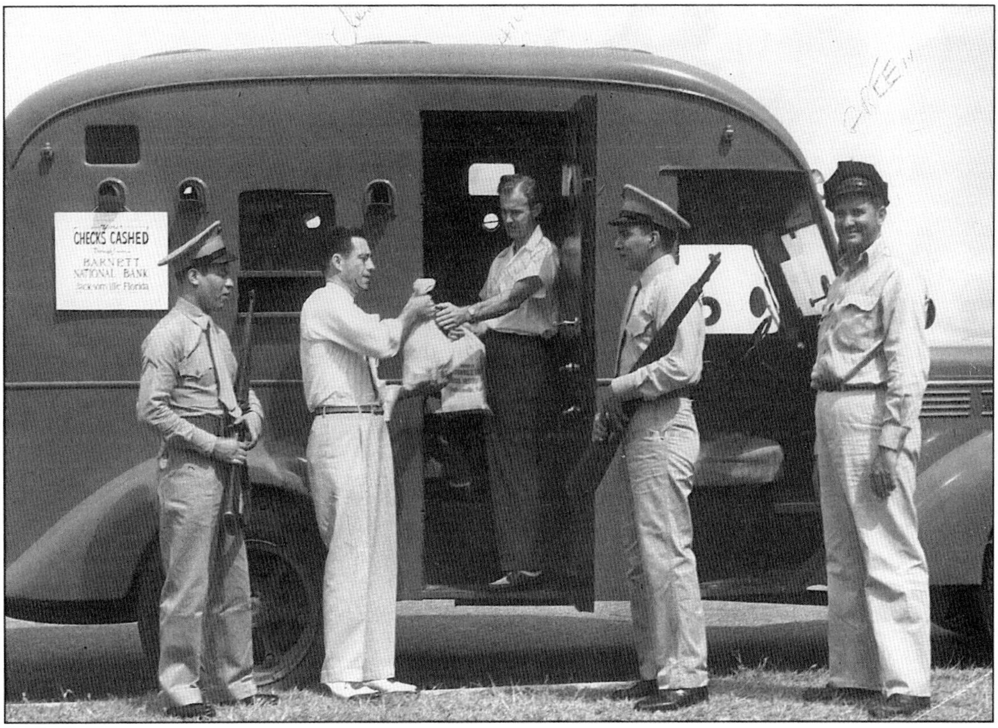

NAS manager Ed Clements loads an armored truck in October 1948. The truck traveled around the base to cash checks on paydays. Clements, who had begun working at Barnett in 1925, was named manager of the NAS office when it opened in 1943 and continued to manage the facility until his retirement in 1969. (Courtesy of U.S. Navy.)

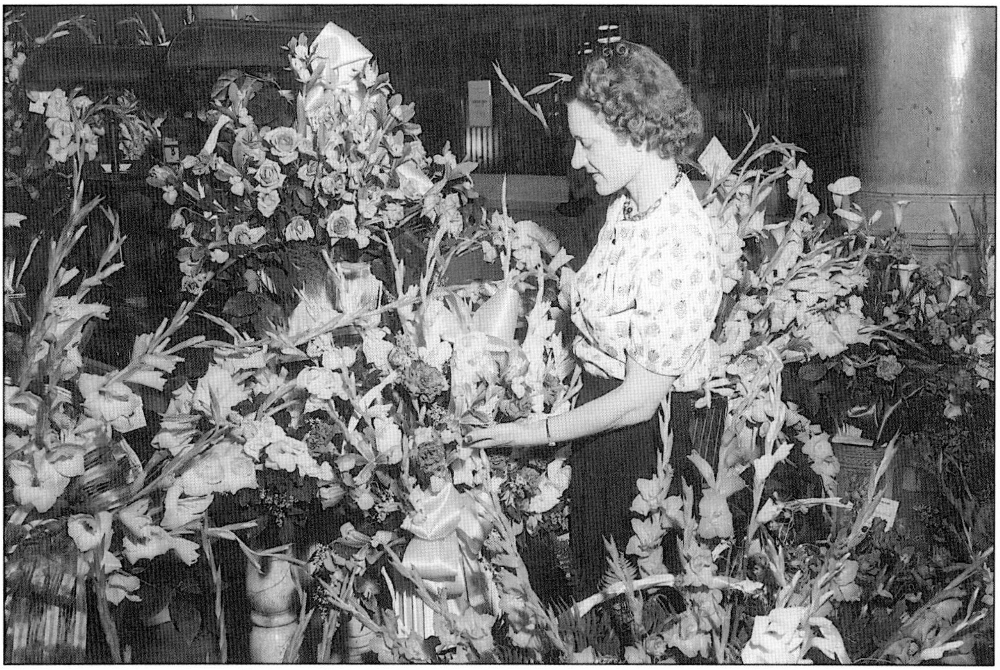

O. Kathryn "Kitty" Bell joined Barnett in 1937 as a stenographer. In 1947, the bank elected Miss Bell as assistant cashier, its first woman officer. She was very active in the National Association of Bank Women and other banking organizations. She was one of four women officers who were the first graduates, in 1955, of the School of Banking of the South at Louisiana State University, the first graduate-level banking school to admit women. (Photo by C.H. Brown Co.)

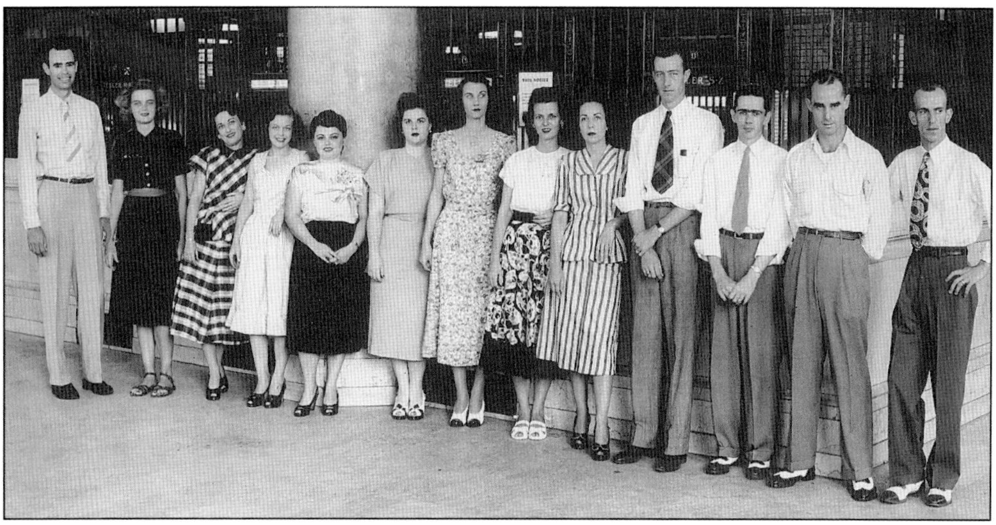

Charles T. Robinson (far left) headed Barnett's staff of tellers in the mid-1940s. From left to right are Robinson, Kathryn Regas, Eileen Masser, Ruby Lane, Ester Tucker, Charlotte Patterson, Gladys S. Hornage, Jeanne Cox, Betty Armstrong, Robert Brown, Eugene Stanley, Robert Oliver, and Duane Borman. Several years afterwards, Robinson was promoted from head teller to assistant cashier in the correspondent bank department. He later headed the correspondent division and, in the early 1970s, was BBFI vice president of commercial loans.

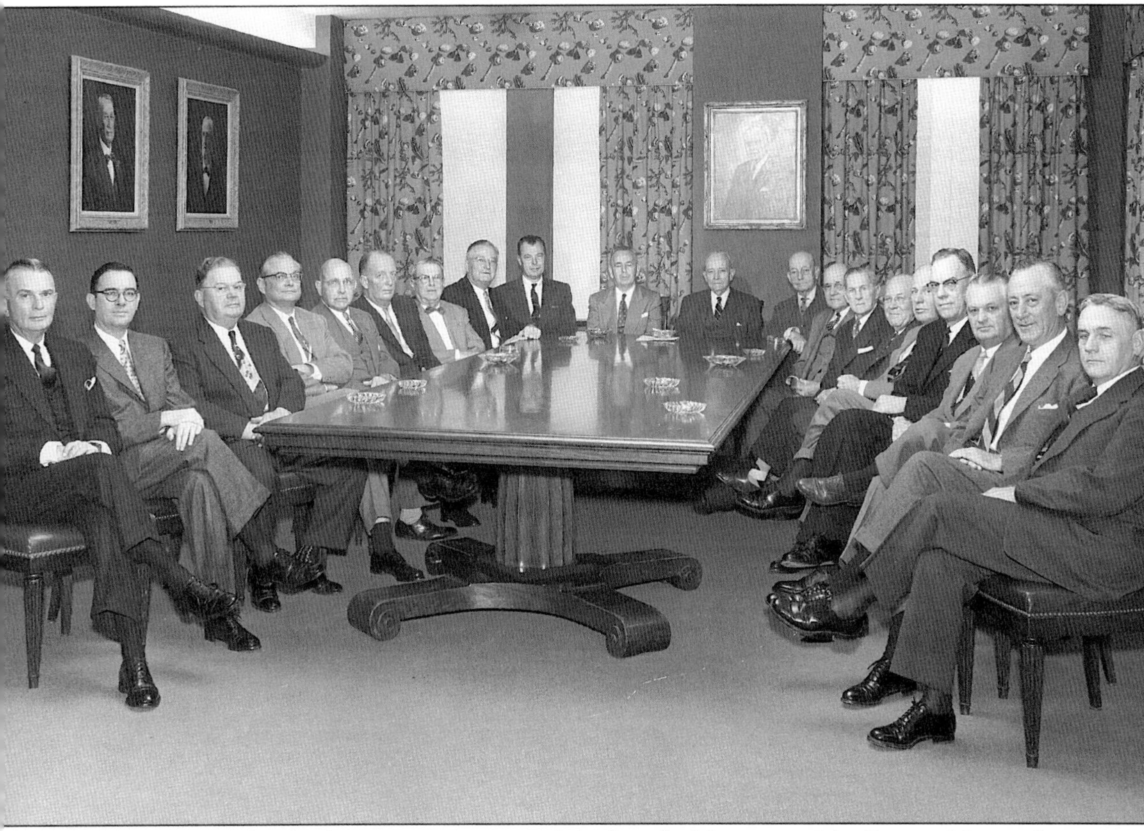

Some of Jacksonville's leading citizens comprised the board of directors of the Barnett National Bank. Pictured in this December 1955 photo, from left to right, are Clifford G. Schultz (Greyhound Corp.), Guy W. Botts (attorney), C.G. McGehee (Jacksonville Paper Co.), Lloyd Smith (attorney), Frank D. Bisbee (Bisbee-Baldwin Corporation), Philip G. Howe (Florida Greyhound Lines), Carl S. Swisher (John H. Swisher & Son, Inc.), Paul E. Reinhold (Foremost Dairies, Inc.), W.R. Barnett, Frank W. Norris, W.R. McQuaid, M.L. Fleishel (St. Joe Lumber & Export Co.), E.D. Treadwell (attorney), I. Beverly Nalle (I. Beverly Nalle, Inc.), James C. Merrill (Merrill-Stevens Dry Dock & Repair Co.), Walter A. McRae (Duval Motors Co.), Olin E. Watts (attorney), Blair Burwell (Burwell Motor Company), W.B. Hicks (Wilson & Toomer Fertilizer Company), and Randall Chase (Chase & Company). (Photo by Bodden Fotos.)

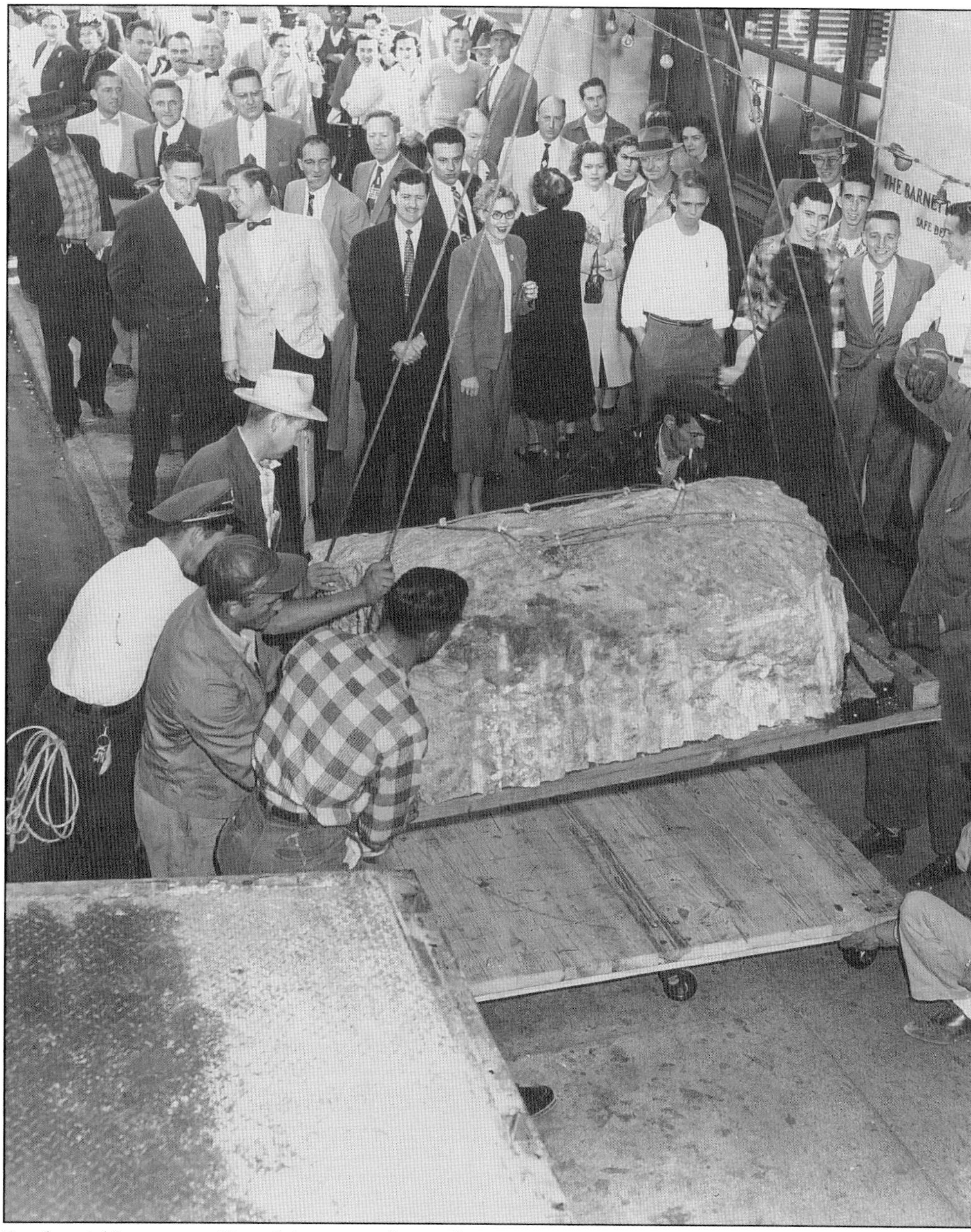

Prudential Insurance Co. of America planned to open its 22-story South Central Home Office in Jacksonville in May 1955. To commemorate the event, British counsel D.W. Hennessy of Miami arranged for 2 tons of the Rock of Gibraltar, "a piece of the rock," to be sent to Jacksonville. Arriving in January 1955, the Rock of Gibraltar was maneuvered into the main lobby of the Barnett National Bank, where it was displayed to the public. (Courtesy of *Jacksonville Journal.*)

By the time Bion Barnett finally retired in 1952, William R. McQuaid (right) had been running the bank for years. He now succeeded the elderly Barnett as chairman and chief executive officer. McQuaid was already 71 and had worked for the bank for 53 years. He served as chairman from 1952 to 1958 and thereafter continued as a director until his death in 1965. (Photo by Dishinger Studio.)

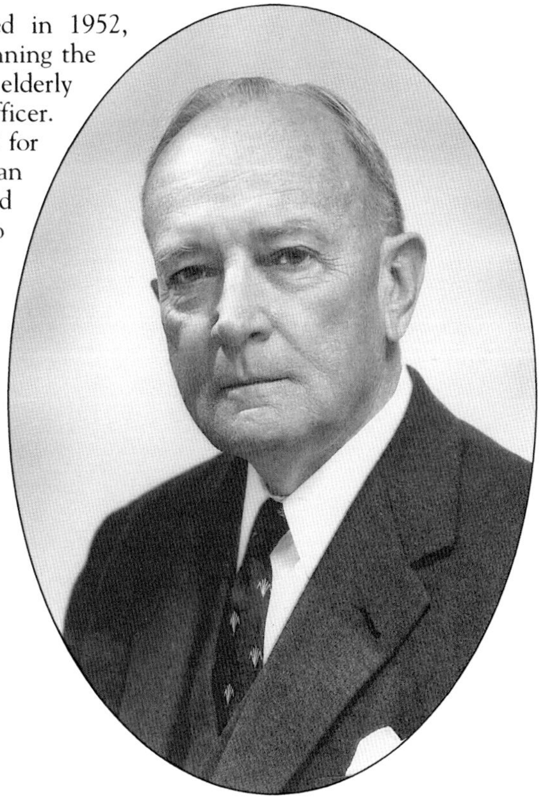

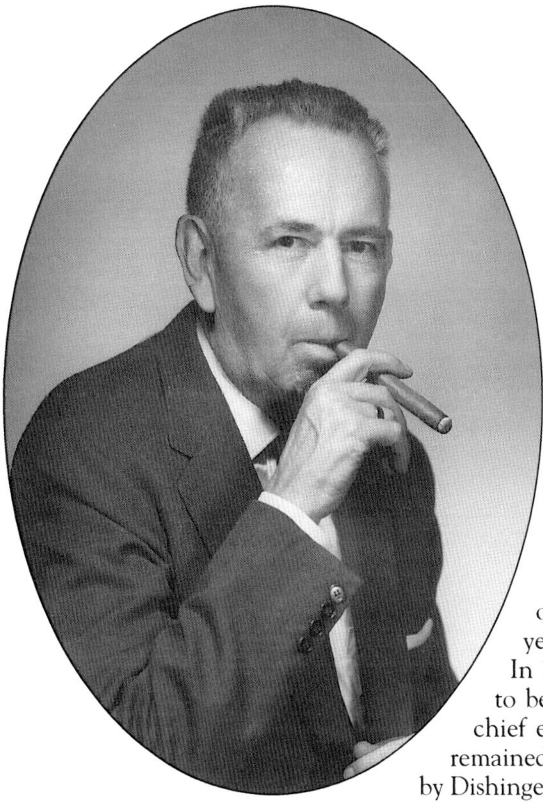

With McQuaid elevated to chairman, Frank W. Norris (left) became president of Barnett National Bank in 1952. Six years later, he became chairman and CEO. In 1963, he directed the election of Guy Botts to be president and his successor as the bank's chief executive. Until his death in 1970, Norris remained a member of the board of directors. (Photo by Dishinger Studio.)

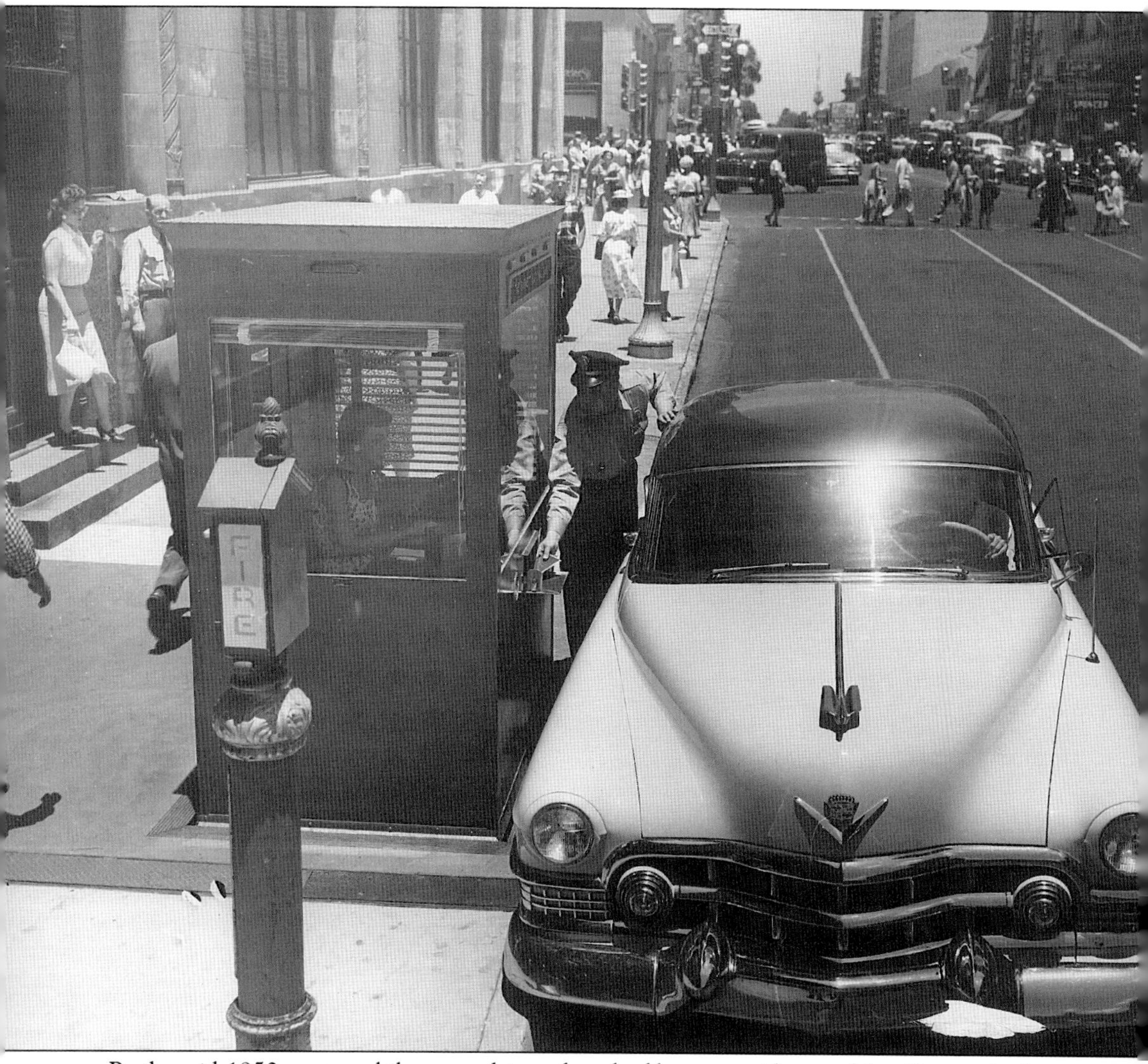

By the mid-1950s, automobile ownership and use had become widespread, but Barnett had space limitations for installing drive-ins, not to mention the city's confusing maze of one-way streets and limited parking options. In 1955, the bank installed a "Jack-in-the-Box" curbside teller along the Laura Street side of the bank. An air-conditioned, bullet-proof booth was constructed under the sidewalk and mounted on a hydraulic elevator. At 9:30 a.m., when the bank opened, the teller compartment was raised, with a teller already stationed inside, linked to the main office by telephone. An off-duty policeman, hired by the bank to direct traffic (and to clear the sidewalk before raising the booth), also assisted customers, since Laura Street was a one-way street and the "Jack-in-the-Box" was set on the passenger side. At closing time, 1:30 p.m., the booth was lowered back to the basement under the sidewalk. When it first opened on May 31, 1955, Bion Barnett, driven by his granddaughter, was the first customer to use the new curbside teller. (Courtesy of *Jacksonville Journal.*)

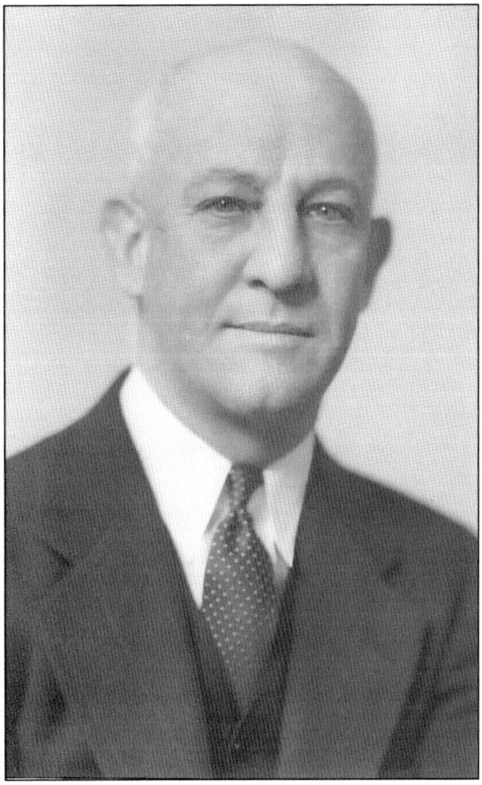

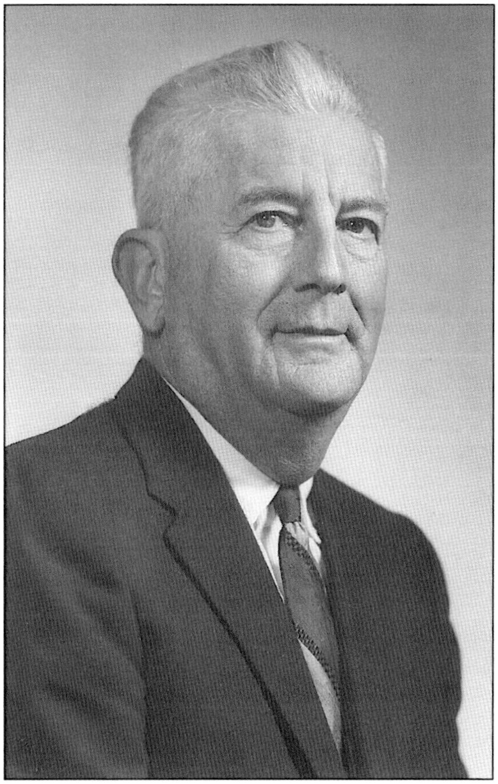

The 1950s and 1960s saw the retirement of many longtime employees. P.L. Walton (upper left), cashier, retired in 1954 after 43 years; A.B. Davis (upper right), vice president and head of the Credit Department, in 1961 after 35 years; and Raymond W. Cushman (lower right), cashier, in 1961 after 42 years. Cushman's service with the bank included nearly six years of military duty—he resigned as chief clerk in 1942 to become a major in the Army Air Corps and continued to serve with the post-war occupation forces, not returning to the bank until 1948. (Photos by Dishinger Studio.)

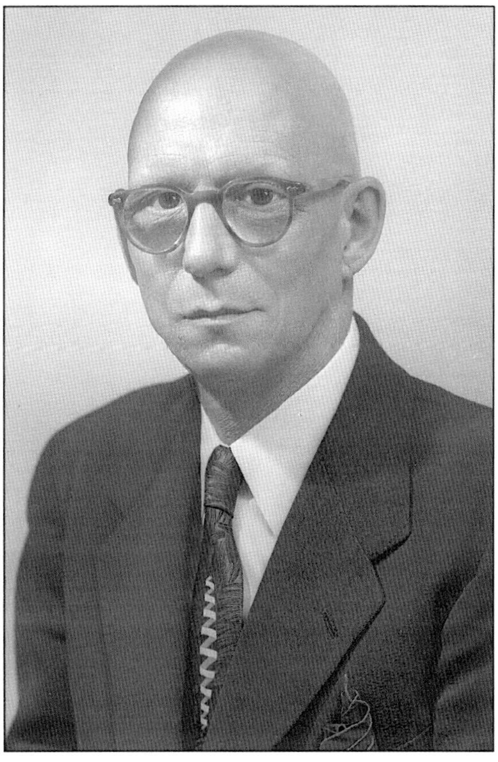

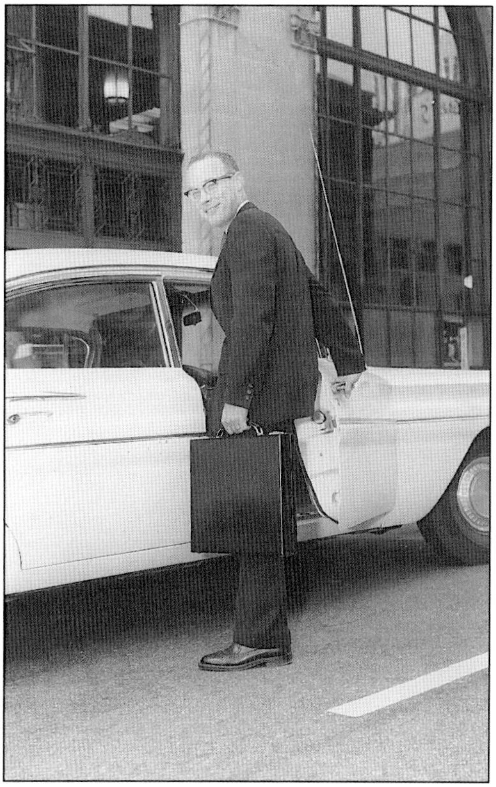

John T. Cannon III worked for Barnett for nearly 40 years. The son of a Barnett banker (his father was president of the DeLand affiliate), he started as a management trainee in 1950. At the time of this 1962 photo, he was an assistant vice president and corporate secretary to the board of directors. He later served as president of the San Jose, Cocoa, and Polk County affiliates. (Courtesy of *Florida Times-Union*.)

R. Boone Lipscombe started with Barnett in 1918. He went to DeLand to help establish that new affiliate in 1929. Returning to the Jacksonville bank in 1946, he managed correspondent banking and, later, all of the commercial banking functions, rising to the position of vice chairman. He was chairman of the board of the Barnett National Bank of Cocoa for nearly 20 years and served on the board of directors of the Barnett National Bank of Jacksonville from 1956 to 1968. (Photo by J. Gordon Spottswood.)

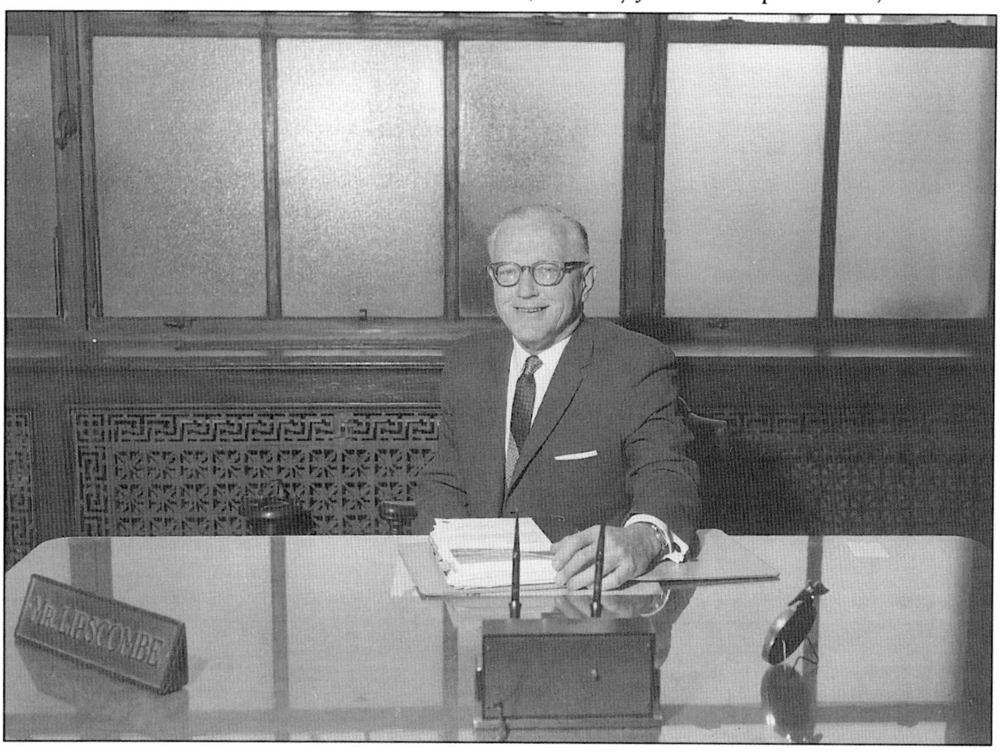

In 1956, the bank launched an employee publication *BANABA* (BArnett NAtional BAnk). On the cover of its December 1959 issue is Jackie Kelly running the bank's Christmas Club booth, with Ann Hayes opening her club account. According to *BANABA*, "The appearance of our Christmas Club booth is one of the first reminders that we must start making our holiday plans for this year and next. True—it is a bit early for that intense emotional spirit of Christmas, but the spark has been ignited."

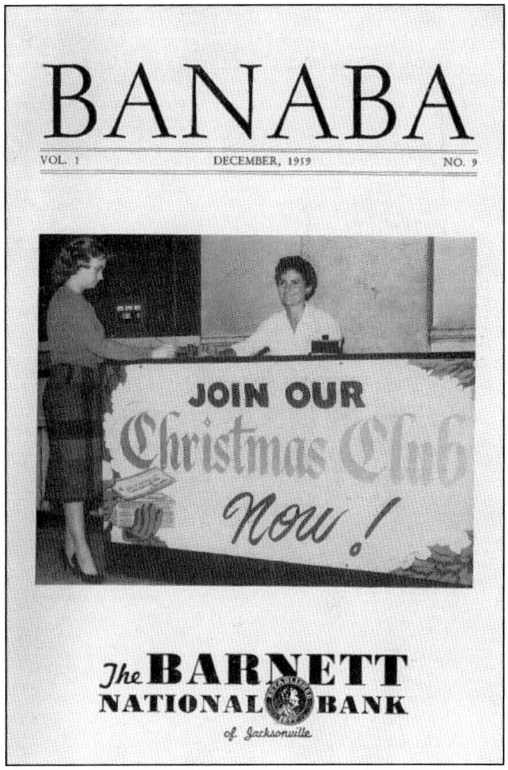

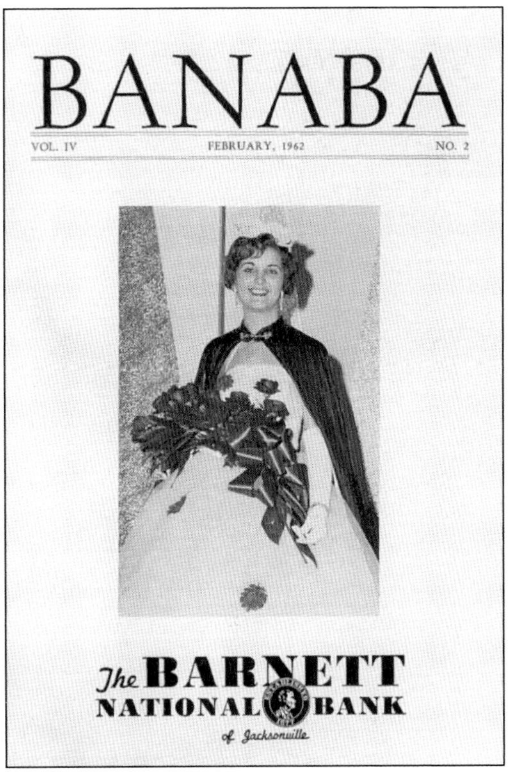

BANABA continued as the bank's monthly communication magazine, filled with employee profiles, birthday listings, cartoons, and "chatter matter," until 1964. On the cover of the February 1962 issue is Katherine Spikes of the Transit Department, Barnett's candidate in the annual Sweetheart Contest sponsored by the Jacksonville chapter of the American Institute of Banking (AIB). *BANABA* reported, "Katherine captivated the audience and the judges" to be chosen AIB Sweetheart.

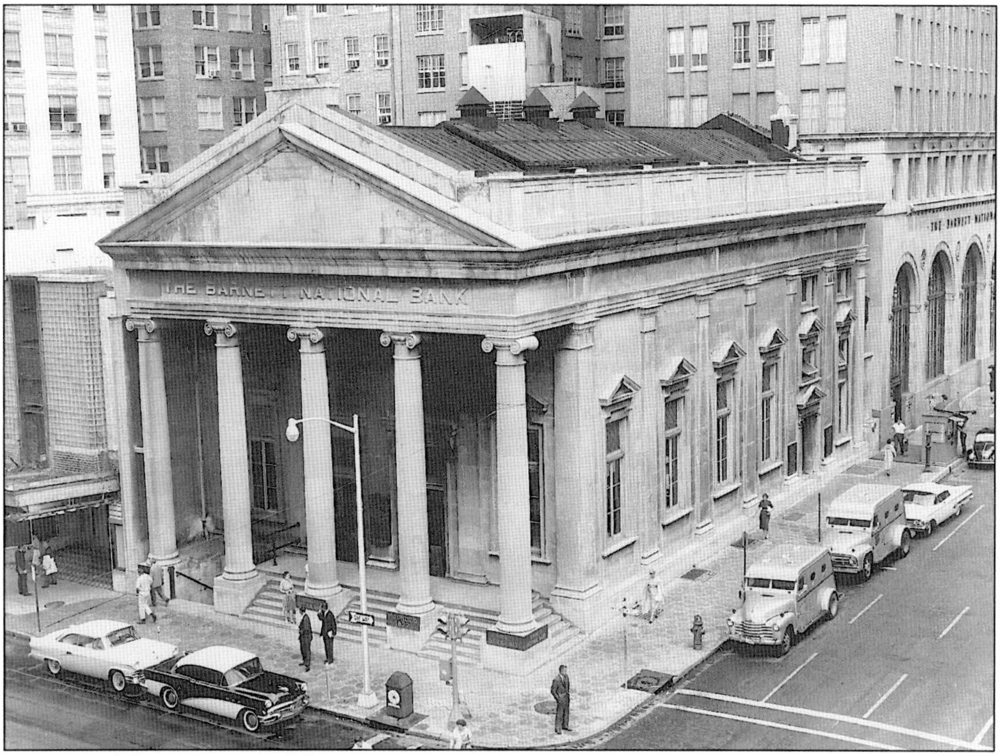

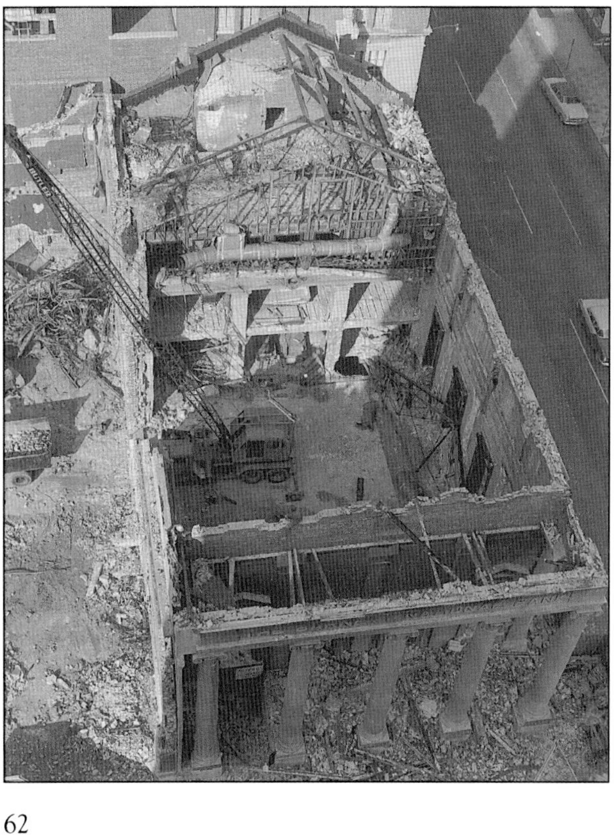

The Barnett National Bank complex (the 1898 bank building in the foreground, with the 1927 18-story building behind it) is seen here in 1961. Note the "Jack-in-the-Box" teller along Laura Street and the vacant movie theater to the west of the bank building along Forsyth Street. (Photo by Lou Egner.)

The demolition of the 1898 building began in 1961. Sentimentality and historic preservation concerns for the only banking office to survive the 1901 fire did not seem to have been considered, only the need to move forward with construction of a more modern, up-to-date office building. (Courtesy of *Florida Times-Union*.)

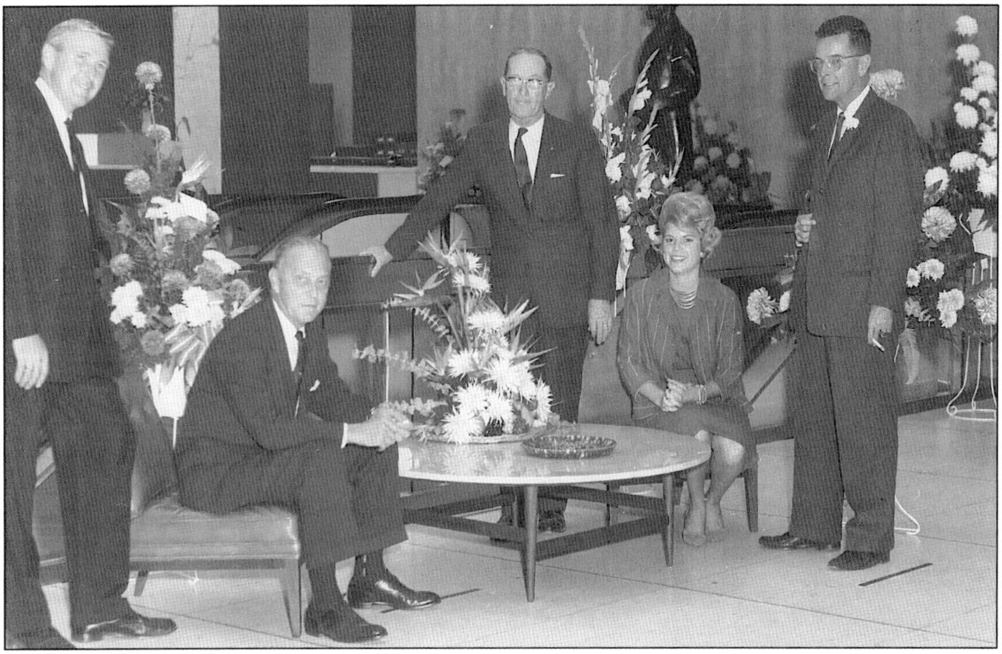

Barnett's banking lobby in the new ten-story headquarters building opened on November 5, 1962. In the lobby, from left to right, are Bob Fennel (assistant to the building manager), Powers Williams (head of the Investment Department), Arthur Irving (building manager), Carol Cortadellas, and Downing Nightingale (vice president of the New Business Department). (Photo by J. Gordon Spottswood.)

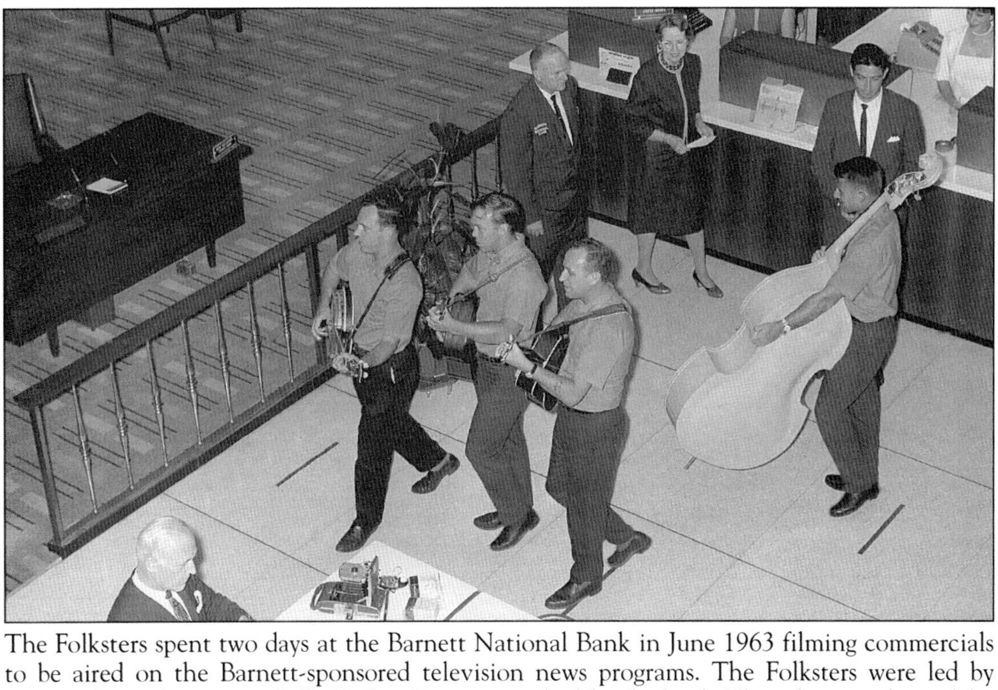

The Folksters spent two days at the Barnett National Bank in June 1963 filming commercials to be aired on the Barnett-sponsored television news programs. The Folksters were led by Ken Hodges, whose sister Sally Hodges Doering worked for the bank. The other members of the popular group were Fred Williams, Gary Scott, and Lefty Baker.

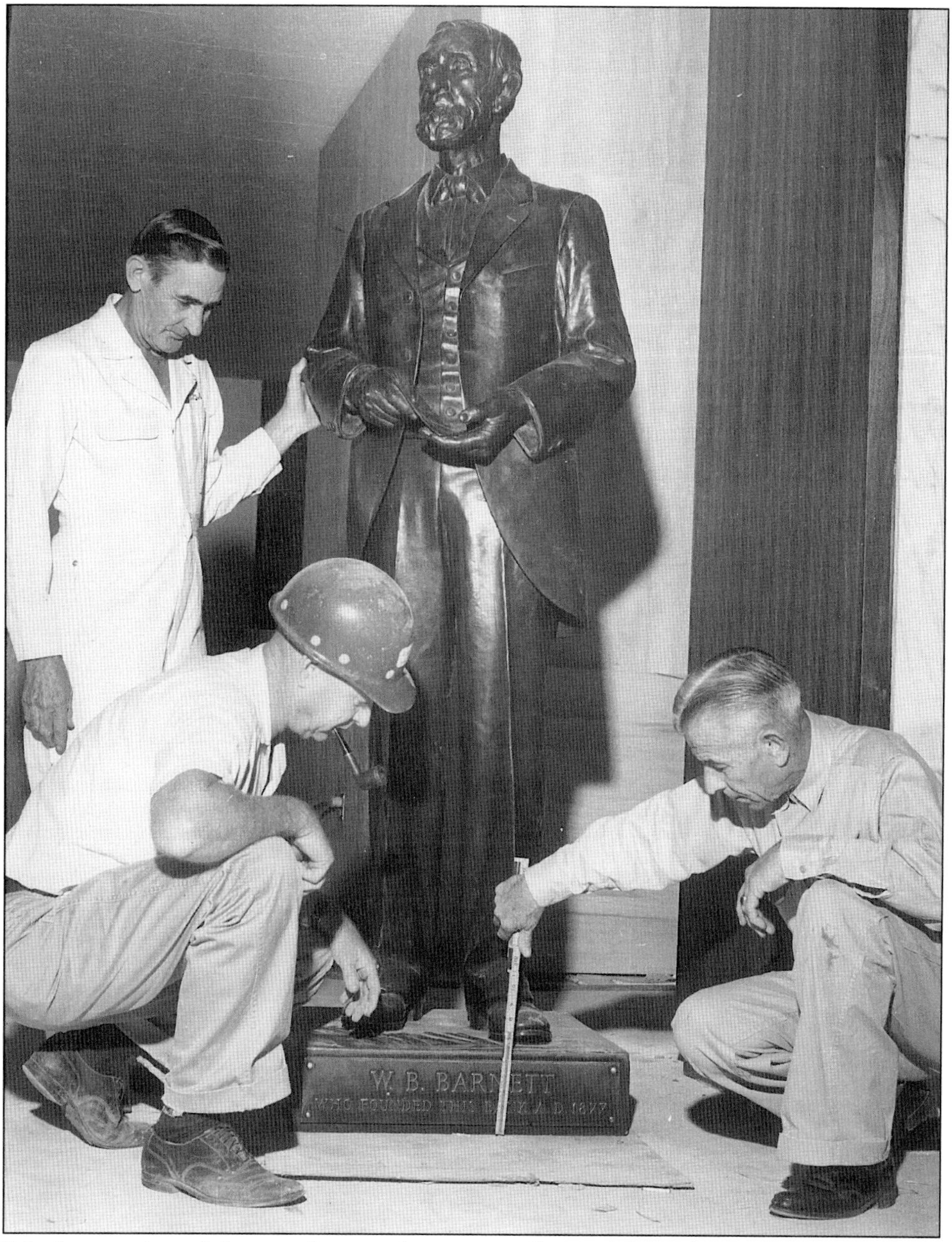

With the opening of the new Barnett downtown office in November 1962, M.G. Pinkston, Ralph McKinney, and Fred Rouse prepare to move the bronze statue of the bank's founder, W.B. Barnett, to its new home. From 1931 through 1998, the statue was housed in three separate "main" bank offices in Jacksonville. In 1999, the statue was given to the Solomon Lodge. This Masonic organization is situated in the Springfield section of Jacksonville at 25 East First Street, in a two-story brick Colonial house that W.D. Barnett built following the 1901 fire. His father, W.B., lived there prior to his death in October 1903. The funeral, with a full Masonic ceremony, was held at the home. W.B. Barnett had been active in the Masons for more than 50 years, and his sons also were involved in the Masonic order. In 1941, Bion Barnett, as trustee for his brother's will, sold the family home to the Solomon Lodge.

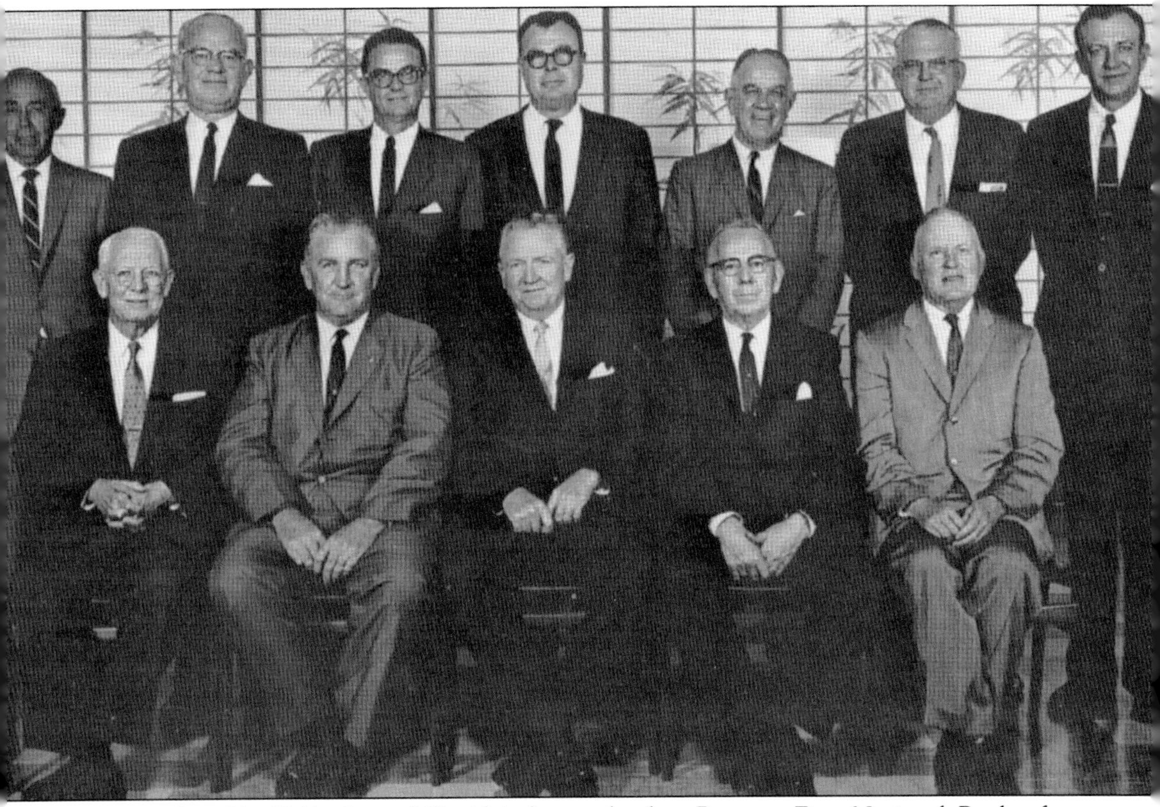

On November 29, 1961, four of Florida's largest banks—Barnett, First National Bank of Miami, First National Bank at Orlando, and Exchange Bank of Tampa—announced that they were combining to form a new bank holding company, First Bancorporation of Florida, Inc. The proposed 12-member board of directors, three from each bank, included some of the most prominent names in Florida banking. From left to right are (seated) Linton E. Allen, Orlando; William H. Dial, Orlando; Comer J. Kimball, Miami; Frank Norris, Jacksonville; and G.R. Griffin, Tampa; (standing) William J. Capehart, Orlando; Ralph W. Crum, Miami; Harry Hood Bassett, Miami; William R. Barnett, Jacksonville; F. Elgin Bayless, Sebring; Fred J. Woods, Tampa; and Chester H. Ferguson, Tampa. On July 30, 1962, the Federal Reserve Board announced that it had rejected the application from First Bancorporation.

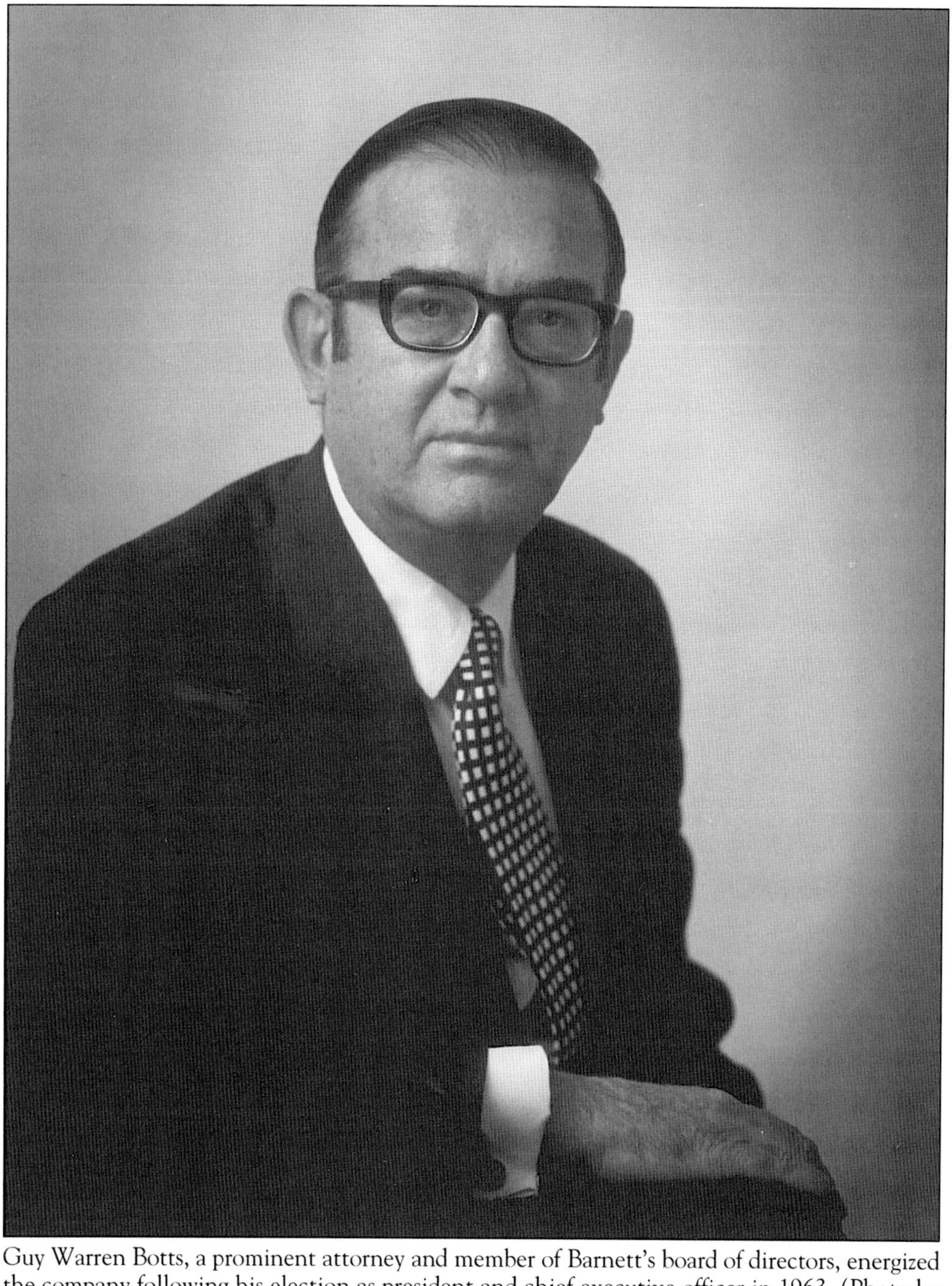

Guy Warren Botts, a prominent attorney and member of Barnett's board of directors, energized the company following his election as president and chief executive officer in 1963. (Photo by Charles Smith Studio.)

Five

The Guy Botts Era: 1963 to 1979

In June 1963, Barnett's board of directors elected one of its members, attorney Guy Warren Botts, as the company's new president and chief executive officer. Botts was a truly remarkable man, with a Horatio Alger, rags-to-riches saga from the rural poverty of west Florida to the head of one of Jacksonville's most prestigious law firms. A quiet, soft-spoken man, who spent his leisure hours growing orchids and sculpting miniature bonsai trees, Botts developed an aggressive, far-reaching strategic vision to transform Barnett into a major statewide banking organization.

Botts had no banking background, although he had served on the bank's board since 1955. He spent his first few years as president devising a ten-year plan with two fundamental goals. First, Barnett would create a statewide franchise, with banking offices in all major markets in the state. With the Federal Reserve's recent rejection of the First Bancorporation application and Florida's legal prohibition against operating branch offices, the only option left for Botts to pursue was an aggressive acquisition campaign directed toward the small, independent banks scattered throughout the state. Second, Barnett's network of banks would maximize long-term earnings at a rate faster than any other major banking group in the country. To achieve this goal in deposit-rich Florida would require implementation of a two-pronged strategy—increasing Barnett's lending efforts and offering expanded banking services, while simultaneously taking advantage of projected economies of scale to cut costs as the number of banking units and volume of business increased.

Botts's first step involved restructuring the Barnett National Securities Corporation, which had been largely dormant since the 1930s. In 1965, Botts announced a plan for the Securities Corporation, which had been a subsidiary of the Jacksonville bank, to become the parent company by purchasing the stock of the Barnett First National Bank of Jacksonville. This transaction, completed early the following year, gave Botts greater flexibility in using the holding company to purchase additional banks. In the meantime, Botts had already begun negotiations with several potential acquisition candidates. Botts soon announced agreements with The First Bank & Trust Company of Pensacola and, shortly thereafter, The First National Bank at Winter Park. After receiving regulatory approval from the Federal Reserve, the Barnett National Securities Corporation completed the purchase of both banks on October 10, 1966. They became the first in a series of acquisitions. Within the next decade, Barnett purchased 34 separate banks and obtained new banking charters to open 19 more.

As the number of Barnett affiliates grew, Botts launched a corporate identification program to create a "one family look." He disliked the name of the holding company, advocating that it "should include Florida and should identify the business we are in, and also identify our group to the extent possible." Thus, in 1969, the Barnett National Securities Corporation became Barnett Banks of Florida, Inc. (known as BBFI). At the same time, the company adopted a corporate logotype with the words Barnett Bank inside of a green rectangle with rounded corners—a symbol that appeared on bank signs and advertisements throughout the state and became widely known as the Barnett lollipop. Then, each of the affiliates became linked by a common nomenclature, with the individual bank names all changed to Barnett Bank of (city or county).

While Barnett launched a major advertising campaign to promote its new same-name statewide image, the company aggressively sought to become the major consumer lender in the state. A key component of this strategy was the introduction of bank credit cards. Botts obtained the exclusive statewide license to operate BankAmericard (now Visa) in Florida. Plans to get the BankAmericard program operational were described as the "single largest project ever undertaken by the Barnett Banks." By the end of 1969, its first year of operation, one million Floridians had received BankAmericards and more than 20,000 merchants had begun accepting credit card purchases.

During the 1970s, Barnett continued to be a leader in new products and services, from the introduction of "Sam the SuperTeller" automated teller machines (ATMs) to the marketing of check verification services for merchants. The expanding scope of operations, together with the growing number of affiliate banks, also led to the formation of a number of non-banking subsidiaries—Barnett Computing Company to coordinate centralized technology support and ensure that common computer systems were used; Barnett Services Company to supply accounting, billing, and other administrative services for BankAmericard; and Barnett Banks Trust Company to standardize bookkeeping, management reporting, and other trust functions.

One area of innovation that did not prove successful was the company's aggressive entry into commercial real estate lending, with the establishment of two real estate investment trusts (REITs) in the early 1970s. The timing of these ventures could not have been worse, with the 1974 oil embargo leading to skyrocketing gasoline prices, record double-digit interest rates, and the onset of a severe recession. The Florida real estate market collapsed. Amidst widespread real estate project defaults, the REITs suffered huge losses. The entire Barnett system faced increasing loan problems, decreasing earnings, and a plummeting stock price—BBFI stock fell from $60\ ^{1}/_{4}$ per share to a low of $8\ ^{3}/_{4}$ in 1974, effectively curtailing the company's acquisition program for the remainder of the decade.

While Barnett struggled to recover from these real estate problems—a challenge that also confronted all other major Florida banks—the company did achieve one of its major objectives in 1975 when the Florida legislature finally passed a bill to permit branch banking. This victory culminated two decades of often-bitter divisions within the state's banking industry and represented a major accomplishment for Botts, who had led the pro-branching lobbying effort. With the legislation effective January 1, 1977, Barnett adopted a two-pronged strategy—merging banks in the same county on a staged basis, with the goal of having a single bank charter in each county, while simultaneously identifying fast-growing markets in which to open new branch offices.

At the beginning of the Botts era, there was no corporate staff in Jacksonville. Several senior officers of the Jacksonville bank had dual responsibilities with the holding company, but not until 1967 did Tom Duer become the first full-time employee of the Barnett National Securities Corporation. The pressures of managing the increasing number of bank and non-bank subsidiaries led to significant increases in the holding company staff during the 1970s. One of the most significant additions to the staff was Charles E. Rice, who had been executive vice president of First National Bank at Winter Park when Barnett acquired it. In 1973, Rice became president and chief operating officer of BBFI. Six years later, when Botts reached the mandatory retirement age of 65, Rice became chief executive officer. Thus ended Botts's 16-year tenure as chief executive, a period of dramatic growth that transformed the Barnett banking organization.

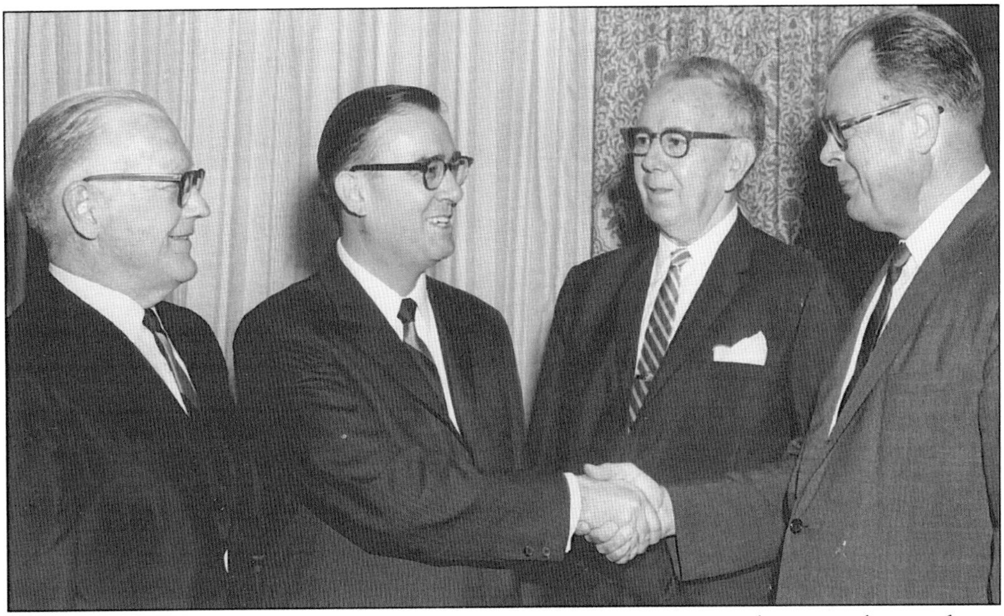

Barnett's senior management team pose for photographs following Botts's election to the presidency on June 11, 1963. From left to right are vice chairman R. Boone Lipscombe, newly elected president Guy W. Botts, chairman Frank W. Norris, and vice chairman William R. Barnett. Norris announced that he would retire at the next annual meeting in January 1964, and he proposed that Bill Barnett succeed him as chairman. (Courtesy of *Florida Times-Union*.)

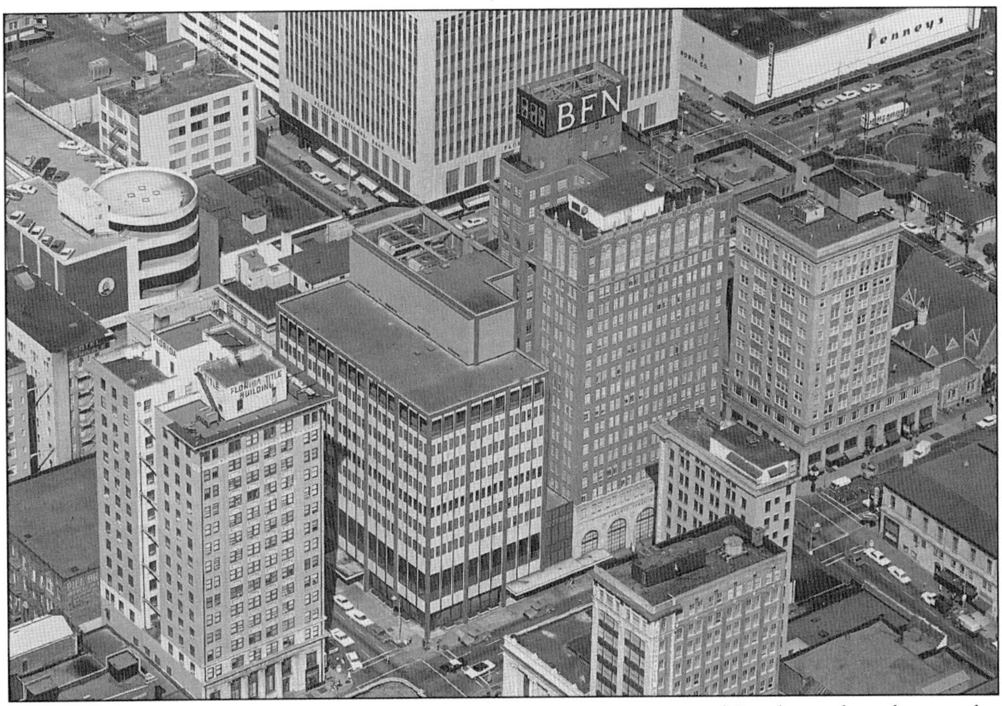

In April 1965, the bank changed its name to Barnett First National Bank to identify it as the oldest bank in the Jacksonville area. It placed the giant letters BFN on the top of its 18-story building. Locals said it stood for "Big Frank Norris." (Photo by Aero-Pic.)

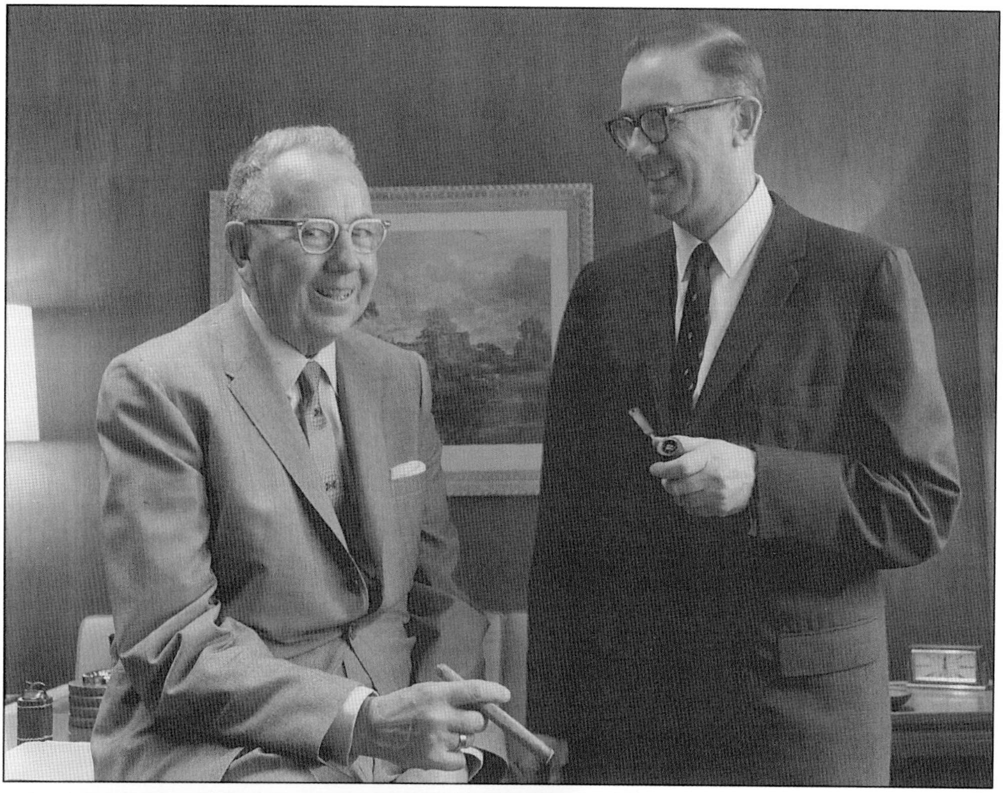

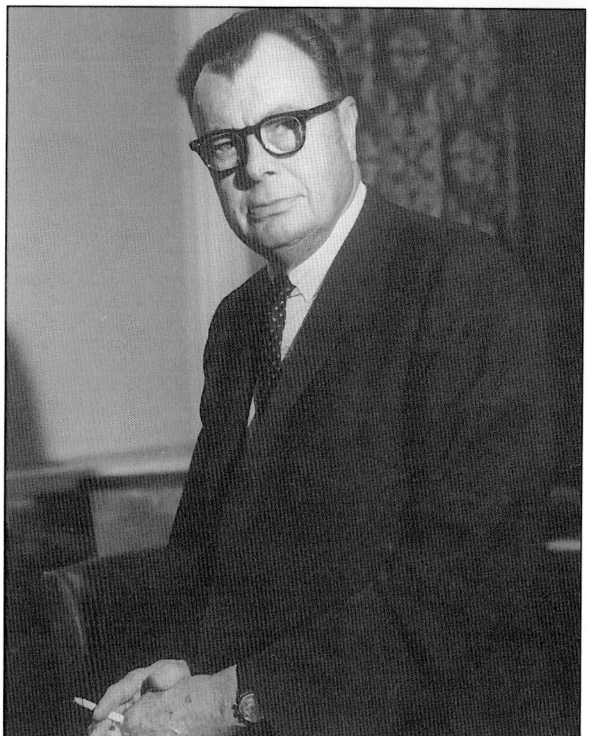

The senior management team at Barnett had different tastes in the 1960s, several decades before smoking was banned in Barnett's downtown banking offices. Above is Frank Norris with his cigar, while Gut Botts favored a pipe. To the left is Bill Barnett with his cigarette. (Photos by Robert R. Favorite.)

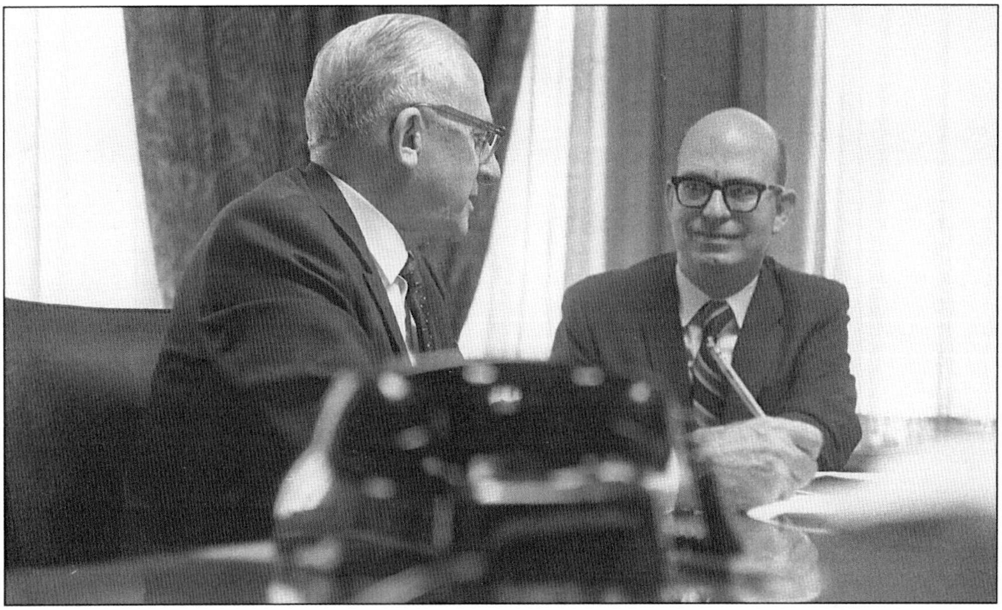

M.K. "Kit" Kittredge (left) was comptroller of the Barnett National Bank for ten years, and then controller of BBFI from 1969 to 1971. George A. Snelling (right) became controller when Kittredge retired. He later was vice president of planning and the first president of Barnett Computing Company. Snelling played an instrumental role in standardizing accounting procedures and developed a "model bank" to compare operating performances among the various affiliate banks.

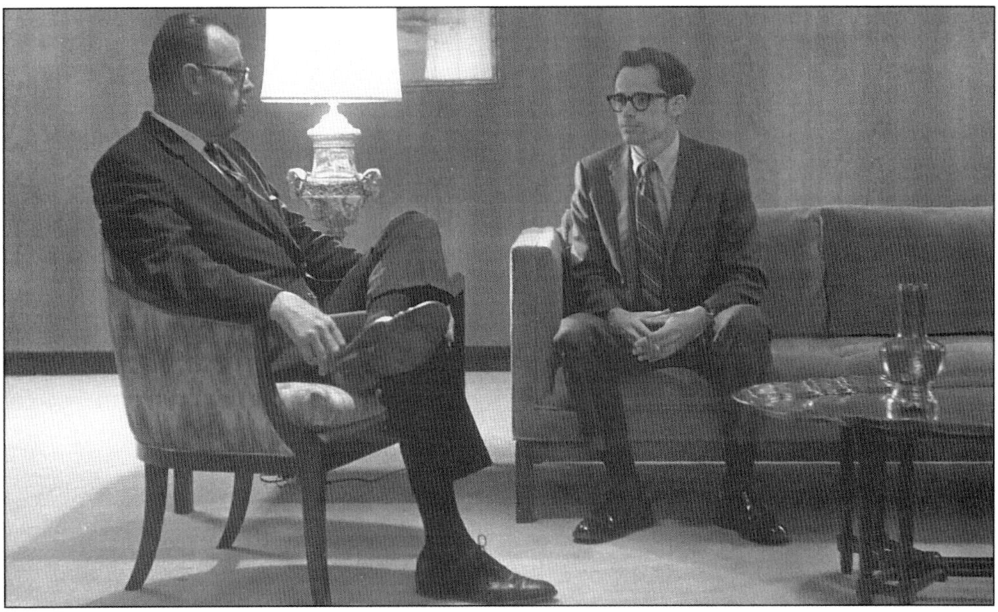

Thomas C. Duer (right) meets with Bill Barnett. Duer was the first full-time employee of the holding company. Quiet and shy, Duer had strong analytical skills concerning financial ratios and projections. He worked closely with Botts identifying potential acquisition candidates, calculating projected returns on investments, and evaluating the financial viability of various expansion alternatives.

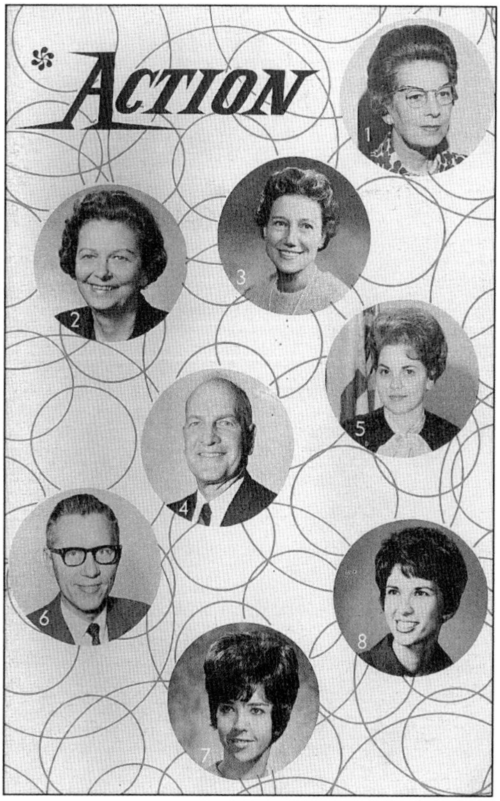

In 1966, Barnett First National Bank began a new employee publication called *BFN Action*. Two years later, it became a statewide publication, renamed simply *Action*. The cover of Volume 1, Number 1 in February 1968 featured the assistant editors who gathered news from affiliates around the state—1. Margaret Enns (Winter Haven and Cypress Gardens); 2. Vera Ferguson (Cocoa); 3. Anna Jillson (Winter Park); 4. Harry Kinne Jr. (San Jose); 5. Judy Moore (Pensacola); 6. Ralph Roberts (Murray Hill); 7. Lori Warensford (DeLand); and 8. Vee Wilson (St. Augustine).

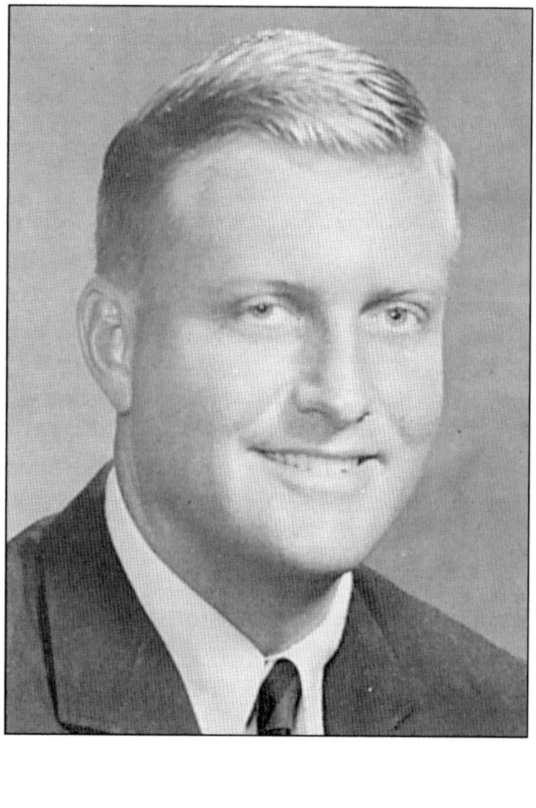

In this same first issue of *Action* was a picture of 32-year-old Charles Rice, who had recently been named president of the First National Bank at Winter Park.

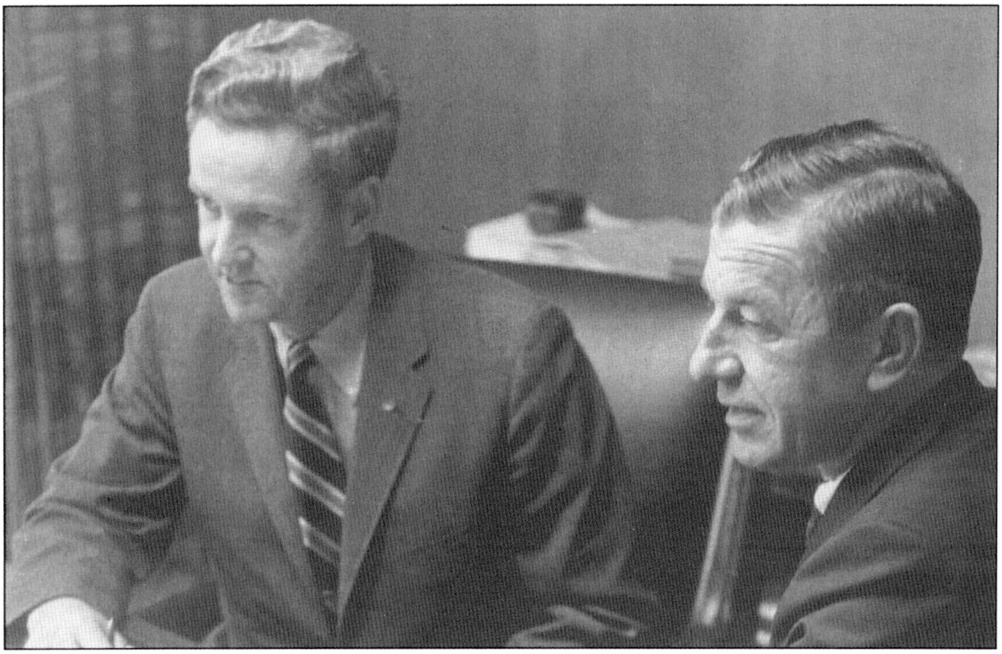

In 1969, BBFI named C. Murray McQuaid (left) as commercial loan coordinator and Harold C. Johnson (right) as consumer credit coordinator. McQuaid, son of former president William R. McQuaid, worked for Barnett for 20 years. Johnson joined Barnett in 1968 to head consumer lending and later served as the company's chief political lobbyist.

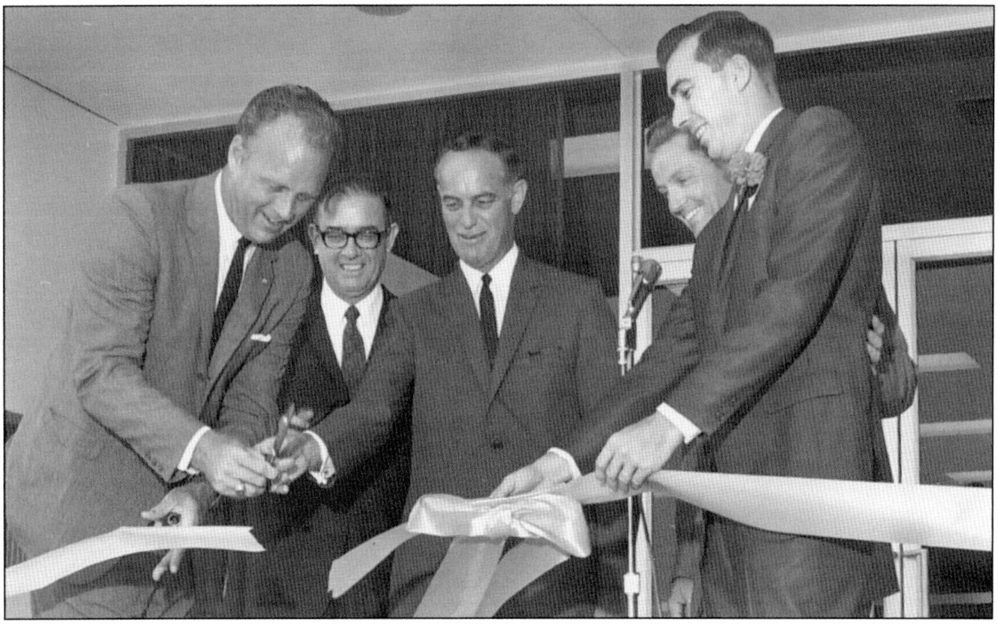

The Regency Square Barnett Bank opened for business in eastern Jacksonville, adjacent to the Regency Square Mall, on July 16, 1968. At the grand opening ceremony are, from left to right, Jacksonville mayor Hans Tanzler, Guy Botts, Florida comptroller (and chief regulator of state-chartered banks) Fred O. "Bud" Dickinson, C. Murray McQuaid (chairman of the board for the new bank), and bank president William M. White (Photo by Berisford.)

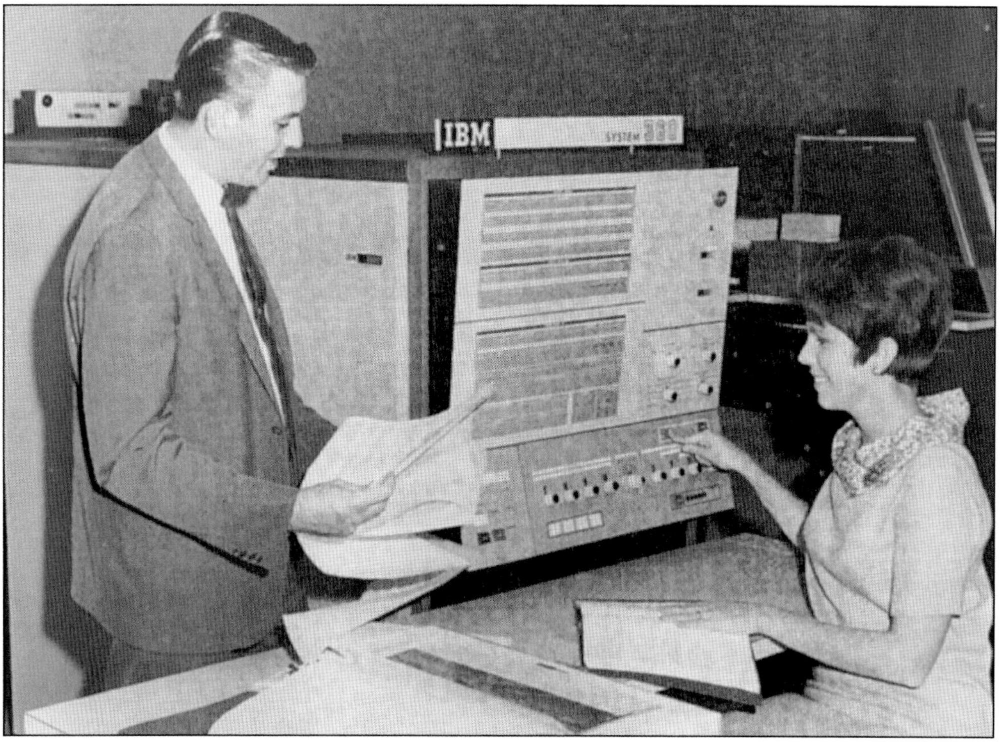

In 1966, Barnett's computer operations were housed on the fourth floor of the downtown Jacksonville bank. The technical staff included three programmers, two of whom are pictured here: Gary Hess and Andrea Mims. Mims spent over 30 years working for Barnett, and in the mid-1990s, she headed Barnett Technology's Y2K program to ensure that computing capabilities would be ready for the year 2000.

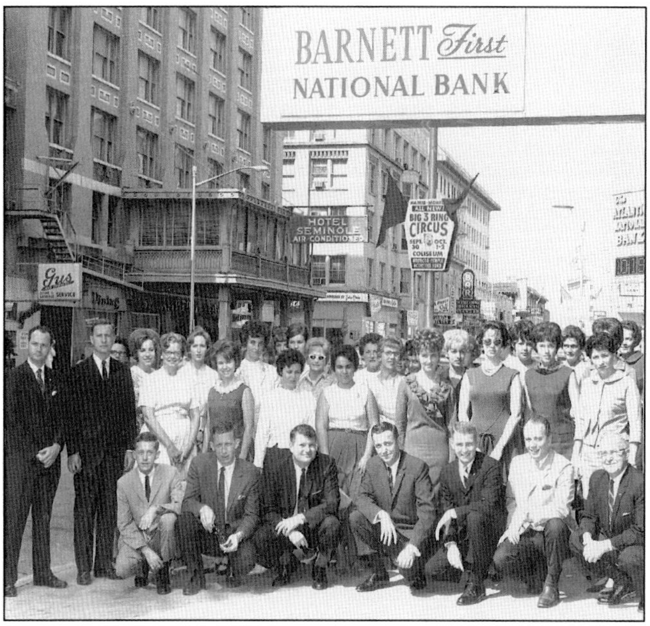

BFN's Data Processing Department began demand deposit processing for the Barnett National Bank of DeLand on September 30, 1966. Forty bankers from DeLand traveled to Jacksonville by chartered bus to tour the computer room and learn about data processing. In this picture of the DeLand staff in downtown Jacksonville, Lowell Edwin Renfroe stands on the far left. He was president of the Volusia County affiliate from 1983 to 1995. (Photo by J. Gordon Spottswood.)

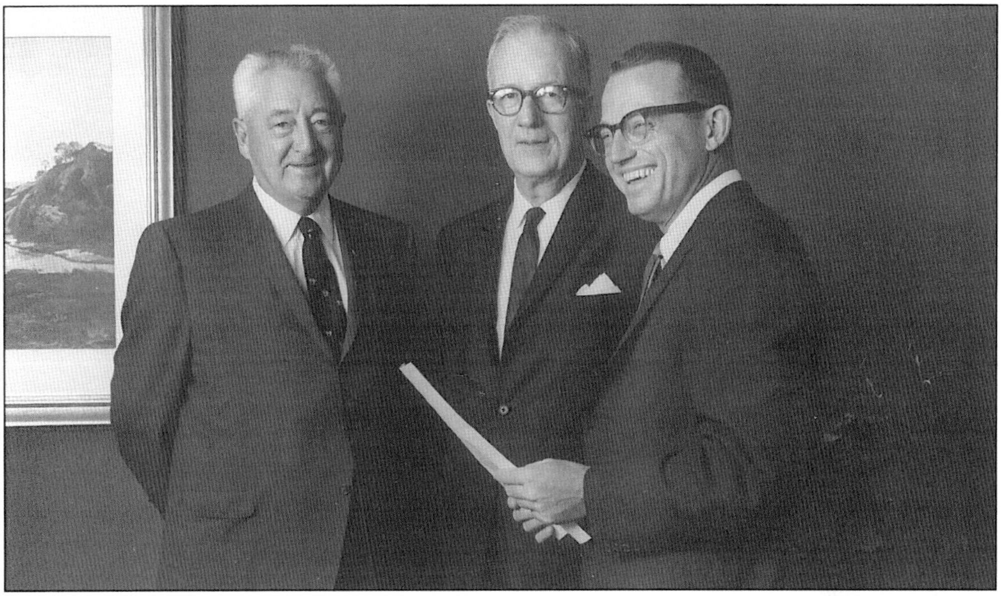

Seen here are Barnett National Securities Corporation directors W.R. Rosenfelt, E. Dixie Beggs, and Jack H. Chambers. Rosenfelt and Beggs both joined the board in 1966 after Barnett's acquisition of affiliates in Winter Park, where Rosenfelt was president, and Pensacola, where Beggs had served on the bank board since 1933. Chambers, a former law partner of Guy Botts, served as the holding company's principal legal counsel. (Photo by Robert R. Favorite.)

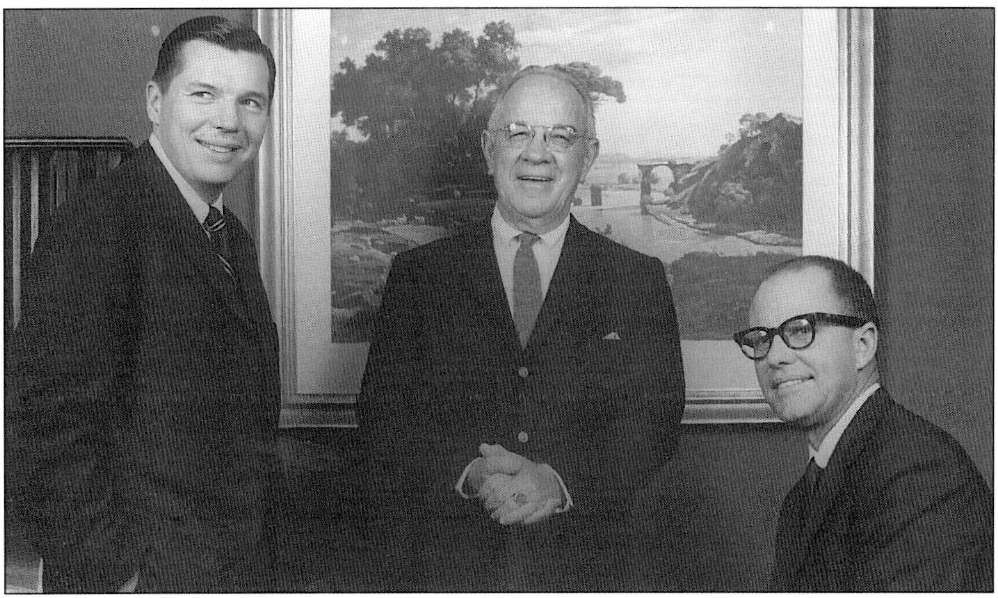

Barnett National Securities Corporation directors Andrew P. Ireland, F. Elgin Bayless, and Frederick H. Schultz are pictured here. Ireland, senior vice president of the Jacksonville affiliate and CEO of banks acquired in Winter Haven and Cypress Gardens, later became a U.S. congressman. Bayless, president of Consolidated Financial Corporation, was one of Barnett's most influential directors. Schultz, a Jacksonville investor and state legislator, served on Barnett's board from 1961 to 1997, with only a brief absence during his tenure as vice chairman of the Federal Reserve Board of Governors. (Photo by Robert R. Favorite.)

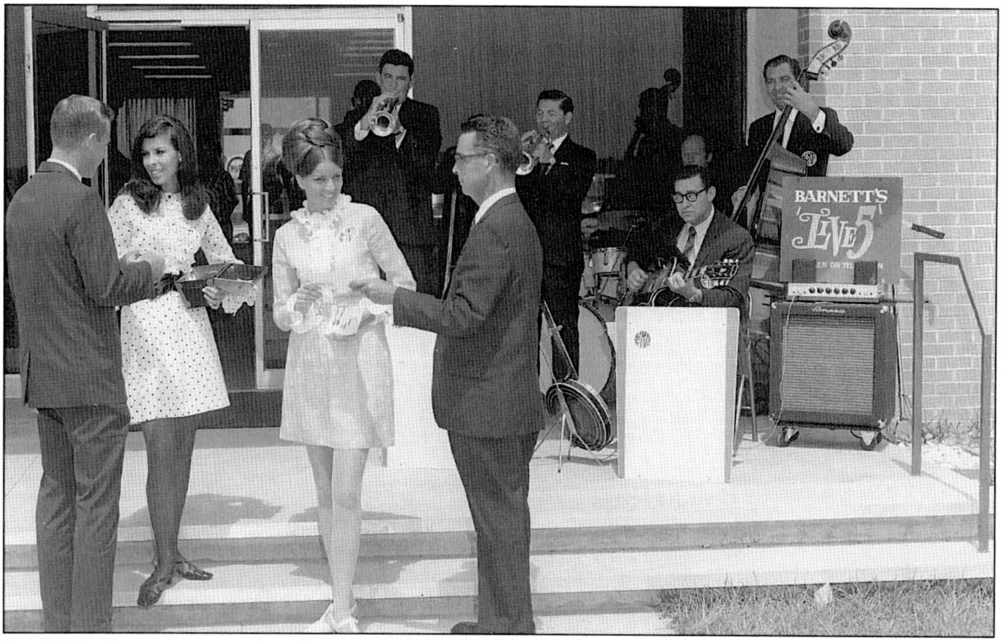

In 1968, Barnett introduced a new 5% savings certificate, along with a major advertising campaign on radio, television, and billboard. A "Live Five" Band played the bank's "new jingle with a modern beat" at the different Jacksonville banking offices, while "Live Five" girls passed out customer brochures. (Photo by J. Gordon Spottswood.)

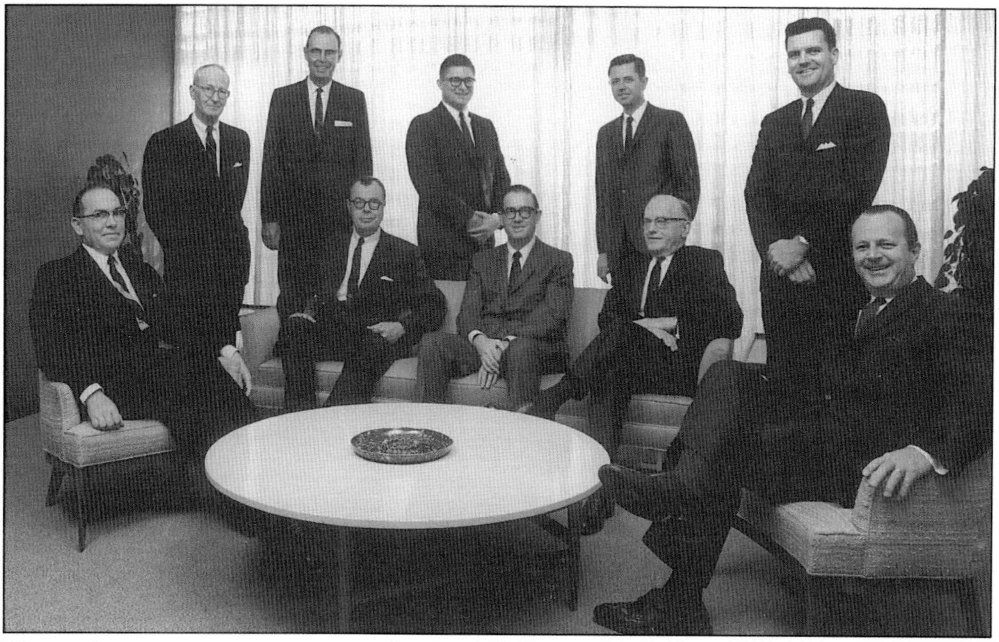

The senior management team in the late 1960s at the Barnett First National Bank of Jacksonville included the following officers, from left to right: (seated) Thomas E. Camp III, William R. Barnett, Guy W. Botts, R. Boone Lipscombe, and W. Ernest Allen Jr.; (standing) William S. Woods, Charles T. Robinson, Edward H. West, Timothy Lane, and Albert J. Brosius. (Photo by Robert R. Favorite.)

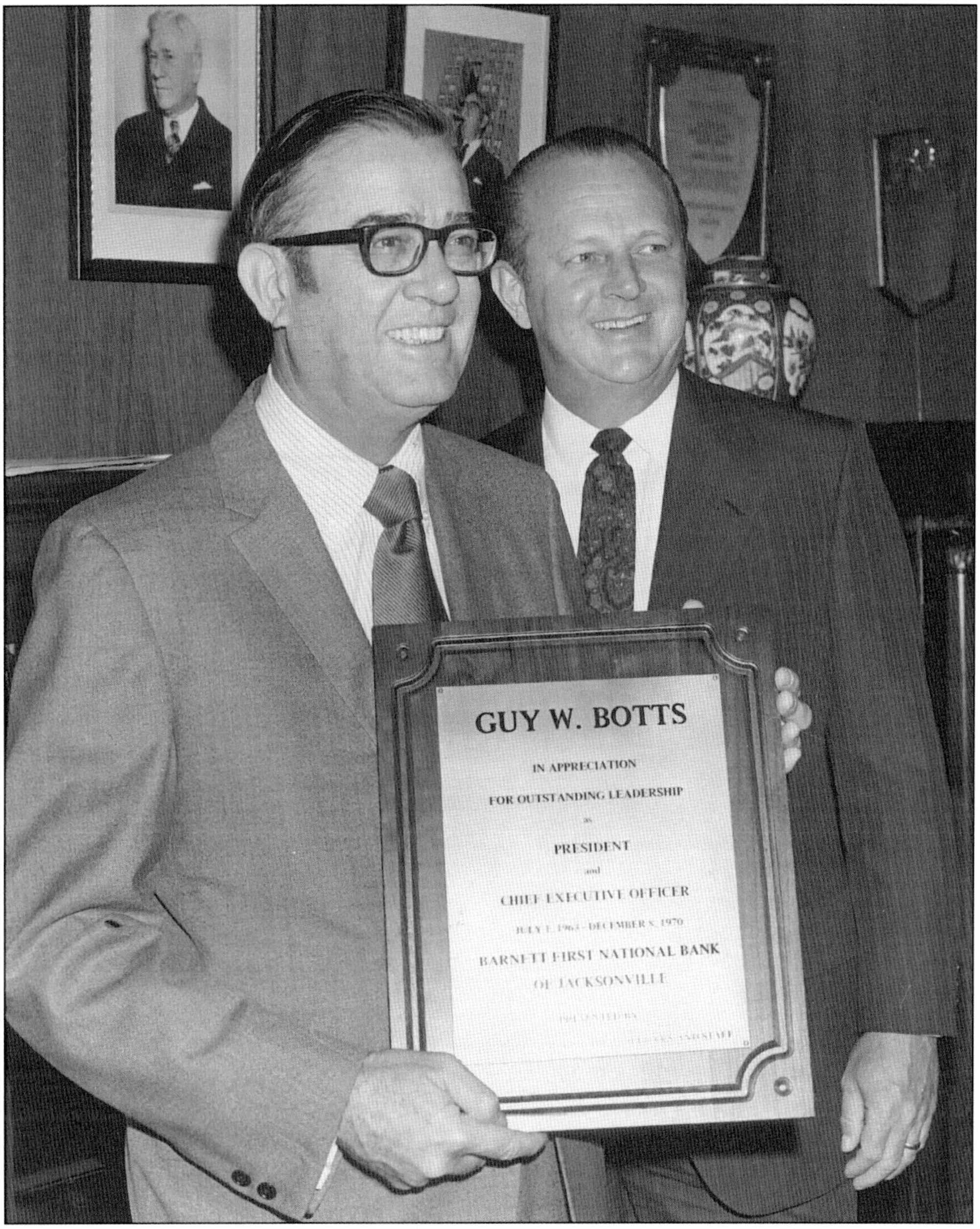

Guy Botts had a dual role as president of both the Jacksonville bank and the holding company. In December 1970, Botts stepped down as bank president, although he remained on the board of directors, and selected Ernie Allen to replace him. A Virginia native, Allen had joined Barnett in 1955 as a member of the Investment Department. When Powers Williams retired in 1965, Allen replaced him as head of the department. He became a trusted advisor to Botts, while simultaneously managing the investment function for both the Jacksonville bank and the holding company. Allen had been elevated to BBFI first vice president before Botts chose him to lead the Jacksonville bank, the company's largest and most important affiliate. In this photo, Allen presents Botts with a certificate of appreciation for his years of service as president of the Barnett First National Bank. (Photo by J. Gordon Spottswood.)

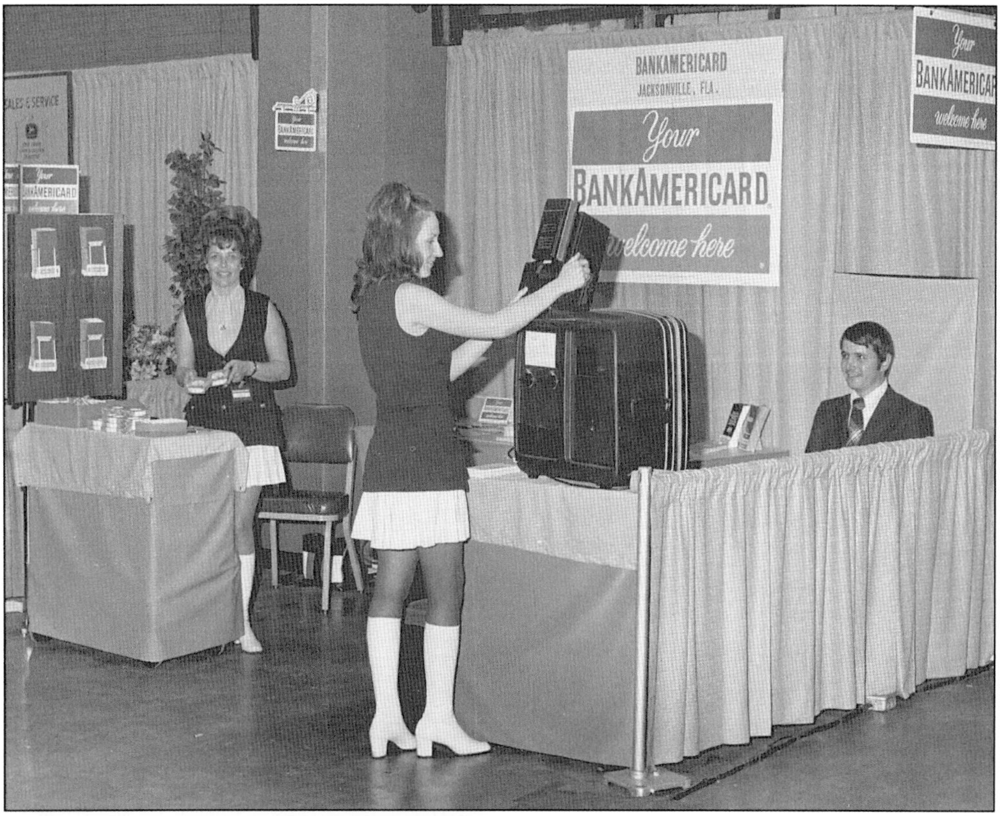

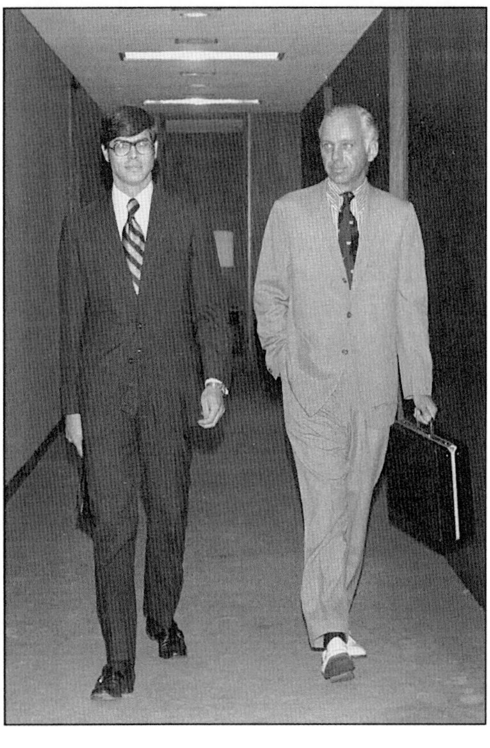

Barnett launched its BankAmericard program in 1969. The following year, the bank introduced a new type of BankAmericard, with a full-color photo of the cardholder. This innovation was designed to reassure customers who might be reluctant to get a credit card for fear of losing it and having it used fraudulently. Cameras were set up in all banking facilities to photograph cardholders so that the cards could be reissued. (Photo by J. Gordon Spottswood.)

Hugh H. Jones Jr., a veteran correspondent banking officer from Chemical Bank, joined Barnett in 1970 as BBFI first vice president and a director. Jones had responsibility for the national calling effort, soliciting corporate customers headquartered outside of Florida, but with stores or business operations in the state. Jones (right) is pictured here with Stephen R. (Bart) Johnson, who assisted him with the out-of-state business development calling. (Photo by J. Gordon Spottswood.)

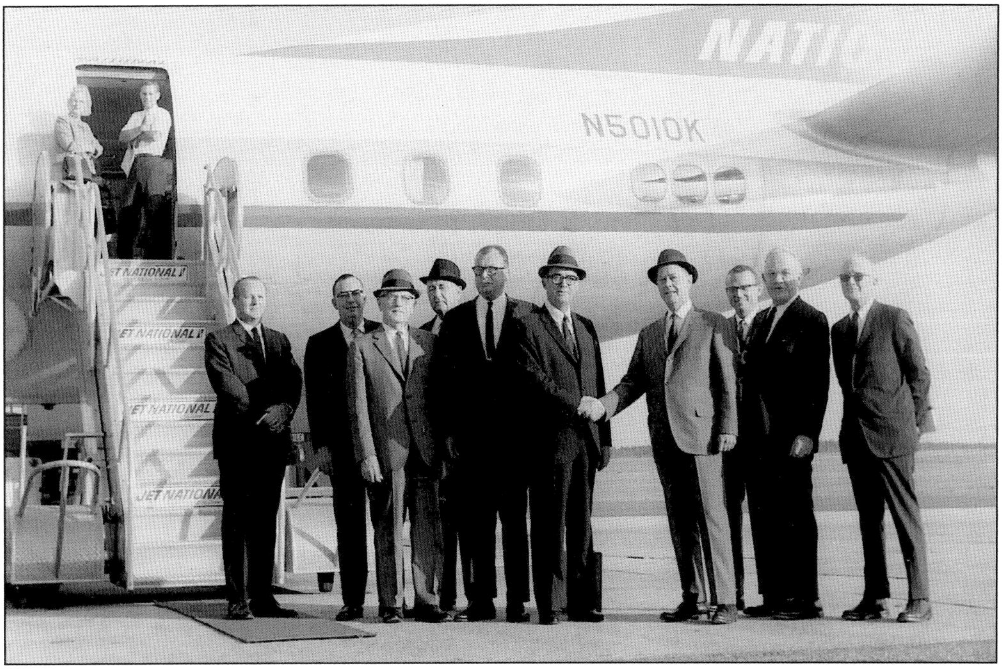

First Bank & Trust Company president F.M. "Son" Turner greets Guy Botts at the Pensacola airport. Barnett directors flew to Pensacola for the holding company's first board meeting to be held outside of Jacksonville, on October 11, 1967. From left to right are Ernie Allen, LeRoy Gardner, Boone Lipscombe, W.R. Rosenfelt, W.R. Barnett, Botts, Turner, Jack Chambers, Elgin Bayless, and William Woods.

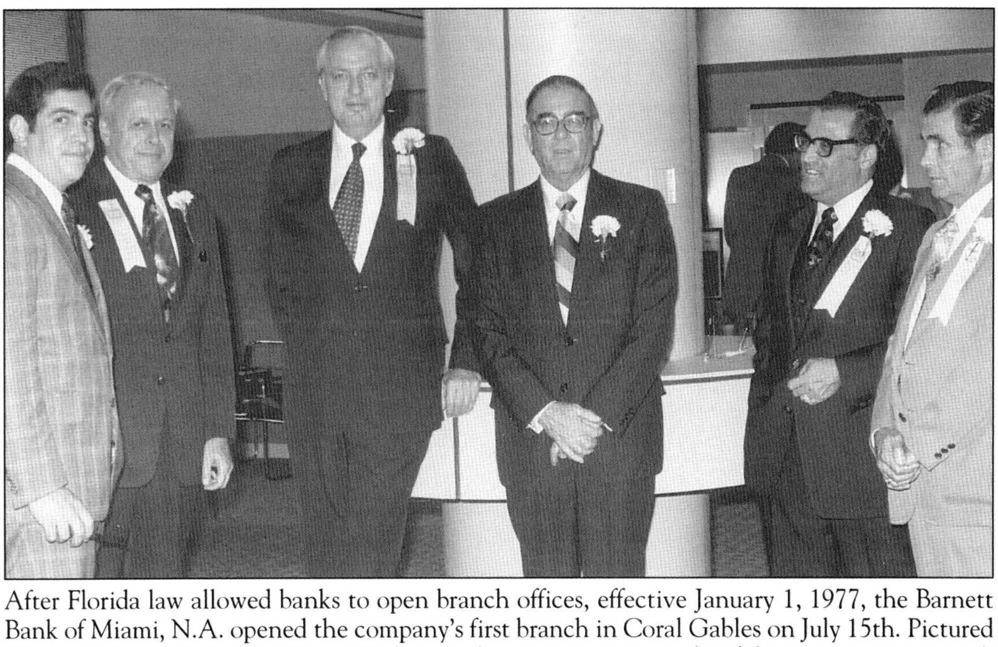

After Florida law allowed banks to open branch offices, effective January 1, 1977, the Barnett Bank of Miami, N.A. opened the company's first branch in Coral Gables on July 15th. Pictured at the branch opening are, from left to right, BBFI vice president/planning Steve Hansel, Joseph Shulman, Miami vice chairman Charles A. Whitcomb, Guy Botts, Miami president Carlos J. Arboleya, and Coral Gables office manager Richard Sankey.

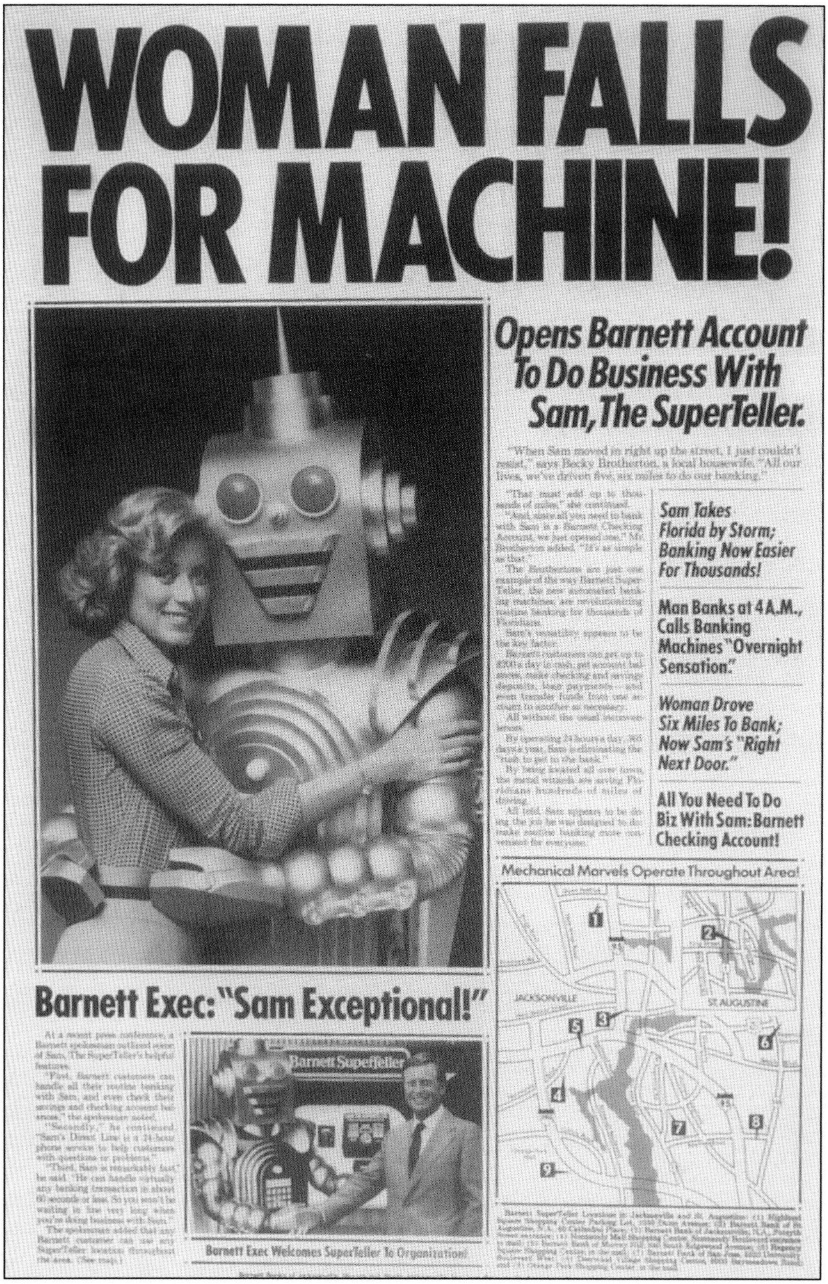

Barnett first introduced automated teller machines, or ATMs, in 1976, with a pilot program in northeast Florida. To promote public acceptance and to market the new service, Barnett sought to humanize its ATM by naming it "Sam the SuperTeller." Barnett contracted to have a "Sam the SuperTeller" costume made, a nearly 7-foot-tall creation of plastic and urethane foam, complete with a low battery voltage pack that powered special lighting effects for its mouth, eyes, and ears. While designed for use during public appearances to promote ATM usage, the suit unfortunately proved so heavy and bulky, with limited mobility, that its use was largely restricted to publicity photos, like the one above.

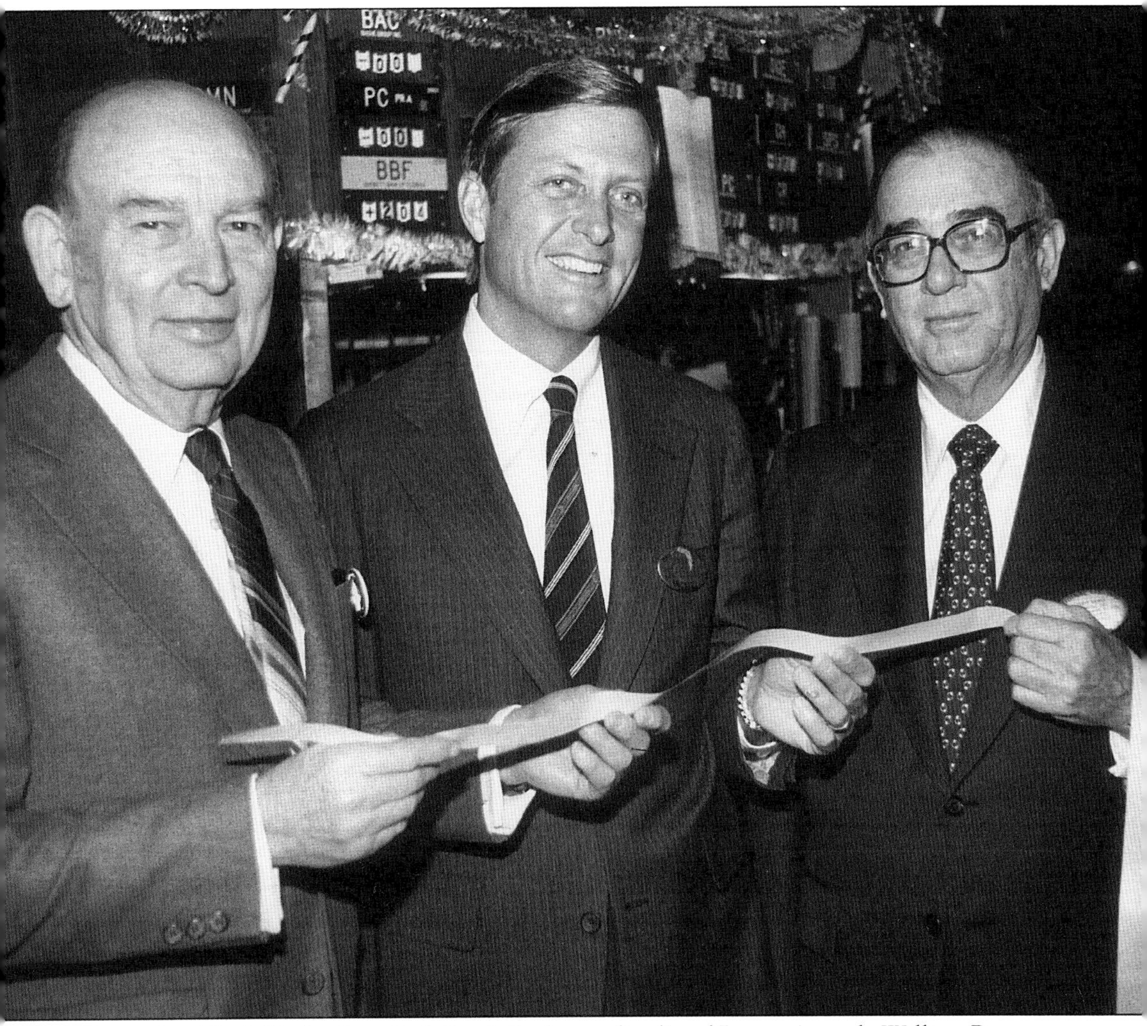

On December 17, 1979, the New York Stock Exchange first listed Barnett's stock. William Batten (left), chairman of the New York Stock Exchange, Barnett president Charles Rice, and Barnett chairman Guy Botts check the ticker tape for the opening trade during listing ceremonies on the Exchange trading floor. Barnett Banks of Florida, Inc., listed under the ticker symbol BBF, opened at 20 1/2. (Photo by Wagner International.)

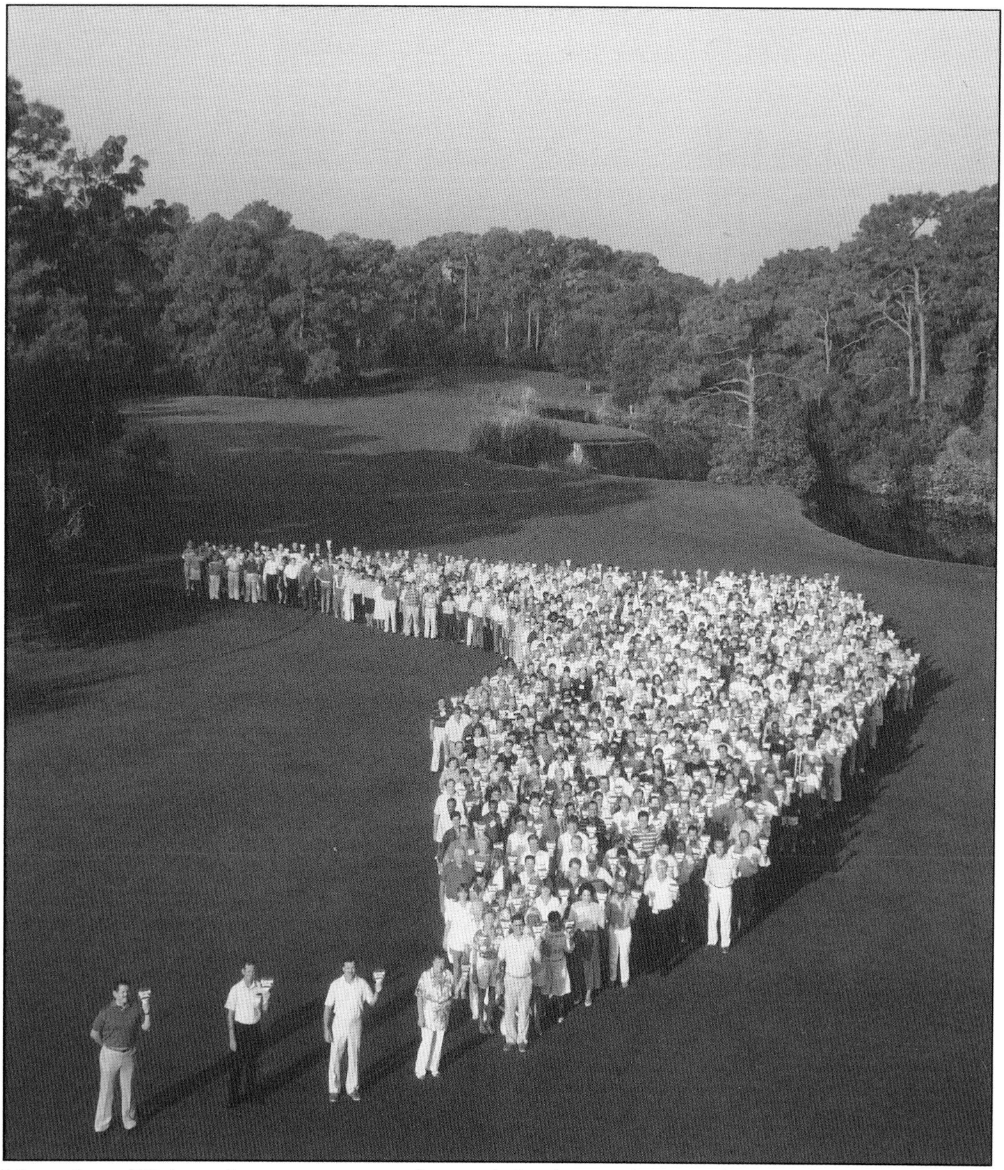

More than 400 branch managers, together with bank presidents and senior holding company staff, gathered for this picture, posed in the shape of the state of Florida, at the 1986 Fall Presidents/Office Managers Meeting at Innsbrook.

Six

The Statewide Franchise

During its first 52 years, Barnett remained an exclusively Jacksonville institution. In the summer of 1929, however, groups of businessmen from DeLand and Cocoa, both left without any banking facilities because of the widespread bank failures sweeping Florida, visited Barnett president William R. McQuaid and other senior officers to urge the Barnett National Bank to open new banks in their cities. Consequently, the Barnett National Bank of DeLand opened on October 24, 1929, and the Barnett National Bank of Cocoa 11 days later. In 1930, Barnett opened a third newly chartered bank in Avon Park and purchased a controlling interest in the St. Augustine National Bank.

Although the Barnett National Securities Corporation owned a majority interest in each of these four affiliated banks, it exercised only minimal supervision. A senior Barnett National Bank officer headed each affiliate as president, while retaining his other responsibilities in Jacksonville. Frank Norris became president at the DeLand bank, Don Barnett at Cocoa and Avon Park, and Camillus L'Engle at St. Augustine, but management of the day-to-day operations of each bank was left to the senior on-site officers. Monthly financial reports were sent to Jacksonville, but as long as no serious problems developed, the parent company followed a largely hands-off policy. In 1937, Barnett added another affiliate, opening the Barnett National Bank of Ft. Lauderdale. Then, expansion stopped. In fact, the Barnett National Securities Corporation actually sold the Ft. Lauderdale bank in 1944 and the Avon Park bank in 1955.

Not until the mid-1960s, with the advent of Guy Botts's plan to have Barnett represented in every major market throughout Florida, did the bank acquisition program resume. Many of these early acquisitions targeted long-established banks. The Munroe and Chambliss National Bank of Ocala, acquired in 1969, had been founded in 1897. First Bank & Trust Company of Pensacola went back to 1914, and First National Bank at Winter Park to 1917. Others had only been in operation for a short time. In an effort to enter the fast-growing Dade and Broward County markets, Barnett acquired 11 banks in the early 1970s. None were large, and the Brickell Bank of Miami had only been in operation for one year.

During the flurry of acquisition activity, Botts remained the central figure. He personally negotiated each of the deals, with Tom Duer providing the behind-the-scenes analysis of financial ratios, growth projections, and return-on-investment calculations based upon the proposed acquisition price. Botts very effectively capitalized on the many contacts he had developed over the years, especially with fellow lawyers who served on local bank boards. He had a soft-spoken, yet direct negotiating style, with a compelling vision for building a statewide confederation of banks. One of his most persuasive arguments centered on his commitment to allow acquired banks to operate relatively autonomously. His management philosophy, which became a key cultural component of the Barnett organization for the next 30 years, placed primary responsibility for operating the bank on the local president and the local board of directors, who best understood local business conditions. As he explained to a group of security analysts, "In the management of our banks our philosophy aims at decentralization with the President being responsible for each bank's performance. This includes pricing, profitability, growth in deposits, and market share of loans and deposits." Only selected support functions, such as audit, accounting, asset/liability management, computer technology, and marketing, required the technical expertise or offered the substantial economies of scale that justified centralization.

When Botts stepped down as chief executive officer in 1979, Barnett Banks of Florida, Inc. had grown to 120 offices, with $3.6 billion in assets. Under his successor, Charlie Rice, the expansion program accelerated. Not only did Barnett continue to buy small banks in communities like Eustis, Lake City, and Niceville, but it began to purchase rival bank holding companies. In the early 1980s it acquired First State Banking Corporation, First Marine Banks, Great American Banks, and Florida Coast Banks, all in the rapidly growing, deposit-rich southeastern Florida market that stretched from Miami to Palm Beach. When attractive acquisitions became scarce, Barnett purchased two savings and loan associations headquartered in Sarasota and Pinellas Counties, successfully overcoming regulatory objections to these unprecedented transactions. In the mid-1980s, after the passage of legislation permitting regional interstate banking for banks headquartered in the Southeast, Barnett acquired the First National Bank of Cobb County , located just outside of Atlanta, and then several other small Georgia banks.

Steve Hansel, and later Hinton Nobles, spearheaded this feverish acquisition effort. Coupled with an aggressive branching strategy that resulted in an average of 27 branch openings per year throughout the decade of the 1980s, Barnett enjoyed phenomenal market share growth. By 1983, Barnett surpassed Southeast Banking Corporation to become the largest bank in Florida. With the 1992 acquisition of Tampa-based First Florida Banks, the last of its large bank acquisitions, Barnett had grown to nearly $40 billion in assets and controlled 27% of Florida's deposits.

In assessing this statewide growth, two important factors must be remembered. First, Barnett Bank of Jacksonville did not dominate the statewide system once the acquisition program got fully underway. While nominally the "lead bank," by 1981 it had ceased to be the largest. With the population growth and business expansion of the Jacksonville metropolitan area considerably slower than other areas of the state, the Barnett Bank of Jacksonville by the mid-1990s represented less than 8% of the company's assets and had fallen to sixth in size.

Second, and perhaps even more important, Barnett affiliates throughout the state operated, within defined parameters, very independently. The management approach instituted by Botts recognized that the different markets in Florida had unique characteristics and that the local affiliates needed autonomy and flexibility to respond to their different opportunities. One size did not fit all, and programs developed in Jacksonville might not be the best solution, without some modification, in a St. Petersburg or a Palm Beach. As a result, affiliate presidents had considerable autonomy and management discretion to get the job done, defined generally as increasing market share and making the profit contribution agreed to at the annual profit planning session. It was this management approach that contributed to a unique entrepreneurial corporate culture.

Thus, it is difficult to understand the Barnett story without looking at the individual banks within the Barnett system and some of the remarkable bankers who made their mark at the local affiliate level.

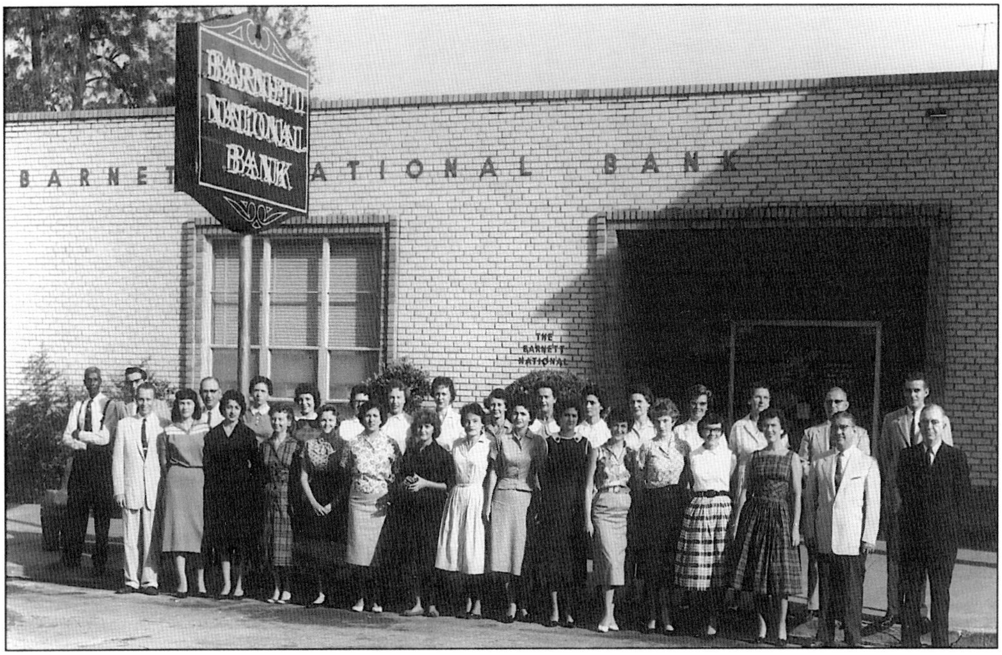

The first Barnett affiliate outside of Jacksonville was the Barnett National Bank of DeLand, founded in October 1929. This photograph shows the staff of the bank outside of its West Indiana Avenue office, to which it moved in 1953.

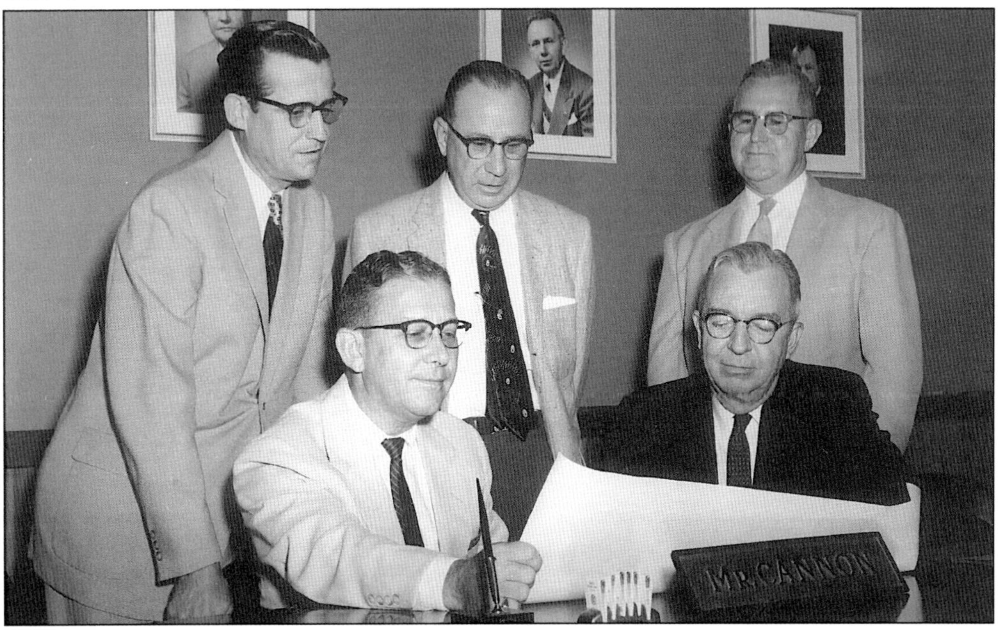

The senior management staff of the DeLand affiliate is pictured here in the early 1960s. From left to right are (seated) John T. Cannon Jr., who joined the bank as a teller in 1930 and became its president in 1956; and vice president Gilmore Anderson; (standing) Allen D. Neckers, who would later become the president of the bank (1971 to 1983); W.C. Holler, who also had joined the bank in 1930 and succeeded Cannon as president in 1969; and cashier Lewis H. Cunningham.

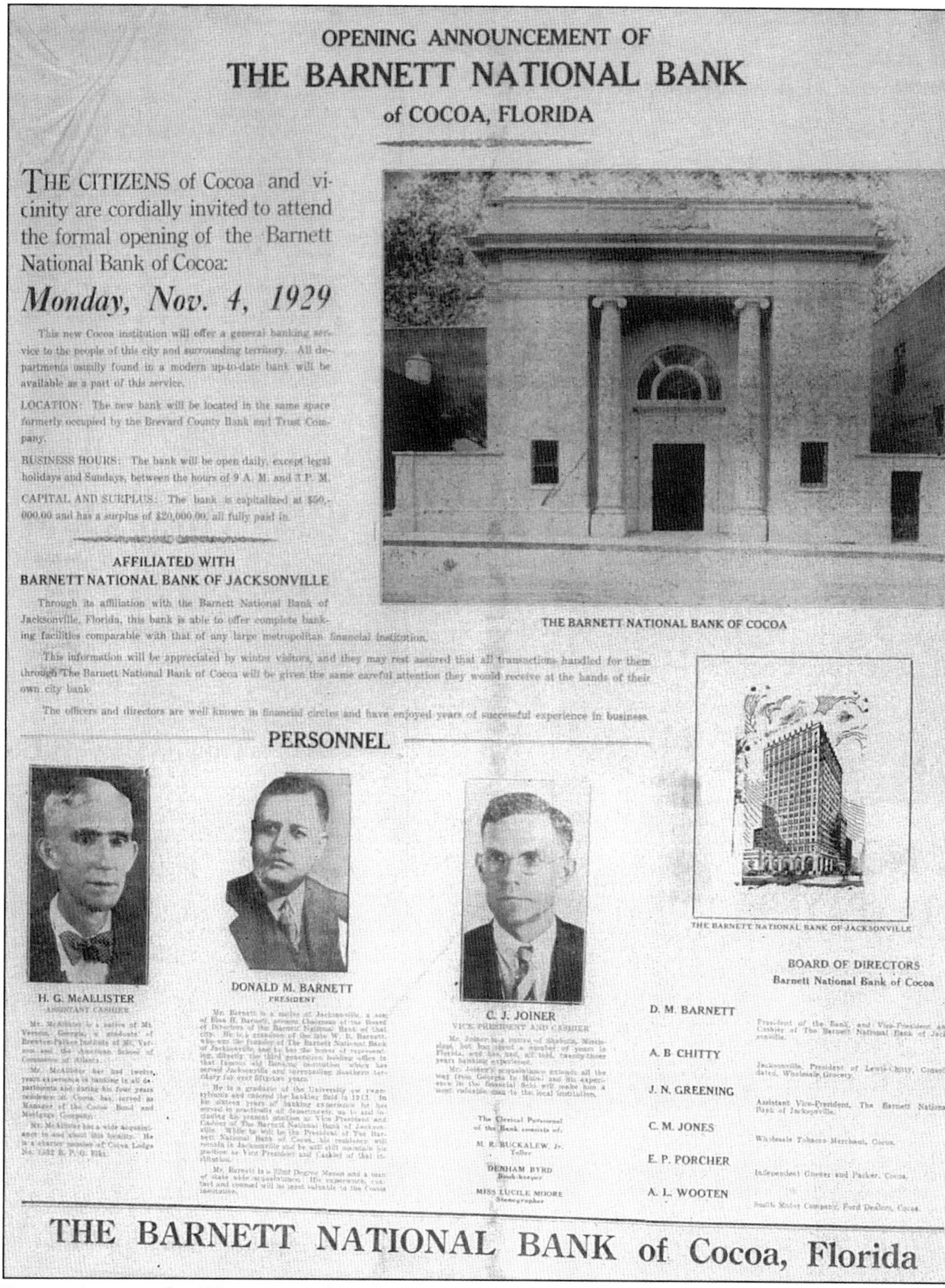

OPENING ANNOUNCEMENT OF

THE BARNETT NATIONAL BANK

of COCOA, FLORIDA

THE CITIZENS of Cocoa and vicinity are cordially invited to attend the formal opening of the Barnett National Bank of Cocoa:

Monday, Nov. 4, 1929

This new Cocoa institution will offer a general banking service to the people of this city and surrounding territory. All departments usually found in a modern up-to-date bank will be available as a part of this service.

LOCATION: The new bank will be located in the same space formerly occupied by the Brevard County Bank and Trust Company.

BUSINESS HOURS: The bank will be open daily, except legal holidays and Sundays, between the hours of 9 A. M. and 3 P. M.

CAPITAL AND SURPLUS: The bank is capitalized at $50,000.00 and has a surplus of $20,000.00, all fully paid in.

AFFILIATED WITH
BARNETT NATIONAL BANK OF JACKSONVILLE

Through its affiliation with the Barnett National Bank of Jacksonville, Florida, this bank is able to offer complete banking facilities comparable with that of any large metropolitan financial institution.

THE BARNETT NATIONAL BANK OF COCOA

This information will be appreciated by winter visitors, and they may rest assured that all transactions handled for them through The Barnett National Bank of Cocoa will be given the same careful attention they would receive at the hands of their own city bank.

The officers and directors are well known in financial circles and have enjoyed years of successful experience in business.

PERSONNEL

H. G. McALLISTER
ASSISTANT CASHIER

DONALD M. BARNETT
PRESIDENT

C. J. JOINER
VICE PRESIDENT AND CASHIER

The Clerical Personnel of the Bank consists of:

M. R. BUCKALEW, Jr.
Teller

DENHAM BYRD
Book-keeper

MISS LUCILE MOORE
Stenographer

THE BARNETT NATIONAL BANK OF JACKSONVILLE

BOARD OF DIRECTORS
Barnett National Bank of Cocoa

D. M. BARNETT — President of the Bank, and Vice-President and Cashier of The Barnett National Bank of Jacksonville.

A. B CHITTY — Jacksonville, President of Lewis-Chitty, Consolidated, Wholesale Grocery.

J. N. GREENING — Assistant Vice-President, The Barnett National Bank of Jacksonville.

C. M. JONES — Wholesale Tobacco Merchant, Cocoa.

E. P. PORCHER — Independent Grower and Packer, Cocoa.

A. L. WOOTEN — Smith Motor Company, Ford Dealers, Cocoa.

THE BARNETT NATIONAL BANK of Cocoa, Florida

Barnett's second affiliate outside of Jacksonville opened in Cocoa on November 4, 1929. Don Barnett was president, with day-to-day operations managed by vice president and cashier C.J. Joiner. This full-page announcement in the *Cocoa Tribune* announced the bank's opening in the building that formerly housed the failed Brevard County Bank and Trust Company. Joiner became president of the bank in 1945. When Joiner retired, H.G. McAllister, who had been an assistant cashier when the bank opened, replaced him as president.

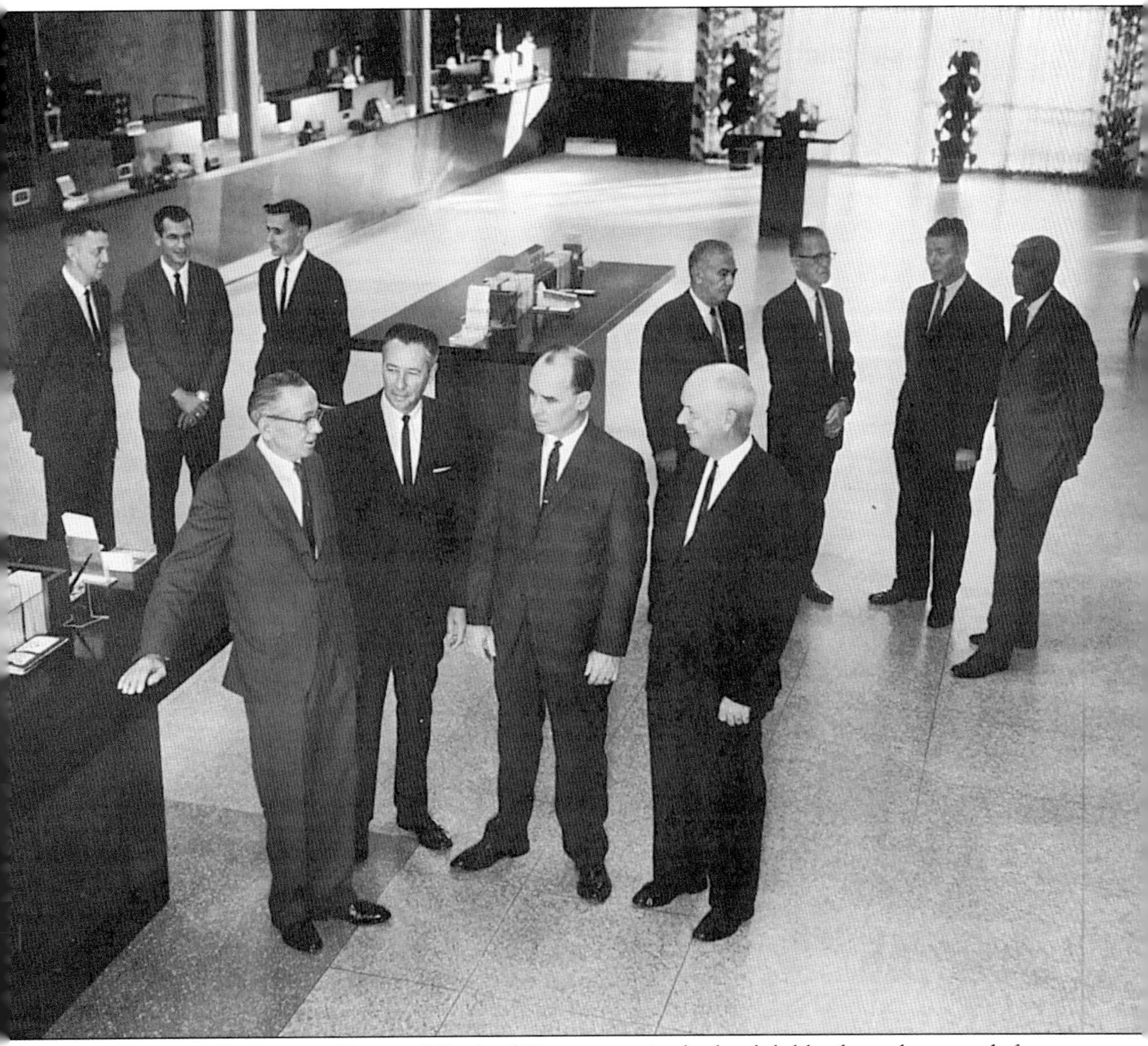

The officers of the Barnett National Bank of Cocoa pose in the bank lobby for a photograph for the 1965 Annual Report. In the foreground is Claude E. "Pappy" Davis (left), who had joined the Cocoa affiliate in 1957 with more than 30 years of banking experience. The following year, he became president of the bank. With Davis are his three principal vice presidents, from left to right, George B. Riley, Robert A. Oliver, and John Denham Bird Jr. When Davis unexpectedly died in 1970, Bird, one of the five original employees of the Cocoa bank, briefly replaced him as president.

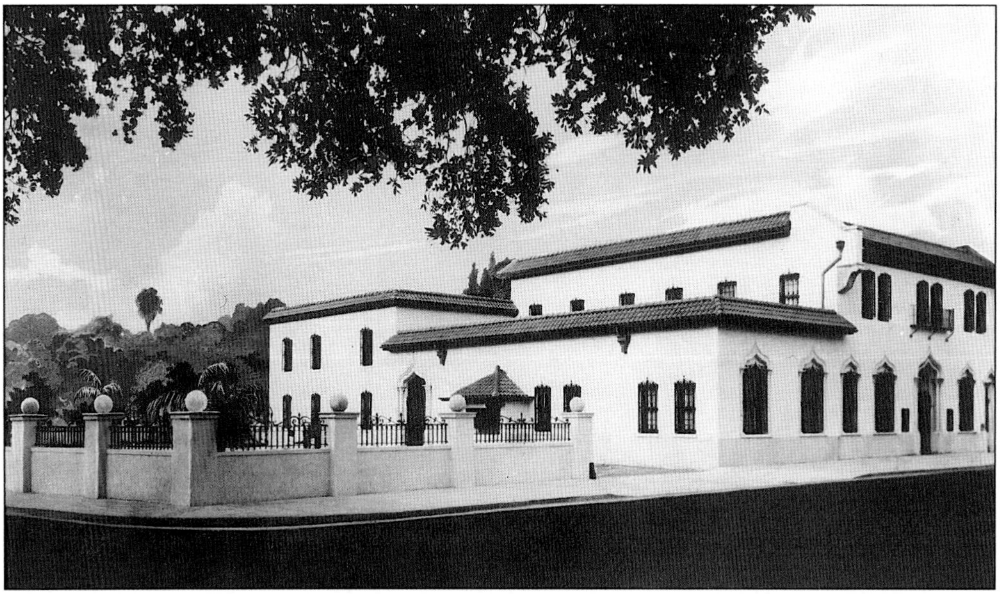

The St. Augustine National Bank opened August 15, 1919, in temporary quarters. It soon relocated to a permanent office at Cathedral and Cordova, situated between the Catholic Cathedral in the center of the city and Henry Flagler's Ponce de Leon Hotel. This location—with several intervening remodelings—remains the bank's principal office to this day. Pictured above is the bank prior to the 1967 remodeling.

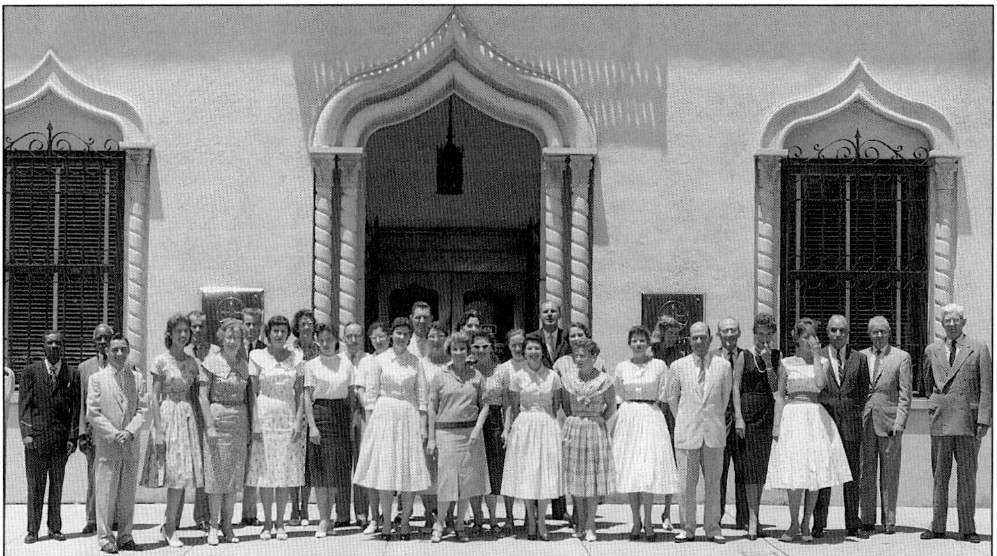

The staff of the St. Augustine National Bank pose outside of the banking office on its 40th anniversary. The second man on the left is Allen Stowball, who joined the bank in November 1919, only months after the bank opened. He worked for the bank until 1973, mostly in custodial work. During his last decade of employment he set his own schedule and became known as a "Lobby Ambassador," greeting customers. He rode his bicycle to work until 1970, when, at the age of 92, he started to take a cab.

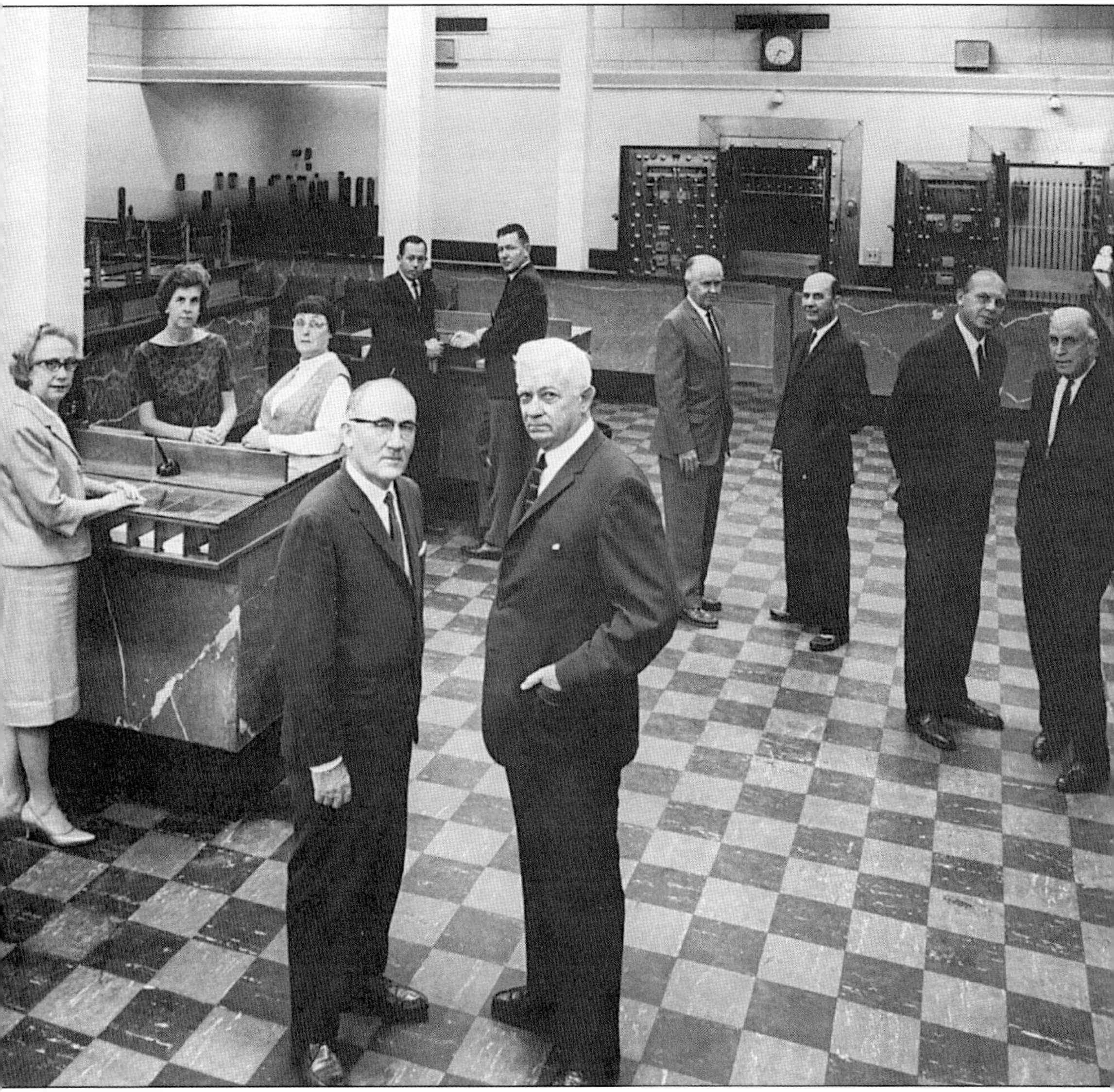

The officers of the St. Augustine National Bank stand in the bank lobby in 1965. In the front are first vice president X.L. Pellicer (left) and president Frank H. Harrold (right), both of whom had been with the St. Augustine bank since its founding in August 1919. Pellicer was the great-great grandson of the leader of the Minorcan colonists who settled in St. Augustine in the 1770s and was an active community leader, an avid proponent of historic preservation, and past president of the Florida Forestry Association. Harrold had been the senior on-site manager of the St. Augustine bank since 1933 and president since 1945. When Harrold retired in 1968, H.A. "Tony" Meitin (far right), who had been born in Havana, Cuba, but raised in St. Augustine, succeeded him as president. Next to Meitin is Edward J. Cosgrove, who became president of the bank in 1970. There is still another future bank president in this photo, Robert E. Hood (back left), who succeeded Cosgrove in 1980.

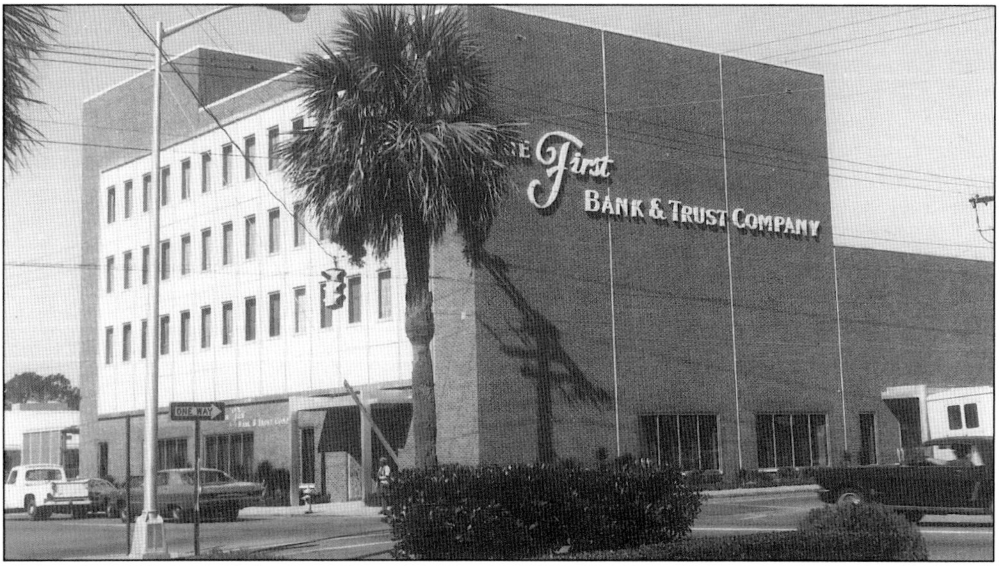

Barnett's first acquisition of the Botts era was the First Bank & Trust Company of Pensacola. The bank had been founded in 1914 as The Banking Savings and Trust Company. One of the three major banks in Pensacola, by 1966 it had $30 million in assets. Pictured above is the banking office at the northwest corner of Garden and Baylen Streets, first occupied in 1963.

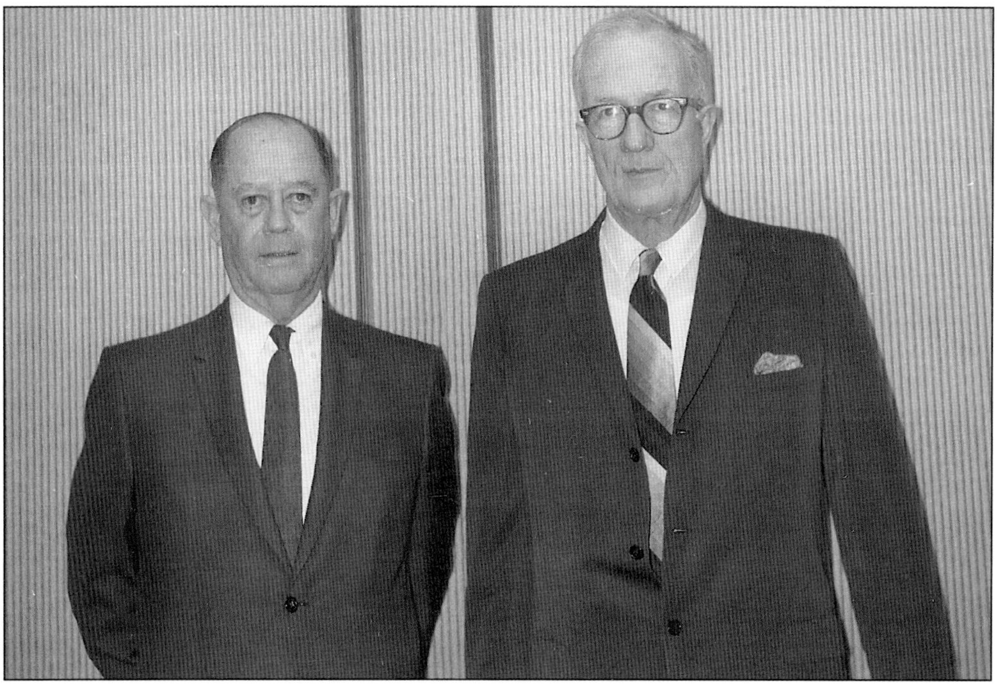

Two representatives from First Bank & Trust joined the Barnett National Securities Corporation's board of directors: Francis M. "Son" Turner Jr. (left) and E. Dixie Beggs Jr. Turner, related by marriage to the Malone family that owned a controlling interest, had been president of the bank since 1947. Beggs, a prominent attorney, had helped Botts get a scholarship in the 1930s to finance his law school studies. Beggs had been on First Bank & Trust's board since 1933 and remained a Barnett director until 1993.

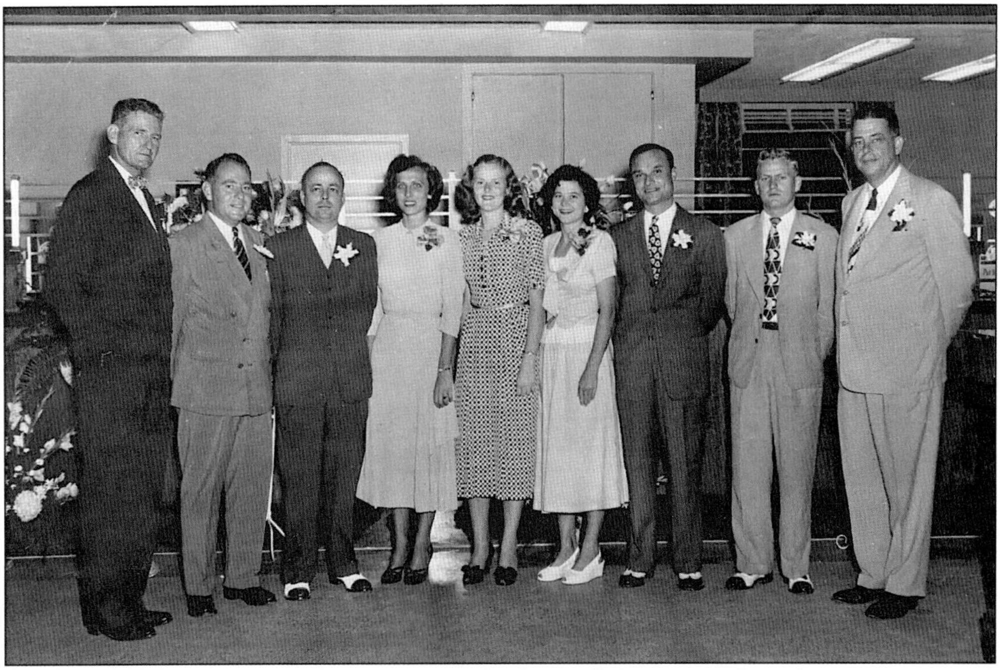

The Tallahassee State Bank (later renamed The Tallahassee Bank and Trust Company) opened on September 1, 1949. The staff of the bank on opening day included, from left to right, chairman Millard F. Caldwell (former governor of Florida), executive vice president Tom N. Humphress, assistant cashier W. Walker Tharpe, Betty Atkinson, Geraldine Murphy, Vernon Andrews Butler, assistant cashier Harman Wheeler, Hershel Stalvey, and president F. Wilson Carraway Sr.

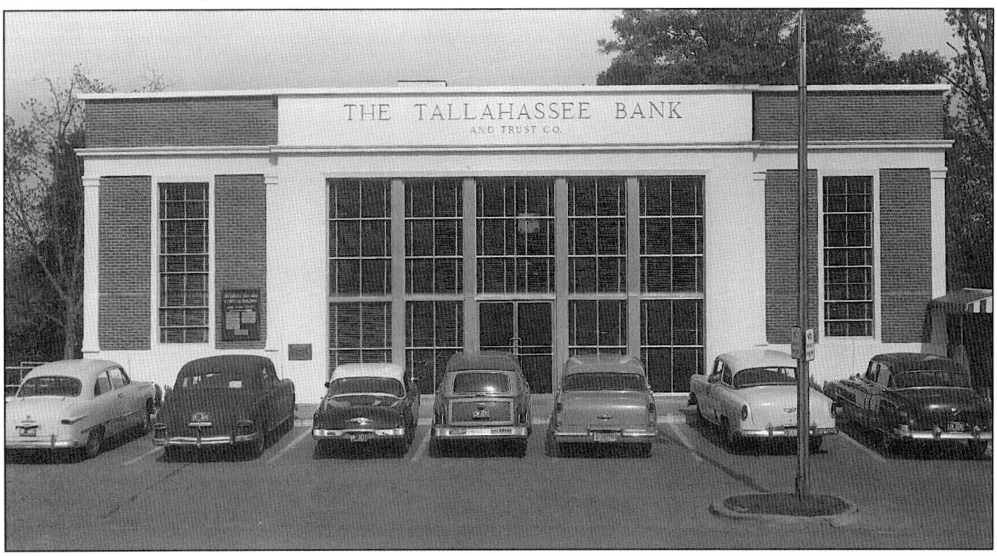

The Tallahassee Bank and Trust Company opened at the southeast corner of Calhoun and Jefferson Streets (above). It remained in this building from 1949 to 1968. Barnett purchased the Tallahassee bank in 1969, and Governor Caldwell joined Barnett's board. The following year, Humphress became president of the bank, later renamed Barnett Bank of Tallahassee, and continued in that position until 1981. (Photo by L'Avant Studios.)

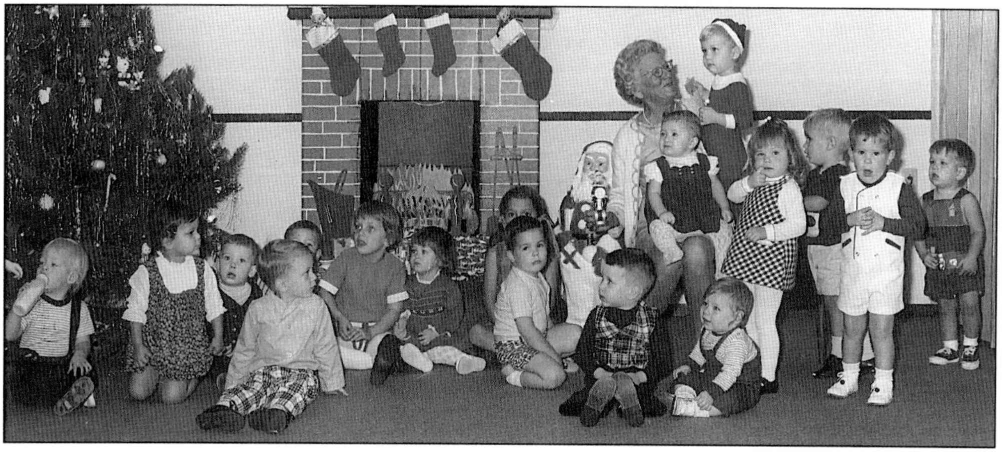

Mamie B. Tooke was Barnett's first woman president. She and her husband, Clarence, opened the Bank of Naples in 1949. Shortly afterwards, Clarence became seriously ill, and Mamie ran the bank during his illness, becoming president after his death in 1955. After Barnett bought the bank in 1974, she continued as CEO of what the locals simply called "Mamie's bank" and also became a BBFI director. Devoted to her staff, Mamie is pictured here hosting her annual Christmas party for the children of the bank's employees. (Photo by Ernest R. Burlingame.)

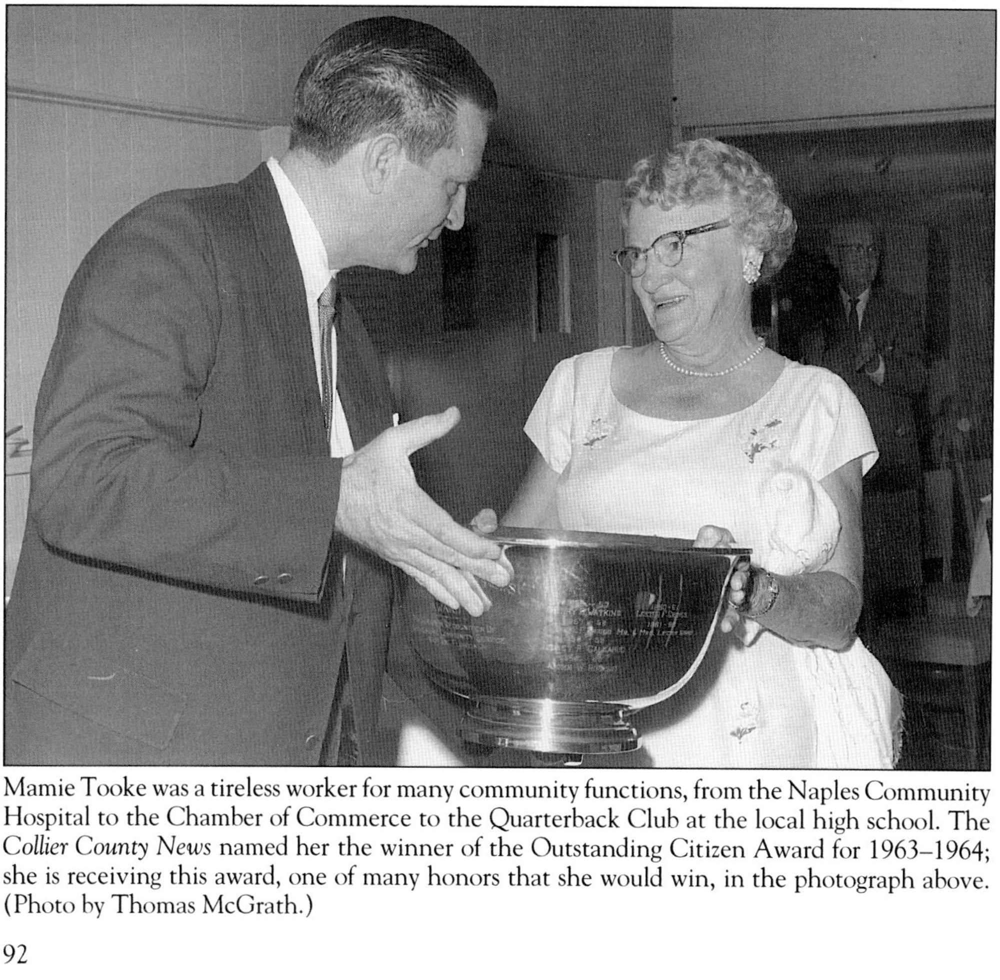

Mamie Tooke was a tireless worker for many community functions, from the Naples Community Hospital to the Chamber of Commerce to the Quarterback Club at the local high school. The *Collier County News* named her the winner of the Outstanding Citizen Award for 1963–1964; she is receiving this award, one of many honors that she would win, in the photograph above. (Photo by Thomas McGrath.)

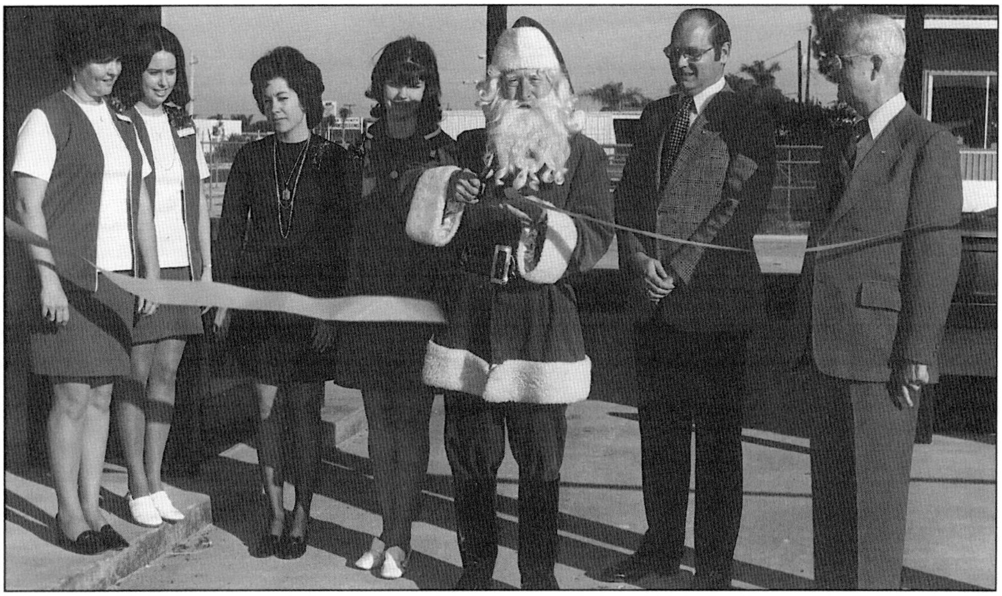

The Barnett Bank of Ft. Myers, N.A. opened its Fowler Street remote facility on December 11, 1975. From left to right are Ruth Carmichael, Karla Davis, Barbara Smallwood, Ruth McDonald, Santa, president Steve Zahorian, and chairman of the board A.W.D. Harris. (Photo by Harmon Photographers.)

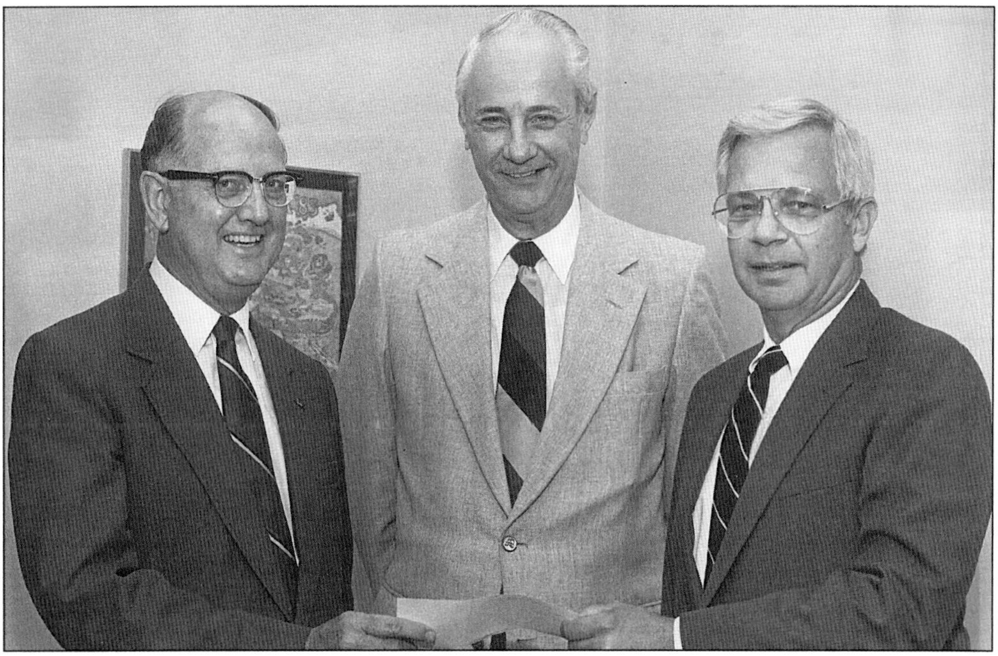

Barnett Bank of West Florida president C. Carl Mertins Jr. presents a check to establish a Barnett scholarship at the University of West Florida, July 16, 1987. From left to right are Mertins, R.C. Einbecker (dean of the College of Business, UWF), and L.H. McDaniel (director of Development and Alumni Affairs, UWF). Barnett was a strong supporter of higher education and funded numerous scholarships and academic chairs at colleges and universities throughout the state. (Courtesy of University of West Florida.)

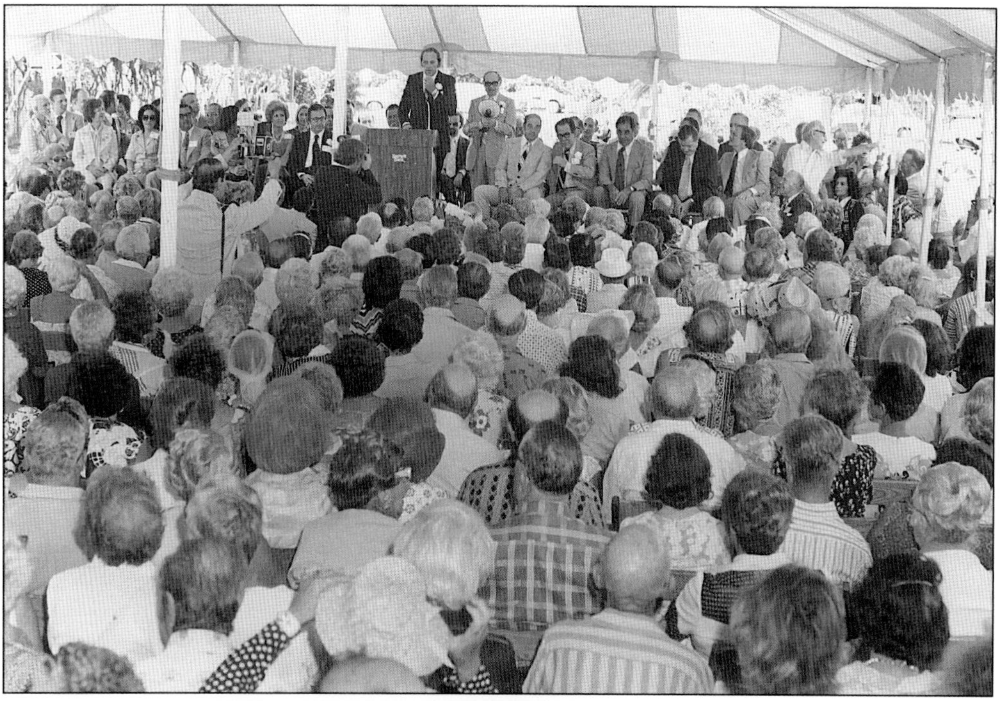

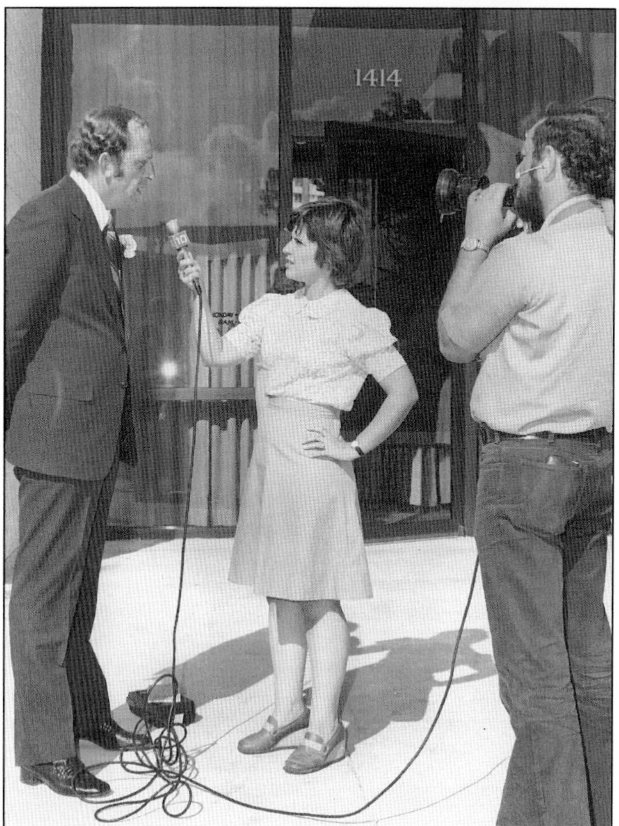

On September 21, 1975, the Barnett Bank of Miami Beach, N.A. opened a Senior Citizens Banking Center at Alton Road. The facility was designed with special features for senior citizens, including ramps (no steps), lowered teller windows, a "free" hotline to the district social security office, and monthly senior citizen health days when medical services such as glaucoma screening and blood pressure checks would be offered. More than 1,000 people came to the grand dedication, attracted by a free fried chicken brunch. Numerous dignitaries attended, including the Miami Beach mayor and the entire city council. Addressing the crowd above is bank president Alan E. Master. Seated on the podium to Master's right is U.S. Senator Richard Stone. To the left, Master is interviewed by a reporter from one of the local television stations. (Photos by Martin Aronow.)

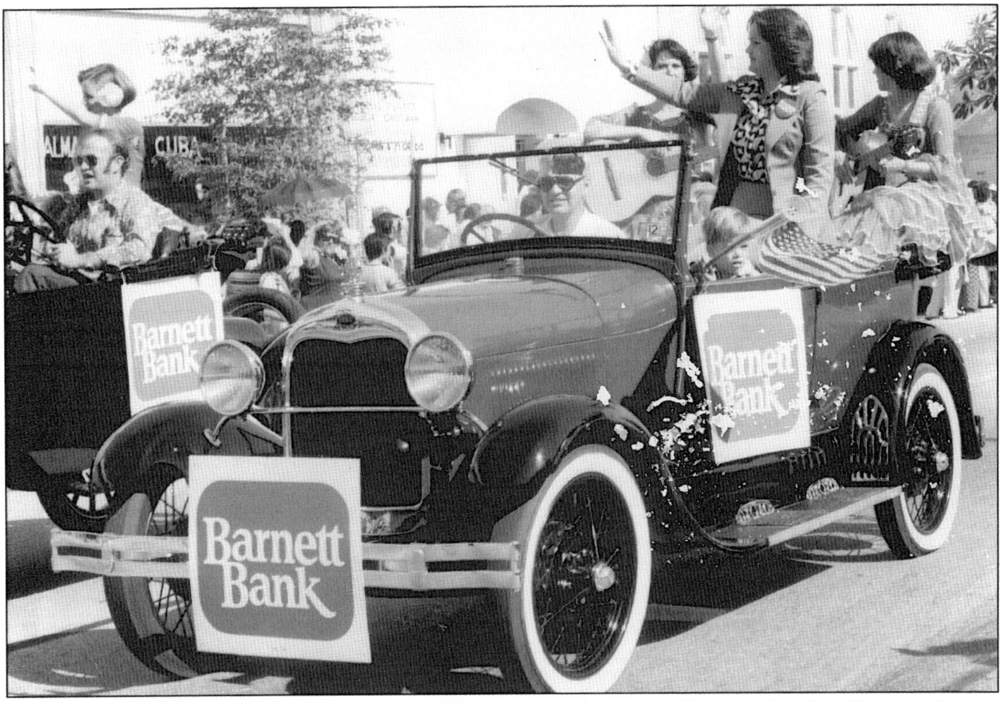

On January 1, 1977, five Dade County affiliates merged to form Barnett Bank of Miami, N.A., the second largest bank in the Barnett system with $230 million in deposits. The following week, the newly consolidated bank participated in Miami's traditional Three Kings Parade, celebrating the Feast of the Epiphany.

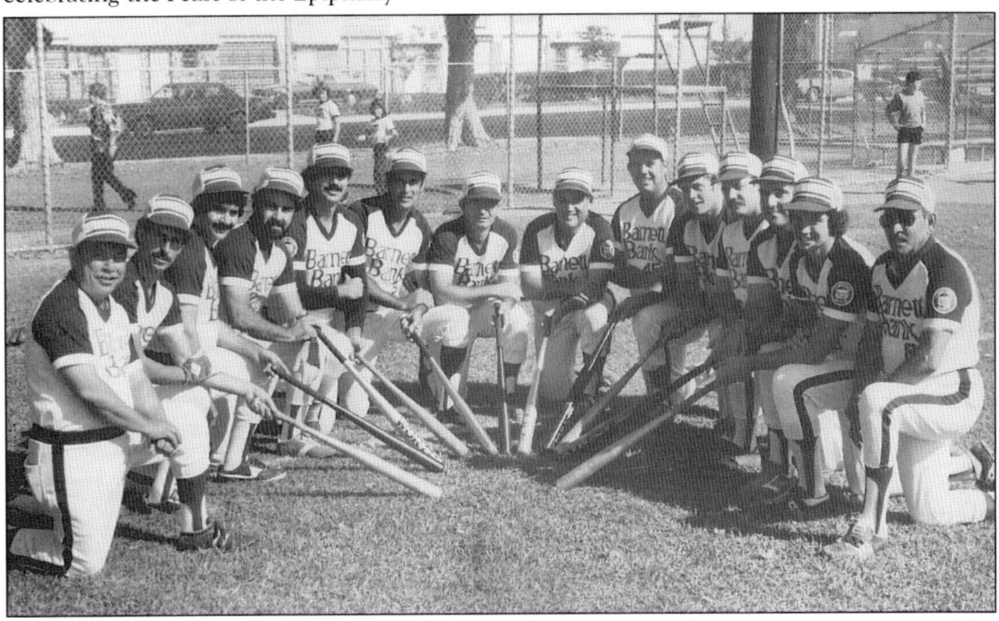
Barnett Bank of Miami's softball team participated in the city softball league in the late 1970s, led by their pitcher and bank president, Carlos J. Arboleya (eighth from left). Among the star players who won eight championship trophies for the "Green Bombers" was former major leaguer Rudy Arias. (Photo by Gort Photo Studio.)

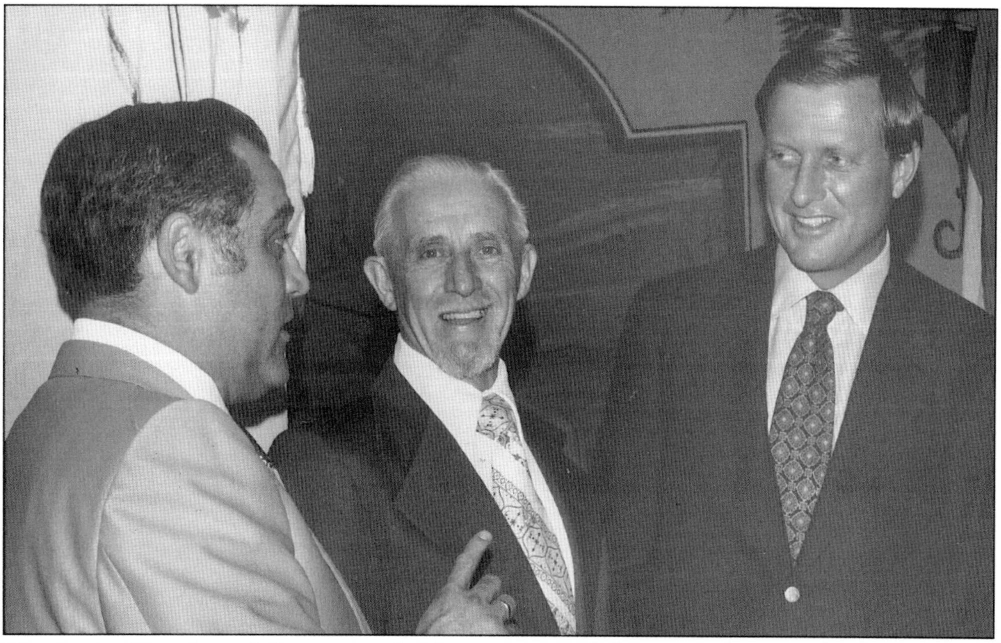

The Latin Chamber of Commerce held a testimonial dinner to honor Charles M. Volk, chairman of the board of Barnett Banks at Westchester, N.A. and Midway, N.A., who was retiring in 1976 after 43 years in banking. Pictured above are "The Three Charles." From left to right, they are Westchester and Midway president Carlos J. Arboleya, Volk, and BBFI president and chief operating officer Charles E. Rice. (Photo by Gort Photo Studio.)

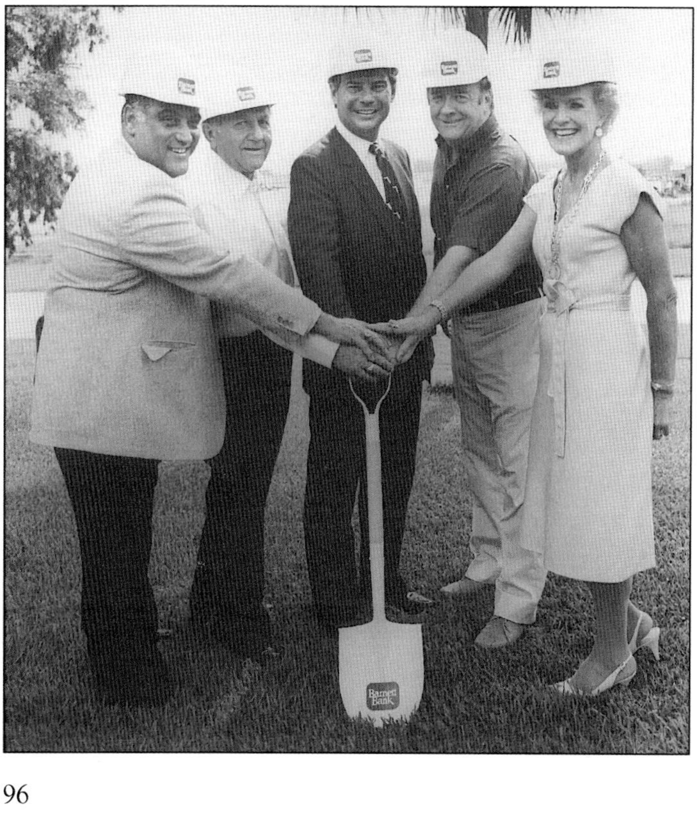

A groundbreaking ceremony for the Barnett Bank of South Florida Operations Center was held in August 1982. From left to right are vice chairman Carlos J. Arboleya, director A.J. Capeletti, Florida governor Bob Graham, president and CEO J. Edward Houston, and director Irma Baker Lyons.

Carlos J. Arboleya was a Barnett president or vice chairman for 19 years. A Cuban refugee who arrived in Miami in 1960 with a wife, a two-year-old son, and $40, he became a community legend. He won countless awards, including the prestigious Horatio Alger Award for succeeding against great odds. Of his many civic achievements, none made him more proud than his involvement with the Boy Scouts, both in the Miami area and on the national level.

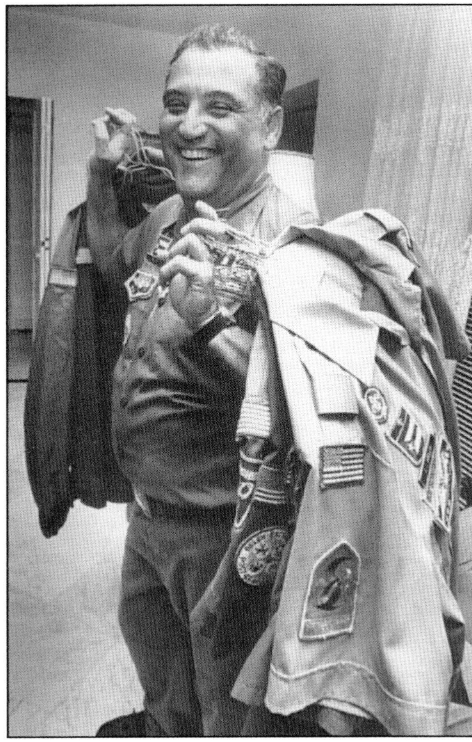

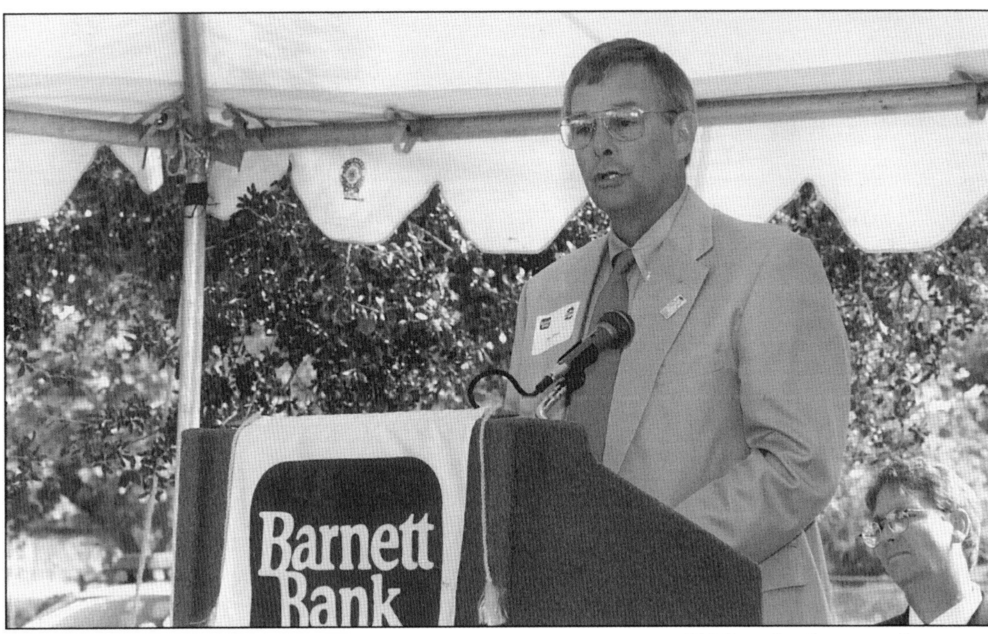

Bill Myers began his Barnett career as a management trainee in 1970 and subsequently rose to be head of the Metropolitan Division of the Barnett Bank of Jacksonville, N.A. In 1982, Myers became president of the Barnett Bank of Manatee County, N.A. and, then in 1990, the Barnett Bank of South Florida, N.A. He headed the South Florida bank, Barnett's largest affiliate with more than $5 billion in assets, from 1990 until the NationsBank acquisition. (Photo by A Woman's Touch.)

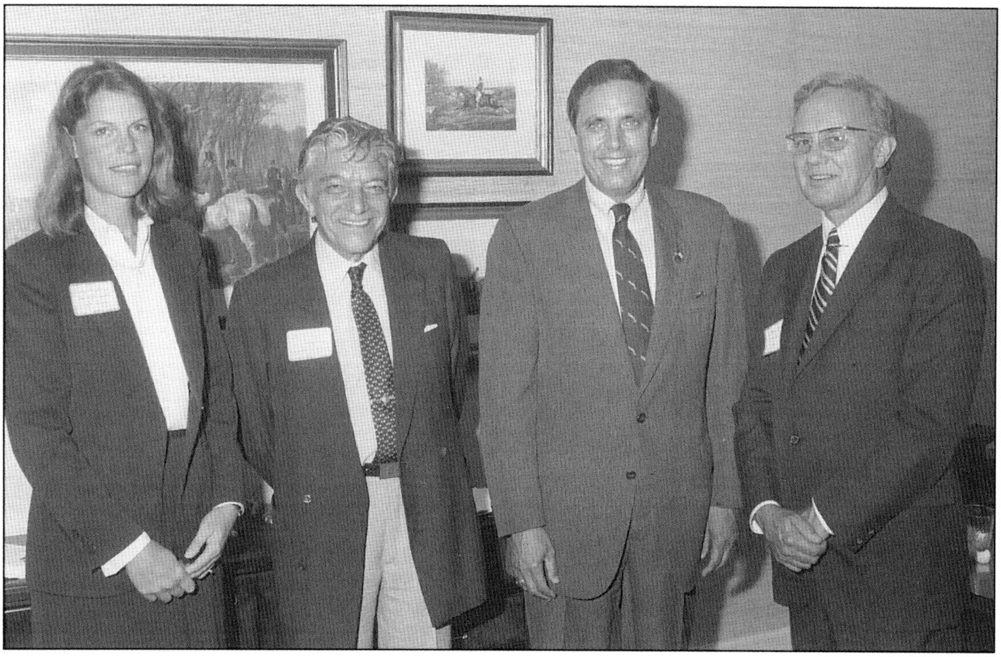

Barnett Bank of Tampa, N.A. hosted a reception on May 7, 1984 for the Honorable Emilio Martin, counsel general of Spain. Pictured, from left to right, are vice president/marketing Maria Henderson, Martin, Tampa mayor (later Florida governor) Bob Martinez, and senior vice president/ marketing Otto Souder. Before joining the Tampa affiliate, Souder had headed BBFI marketing during the 1970s, when Barnett launched its corporate identification program and began annual statewide advertising campaigns.

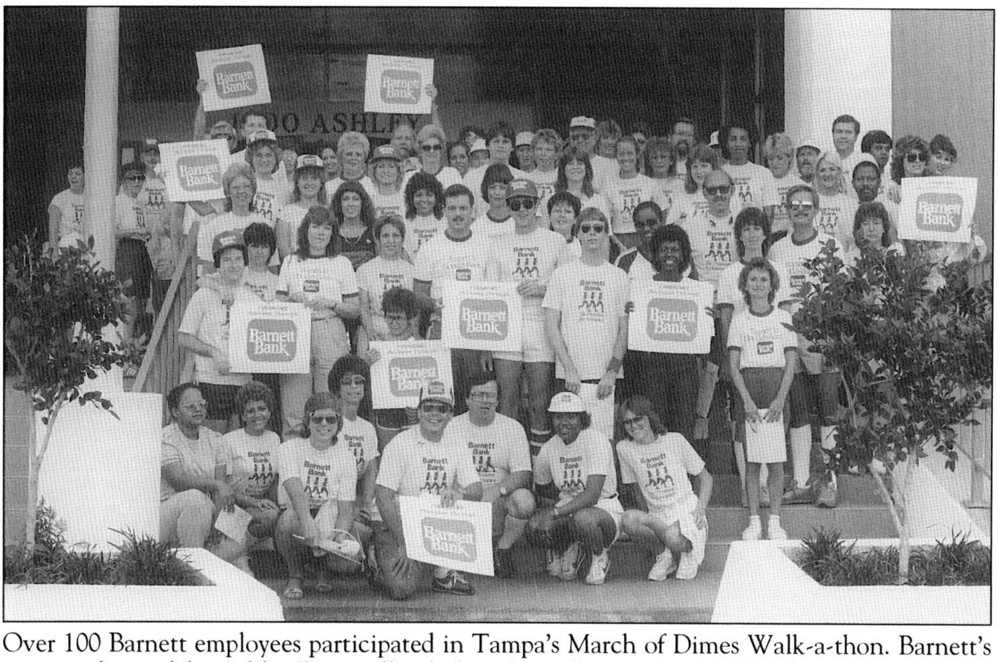

Over 100 Barnett employees participated in Tampa's March of Dimes Walk-a-thon. Barnett's team, in front of the Ashley Drive office before the walk, raised more than $4,000, the second-highest money earner for that April 1984 event.

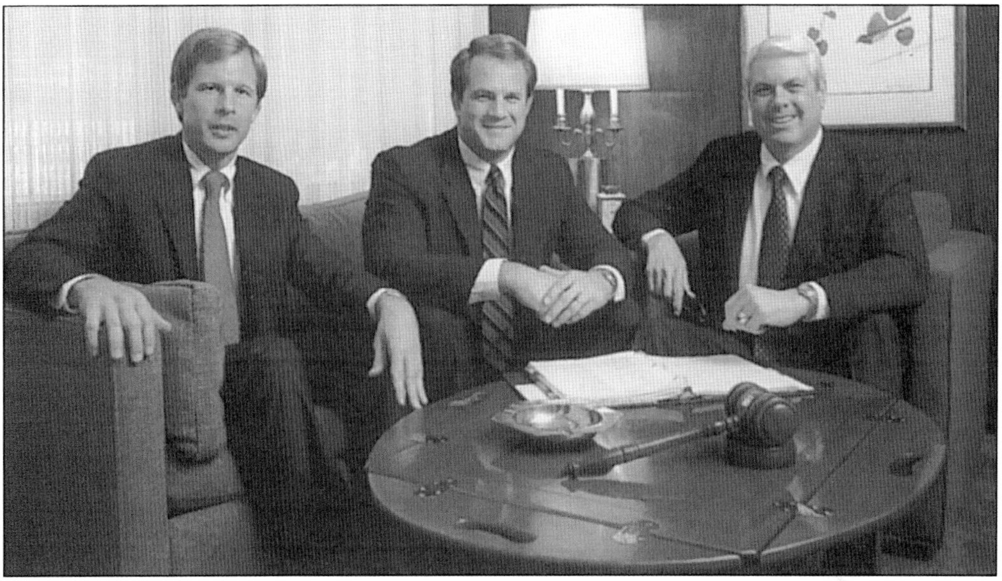

Charles K. "Pete" Cross, a veteran Georgia and South Carolina banker, joined Barnett in 1974 and headed the Central Florida affiliate for the next 19 years. Known for his development of management talent, Cross (right) is pictured here with two of his many successful protégés, Mike Strickland (left) and Rick Anderson (center). Strickland was president of the Barnett Bank of Palm Beach County for many years, while Anderson headed the Naples and Broward County affiliates and later became a regional banking executive.

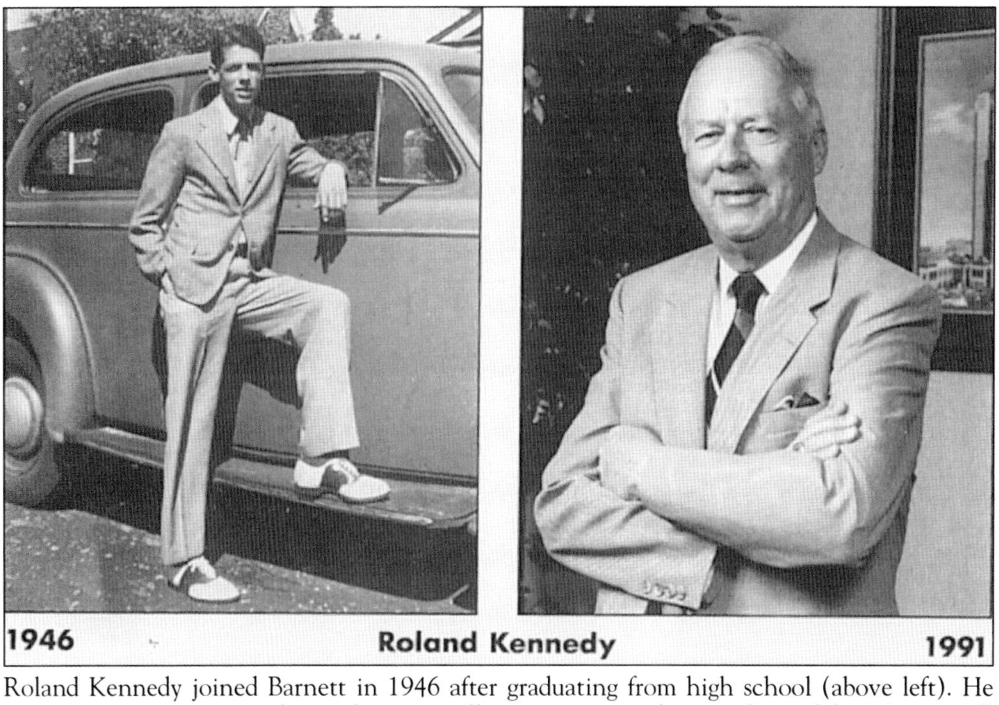

Roland Kennedy joined Barnett in 1946 after graduating from high school (above left). He started wrapping coin in the vault, eventually progressing to be president of the Murray Hill and Jacksonville affiliates. He later became president and CEO of the Barnett Bank of Pinellas County (above right), retiring in 1993 after 47 years of service.

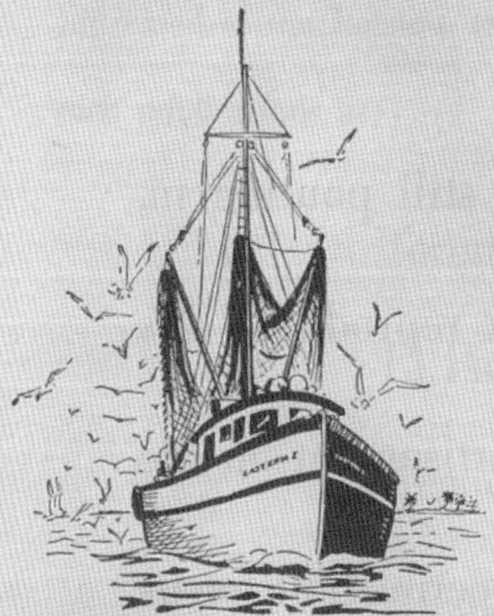

Fight Cancer

Fable of the

GULLIBLE GULL

In our friendly neighbor city of St. Augustine great flöcks of seagulls are starving amid plenty. Fishing is still good, but the gulls don't know how to fish. For generations they have depended on the shrimp fleet to toss them scraps from the nets. Now the fleet has moved to Key West.

The shrimpers had created a Welfare State for the St. Augustine seagulls. The big birds never bothered to learn how to fish for themselves and they never taught their children to fish. Instead they led their little ones to the shrimp nets.

Now, the seagulls, the fine free birds that almost symbolize liberty itself, are starving to death because they gave in to the "something for nothing" lure! They sacrificed their independence for a hand-out.

A lot of people are like that, too. They see nothing wrong in picking delectable scraps from the tax nets of the U. S. Government's "shrimp fleet." But what will happen when the government runs out of goods? What about our children of generations to come?

Let's not be gullible gulls. We Americans must preserve our talents of self-sufficiency, our genius for creating things for ourselves, our sense of thrift and our true love of independence.

The BARNETT NATIONAL BANK
of Jacksonville

Member Federal Reserve System and Federal Deposit Insurance Corporation

"THE OLDEST BANK ON THE PENINSULA OF FLORIDA"

Seven

BUILDING THE BARNETT IMAGE

In 1929, the Barnett National Bank hired Stephen H. Fifield to establish the bank's first public relations and business development department. Over the next 25 years, Fifield directed Barnett's advertising and coordinated efforts by officers and directors to solicit new business, while simultaneously being a tireless worker for a host of civic organizations from the Chamber of Commerce to the Red Cross. Fifield was the first in a series of marketing executives—a list that includes Downing Nightingale (Don Barnett's son-in-law), Otto Souder, Bill Fackler, James Covington, and Susan Blaser—who sought to publicize Barnett and build a positive image about its products and services.

Over the years, Barnett used many different media, from print advertisement in newspapers and magazines to roadside billboards to informational brochures inserted into bank statements. Television became an increasingly important, and expensive, advertising vehicle. In the early 1960s, Barnett used 20-second and 10-second commercials, as well as sponsoring the 15-minute Channel 12 News broadcast every other Friday at 6:30 p.m., which surveys showed had a viewing audience of 47,000 in the Jacksonville area. In the early 1970s, uniform television advertising in all of Florida's major markets became a powerful means of building the company's statewide identity and continued to be a major focus of the annual marketing campaigns. In 1996, when Barnett introduced its new theme, "Ideas For The Way You Live," it launched a TV blitz with 2-minute commercials, featuring an original "Barnett Anthem" musical score, during the news telecasts in all major Florida television markets. With a follow-up campaign of 60-second and 30-second ads, the goal was to reach 10 million viewers.

Barnett's advertising, whether in print, radio, or television, generally either promoted specific products and services or focused on developing a positive "brand" image. In trying to show that Barnett cared about its customers and provided quality service to meet their financial needs, a number of memorable slogans were used—from "The Bank of Your Friends and Neighbors—Make it Yours" in the 1960s to "We Promise Performance" in the 1980s. Perhaps the most successful was the "Barnett Is Florida's Bank" theme introduced in 1984.

Several advertising agencies helped Barnett develop its marketing programs. Stephen Fifield worked closely with the Bacon, Hartman & Vollbrecht agency in St. Augustine, the company that developed the "Gullible Gull" advertisement. After this ad first appeared in the *Florida Times-Union* on April 14, 1950, the Barnett National Bank was inundated with requests for reprints. Eventually, over 400 newspapers throughout the country reprinted this advertisement. Later, Barnett used several nationally recognized advertising agencies, including McKinney & Silver and The Martin Agency. Both agencies, working closely with Barnett's marketing officers, developed television advertisements that received awards from the Bank Marketing Association.

If you ask former Barnetters about their favorite advertisements, you will get many different answers. Maybe it is the Betty White ads, when she and camera crews walked into different branch offices and, unannounced and unrehearsed, she asked questions about the Senior Partners program. Or perhaps it is the "trucks" ad, with bankers of recently acquired competitors being shipped out-of-state on flatbed trucks to their new, far-away headquarters. Or the "Top of the Mountain" ads where the customer is told repeatedly to "Go higher" for an answer to his loan request. There are many memorable ones from which to choose.

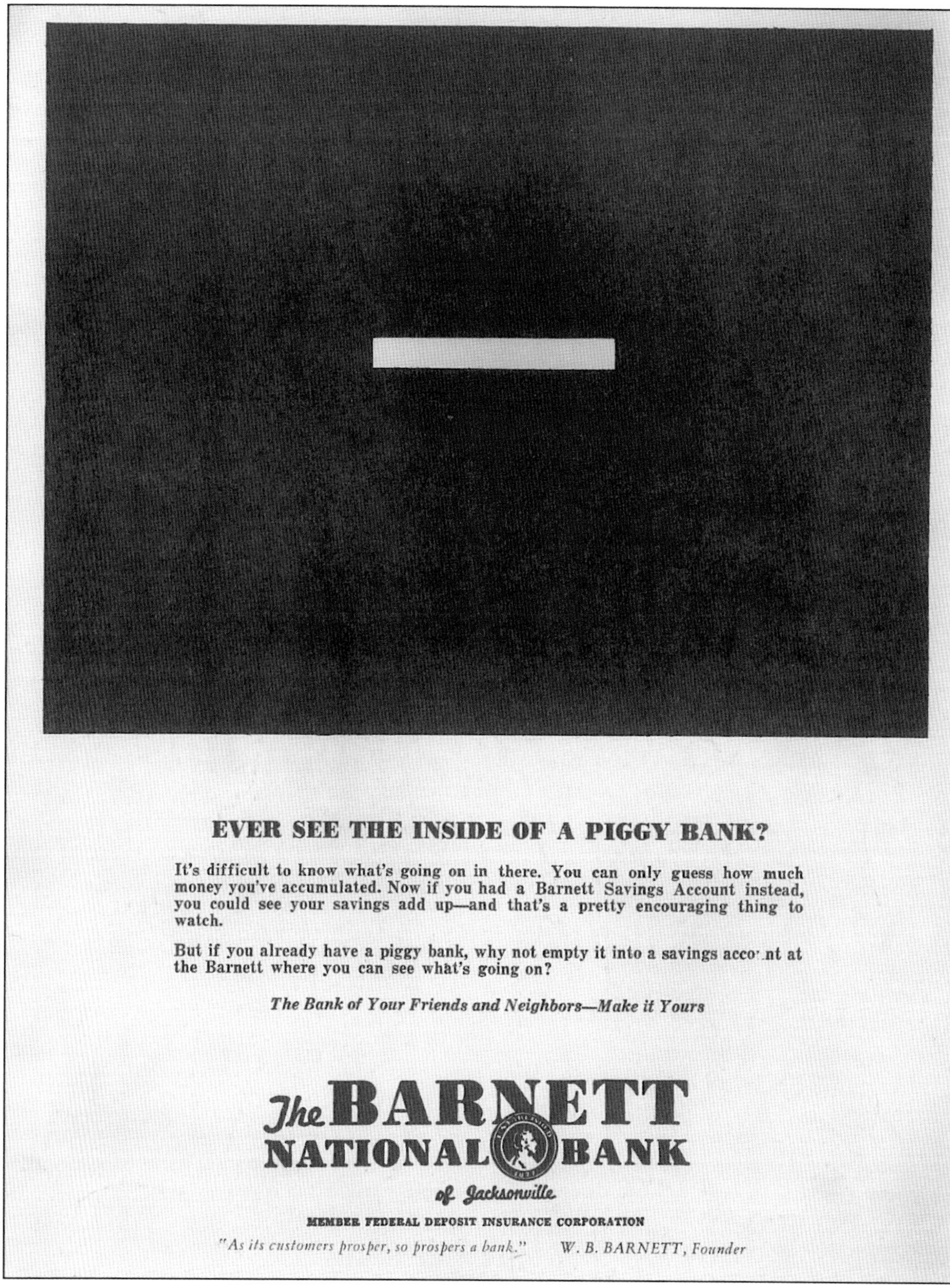

RODNEY DANGERFIELD TELLS HOW HE FINALLY GOT A LITTLE BIT OF RESPECT.

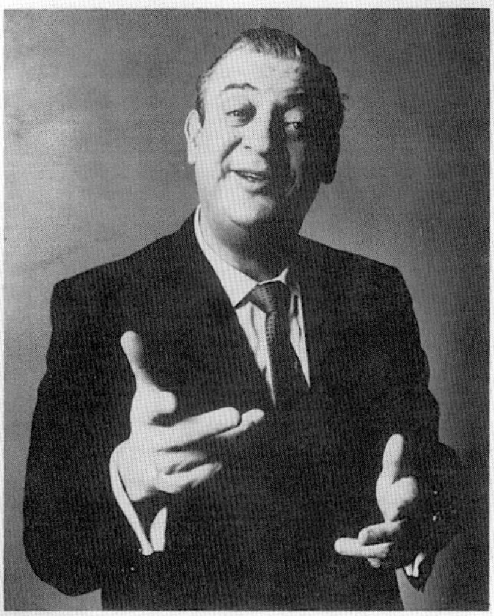

"I don't get no respect. When I was a kid, we played hide-'n-seek. They didn't even look for me.

Last night, my own kid told me to go to my room.

This morning, I had a fight with our dog. My wife said the dog was right.

It's been like this all my life. But the other day, when I was in Florida, something strange happened.

I stopped by this Barnett Bank to open an account. The guard held the door for me. And when I walked up to the teller's window, she didn't snicker; she smiled.

So I asked her, 'What's going on here?'

She said Barnett people treat everybody like a half-millionaire. Because most people do three, four, even $500,000 worth of banking over a lifetime.

That makes each and every customer important to them. So they give everybody respect. Now that's not exactly saying, 'Mr. Dangerfield, I respect you.'

But, me, I take any kind of respect I can get."

Barnett Bank

"I will never forget that cold, rainy night in November when I met Sam."

"It was November 28, 1977.

I remember the date, because it was payday.

I'd worked late, so I hadn't had a chance to deposit my paycheck.

All the banks were closed, and I had nowhere to turn.

I was panicked, until I spotted a green and white glow way off in the distance.

As I got closer, I realized that it was Sam, and that I could use my Barnett SuperCard.

So I made my deposit, got some cash and, in less than sixty seconds, I was on my way.

As I drove along, I thought: If it was that easy, why haven't I been banking with Sam all along?

So now I do. I don't worry about what time of day or night it is, or whether it's a weekend or a holiday.

And, with 11 Sam locations, I don't even worry about where I am. My life's completely changed since I met Sam.

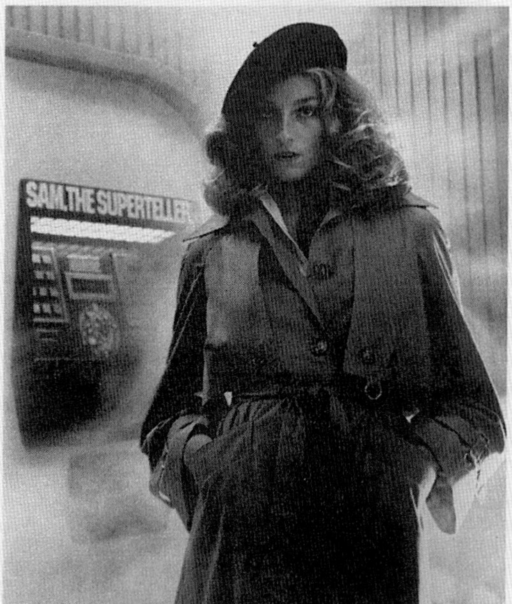

What began as just a casual affair has grown into a meaningful relationship."

There are over 75,000 stories every month about doing business with Sam. This has been one of them.

Sam, The SuperTeller

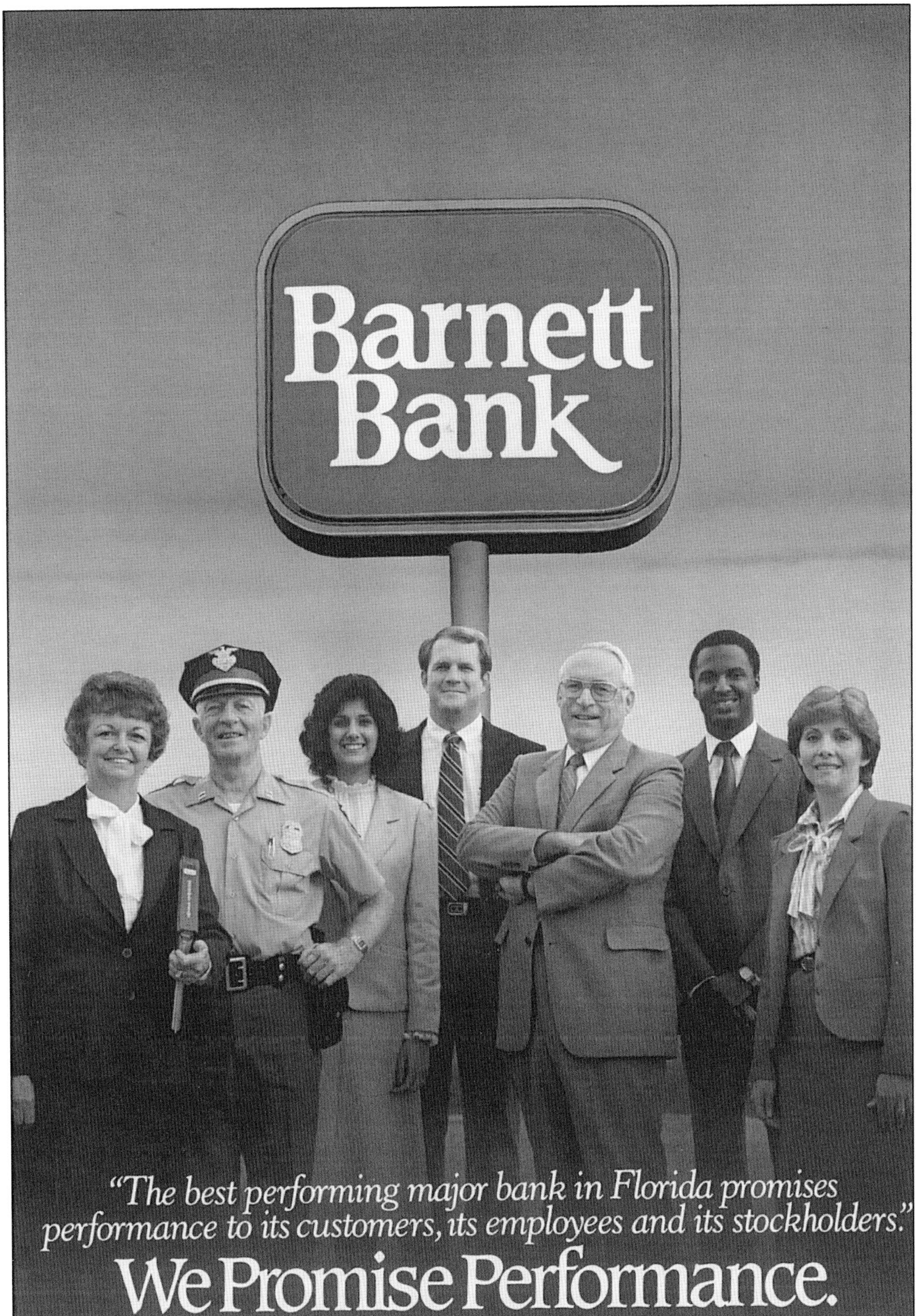
Barnett Bank
"The best performing major bank in Florida promises performance to its customers, its employees and its stockholders."
We Promise Performance.

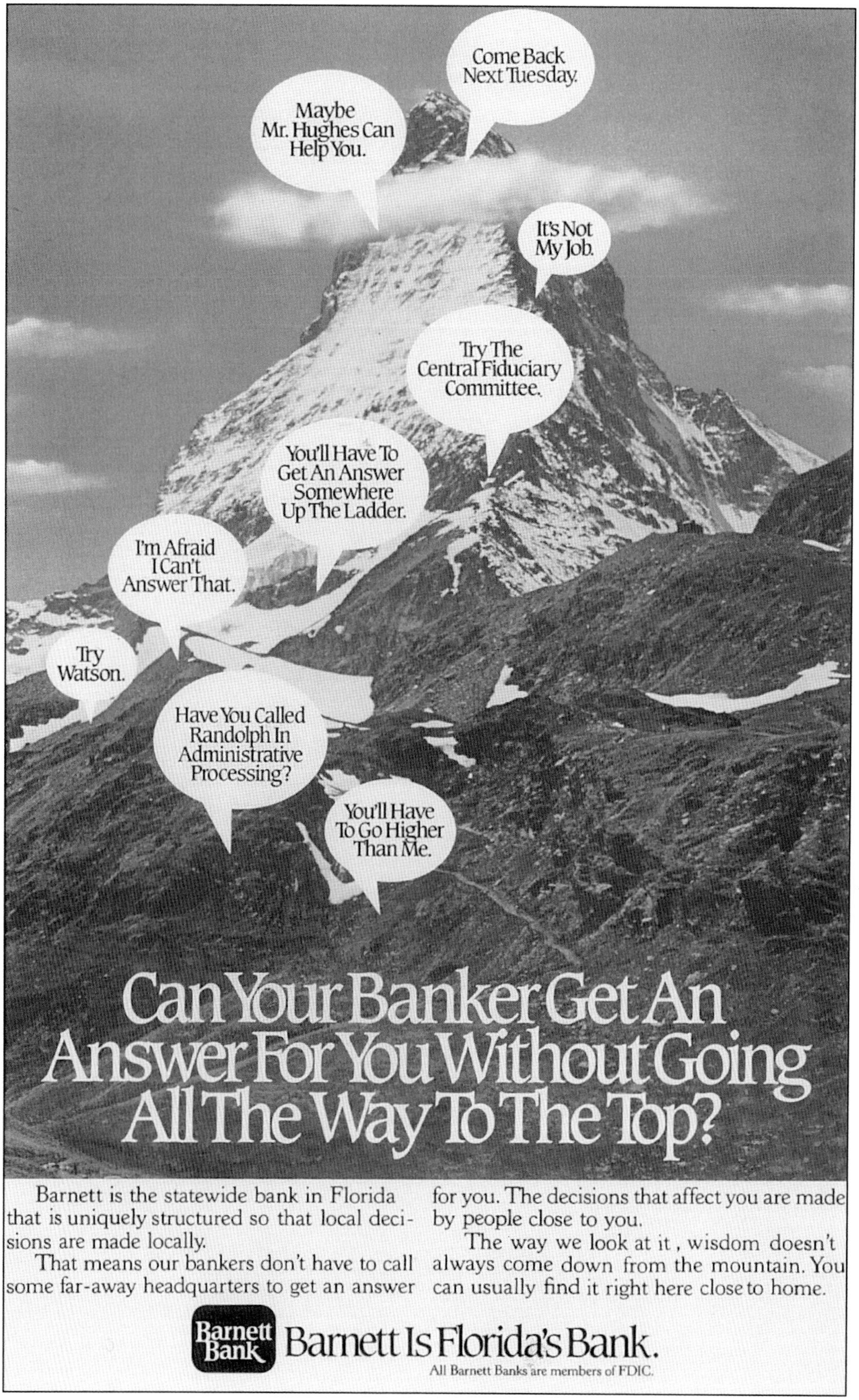
Come Back Next Tuesday.
Maybe Mr. Hughes Can Help You.
It's Not My Job.
Try The Central Fiduciary Committee.
You'll Have To Get An Answer Somewhere Up The Ladder.
I'm Afraid I Can't Answer That.
Try Watson.
Have You Called Randolph In Administrative Processing?
You'll Have To Go Higher Than Me.
Can Your Banker Get An Answer For You Without Going All The Way To The Top?
Barnett is the statewide bank in Florida that is uniquely structured so that local decisions are made locally.
That means our bankers don't have to call some far-away headquarters to get an answer for you. The decisions that affect you are made by people close to you.
The way we look at it, wisdom doesn't always come down from the mountain. You can usually find it right here close to home.
Barnett Bank
Barnett Is Florida's Bank.
All Barnett Banks are members of FDIC.

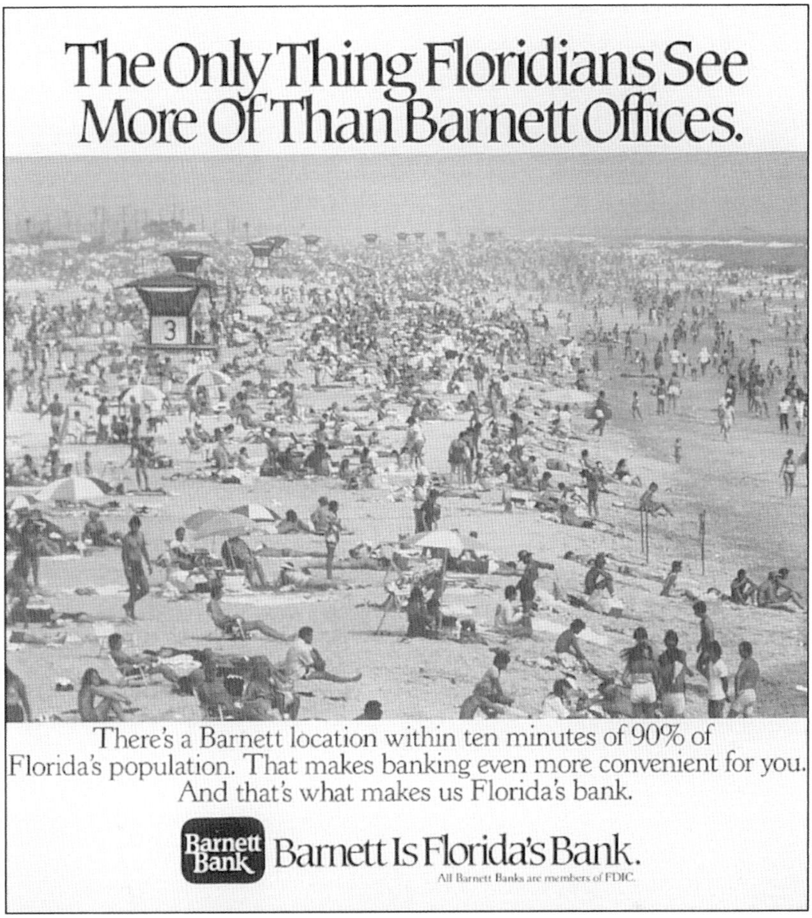
The Only Thing Floridians See
More Of Than Barnett Offices.
3
There's a Barnett location within ten minutes of 90% of
Florida's population. That makes banking even more convenient for you.
And that's what makes us Florida's bank.
Barnett Bank
Barnett Is Florida's Bank.
All Barnett Banks are members of FDIC.

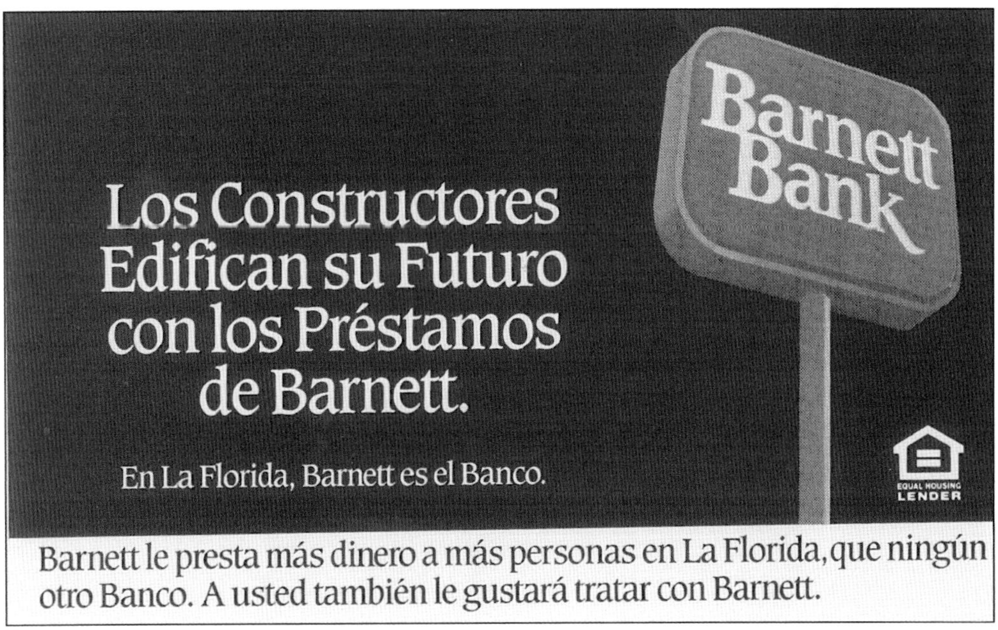
Barnett Bank
Los Constructores
Edifican su Futuro
con los Préstamos
de Barnett.
En La Florida, Barnett es el Banco.
EQUAL HOUSING
LENDER
Barnett le presta más dinero a más personas en La Florida, que ningún
otro Banco. A usted también le gustará tratar con Barnett.

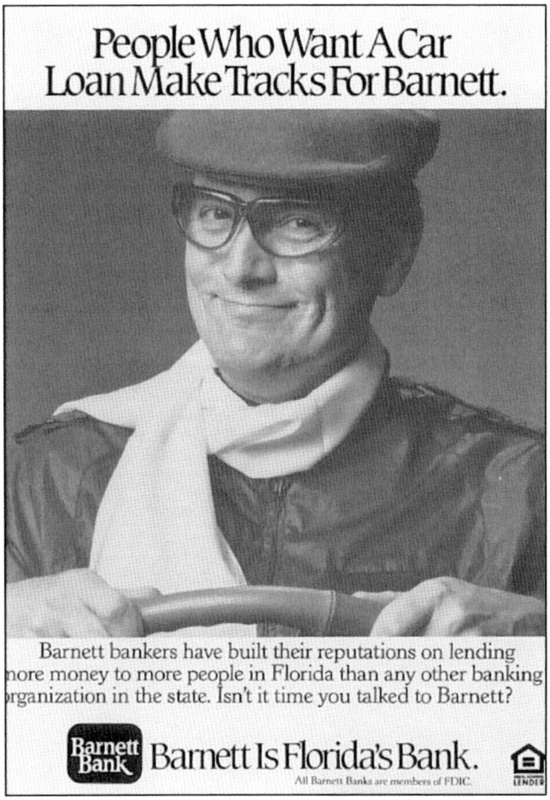
People Who Want A Car
Loan Make Tracks For Barnett.
Barnett bankers have built their reputations on lending
nore money to more people in Florida than any other banking
rganization in the state. Isn't it time you talked to Barnett?
Barnett Bank
Barnett Is Florida's Bank.
All Barnett Banks are members of FDIC.
LENDER

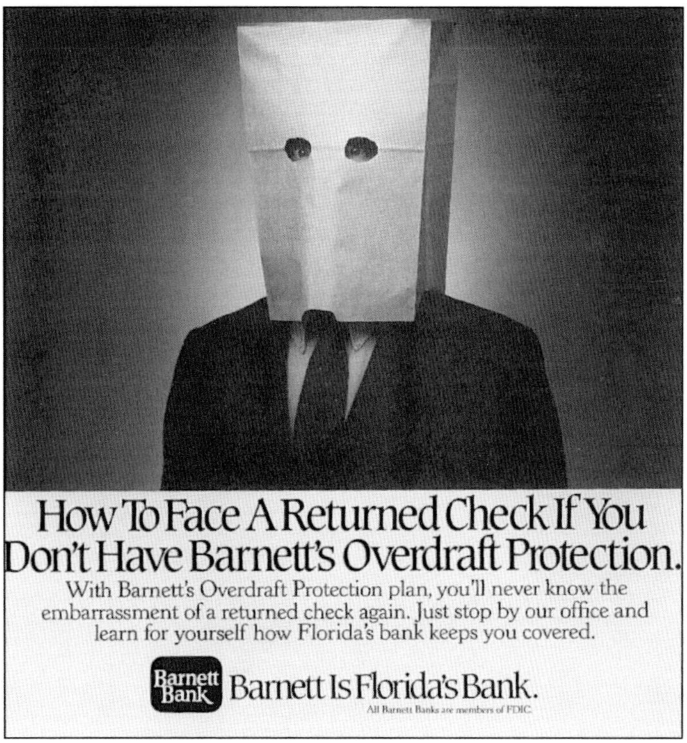
How To Face A Returned Check If You
Don't Have Barnett's Overdraft Protection.
With Barnett's Overdraft Protection plan, you'll never know the
embarrassment of a returned check again. Just stop by our office and
learn for yourself how Florida's bank keeps you covered.
Barnett Bank
Barnett Is Florida's Bank.
All Barnett Banks are members of FDIC.

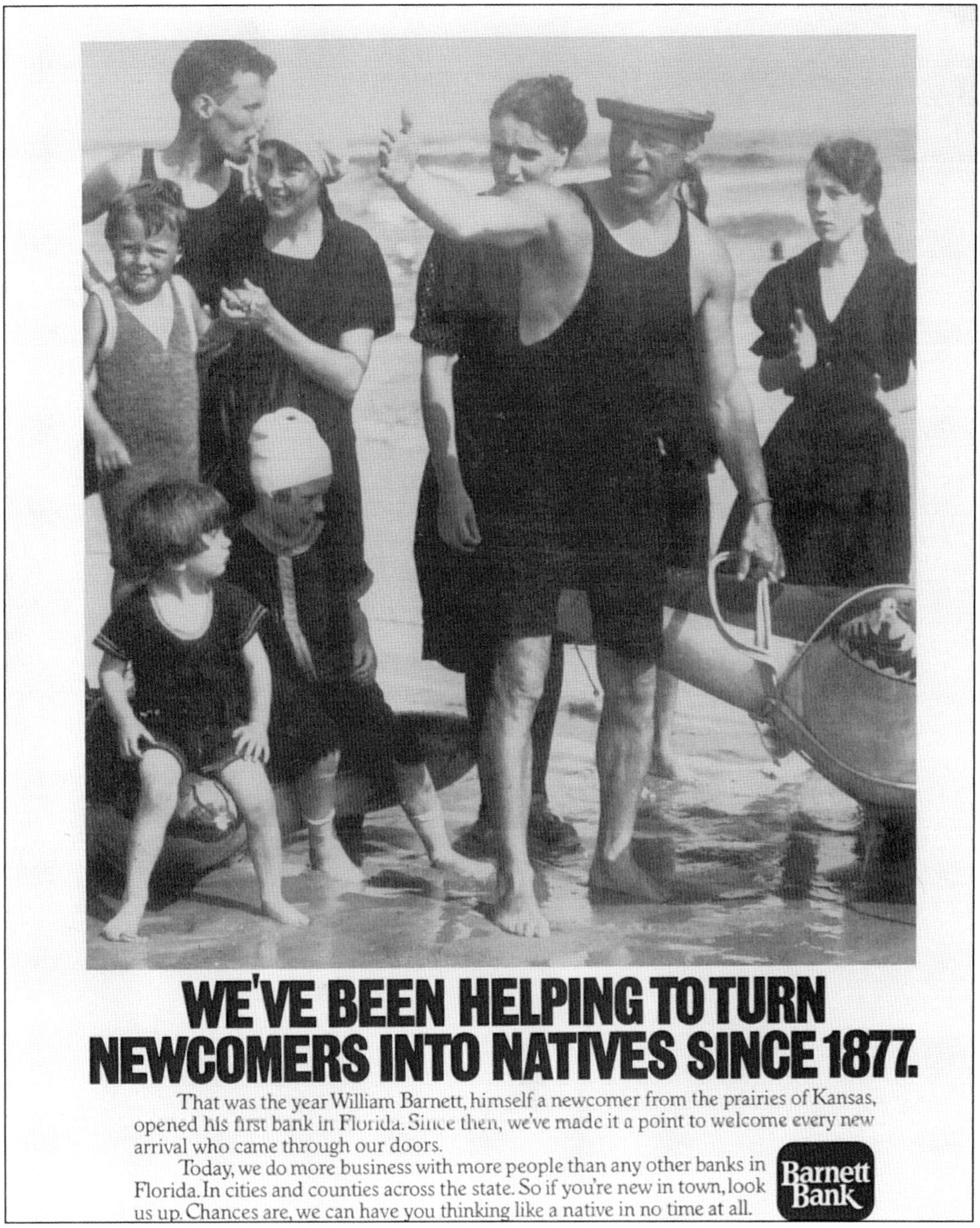
WE'VE BEEN HELPING TO TURN NEWCOMERS INTO NATIVES SINCE 1877.
That was the year William Barnett, himself a newcomer from the prairies of Kansas, opened his first bank in Florida. Since then, we've made it a point to welcome every new arrival who came through our doors.
Today, we do more business with more people than any other banks in Florida. In cities and counties across the state. So if you're new in town, look us up. Chances are, we can have you thinking like a native in no time at all.
Barnett Bank

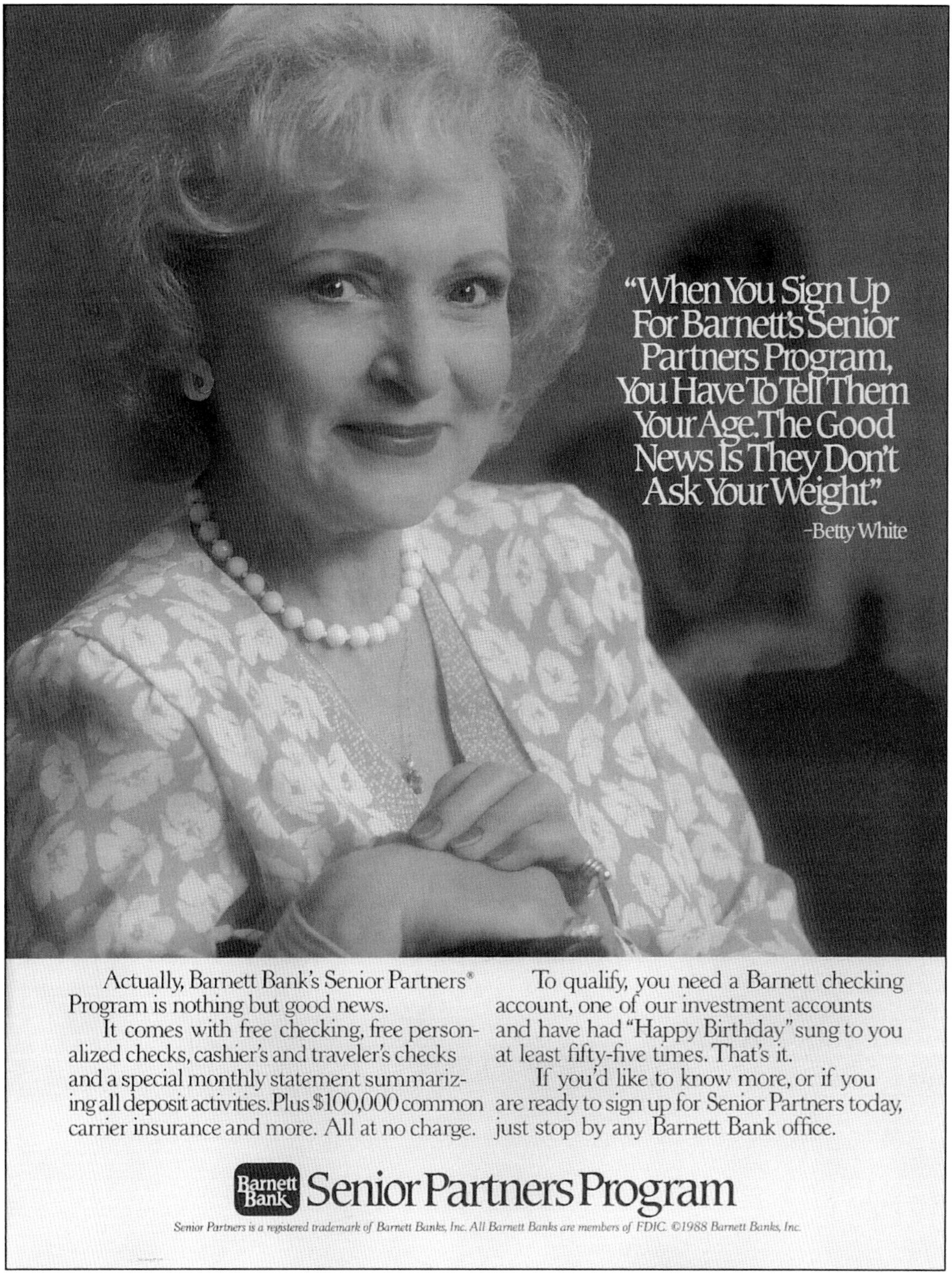
"When You Sign Up For Barnett's Senior Partners Program, You Have To Tell Them Your Age. The Good News Is They Don't Ask Your Weight."
–Betty White
Actually, Barnett Bank's Senior Partners® Program is nothing but good news.
It comes with free checking, free personalized checks, cashier's and traveler's checks and a special monthly statement summarizing all deposit activities. Plus $100,000 common carrier insurance and more. All at no charge.
To qualify, you need a Barnett checking account, one of our investment accounts and have had "Happy Birthday" sung to you at least fifty-five times. That's it.
If you'd like to know more, or if you are ready to sign up for Senior Partners today, just stop by any Barnett Bank office.
Barnett Bank
Senior Partners Program
Senior Partners is a registered trademark of Barnett Banks, Inc. All Barnett Banks are members of FDIC. ©1988 Barnett Banks, Inc.

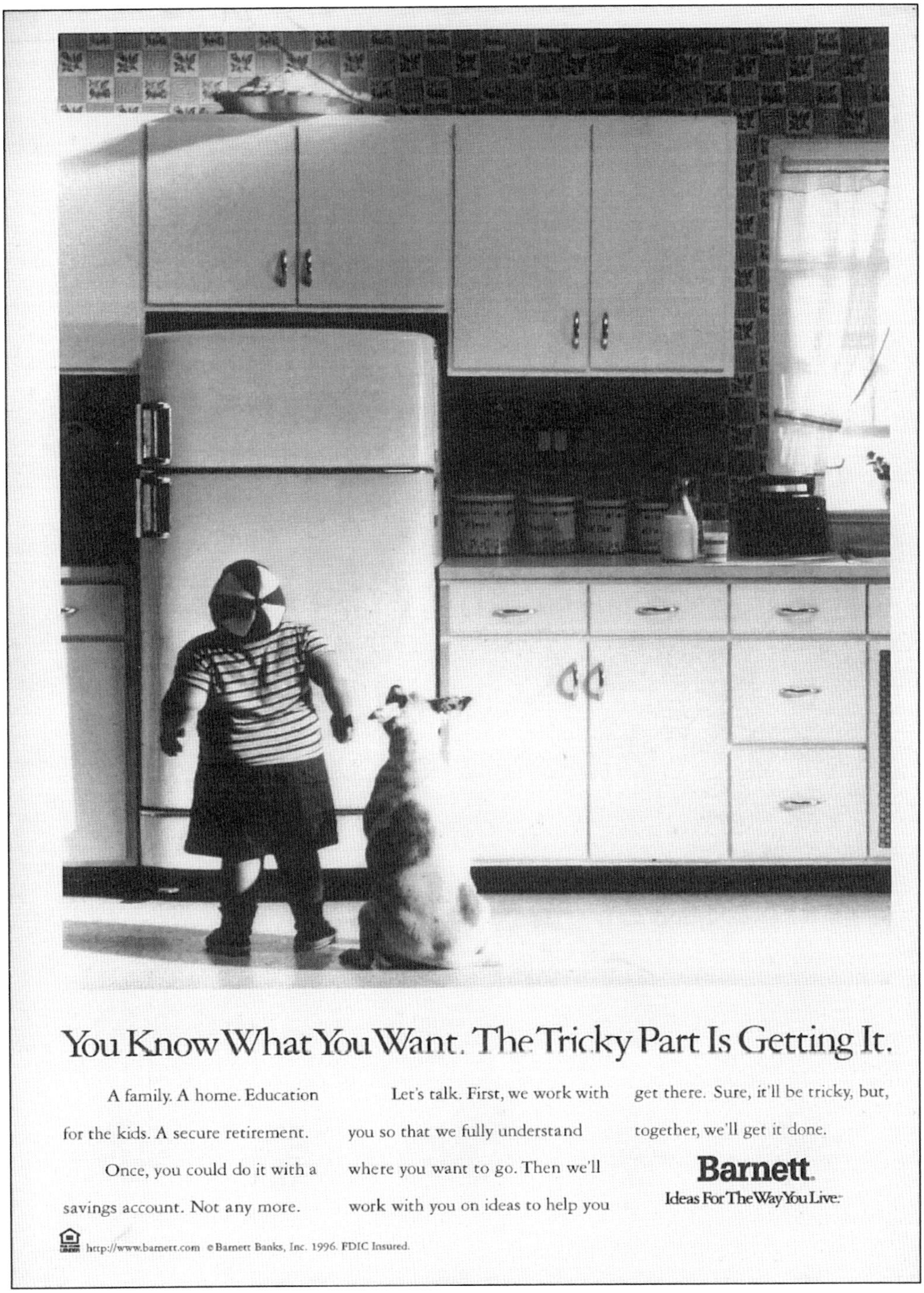
You Know What You Want. The Tricky Part Is Getting It.
A family. A home. Education for the kids. A secure retirement.
Once, you could do it with a savings account. Not any more.
Let's talk. First, we work with you so that we fully understand where you want to go. Then we'll work with you on ideas to help you get there. Sure, it'll be tricky, but, together, we'll get it done.
Barnett
Ideas For The Way You Live.
http://www.barnett.com ©Barnett Banks, Inc. 1996. FDIC Insured.

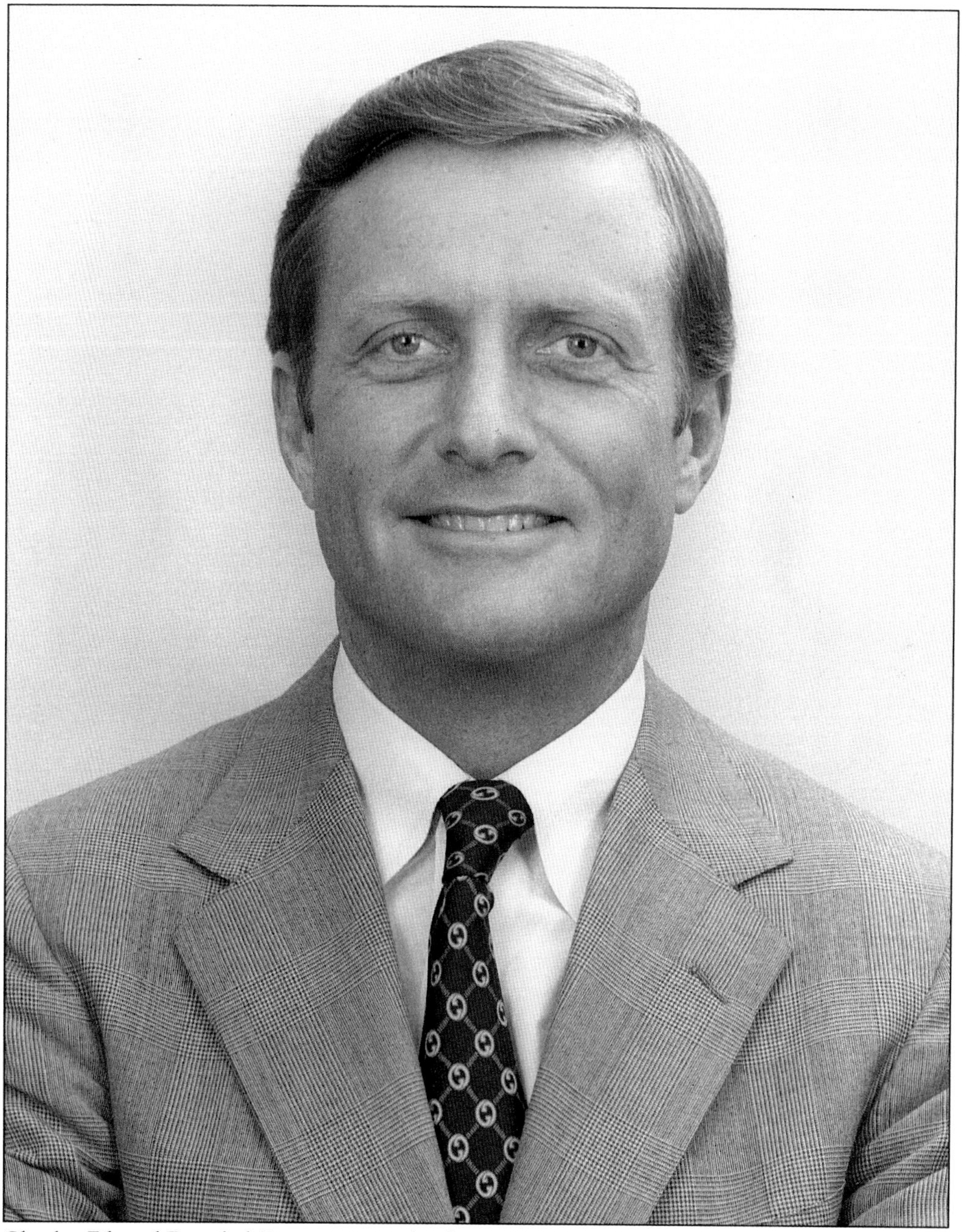

Charles Edward Rice led Barnett as its chief executive officer from 1979 until the company's sale had been finalized in 1998.

Eight

Florida's Bank: 1979 to 1998

When Charlie Rice assumed command in 1979, Barnett had nearly recovered from its earnings problems caused by the real estate troubles of 1974–1975 and was positioned to renew its aggressive acquisition strategies. During his 18-year tenure as chief executive, Rice guided the company's growth from $3.6 billion in assets to more than $40 billion. He oversaw Barnett's evolution from a traditional Florida-focused commercial bank to a national financial services company offering a wide array of products and services.

The 1980s and 1990s proved to be challenging times for Barnett, and for the entire banking industry. There were two national economic recessions, each with significant challenges for bank management—the skyrocketing inflation of the early 1980s that saw the prime lending rate reach an historic high of 21½% and the real estate collapse of the early 1990s that left a trail of failed banks and thrifts. The very nature of the banking industry itself underwent evolutionary, or perhaps revolutionary, changes as technological innovations, government deregulation, and the dynamics of the marketplace broke down long-established geographic and product barriers. Barnett's principal competitors were no longer exclusively Florida banks, but also investment firms like Merrill Lynch, money-center banks like Citicorp, national credit card issuers, and what became curiously known as "non-bank banks."

Barnett found itself at the forefront of several of the most contentious issues. The 1980s saw the advent of regional interstate banking, an idea that Guy Botts had first advocated as an "interim step" to allow banks in the South to achieve the size and sophistication necessary to survive the inevitable onset of nationwide banking. Barnett lobbied the Florida legislature for the passage of regional interstate banking, which finally occurred in 1984, but it had some unexpected consequences. With out-of-state banks anxious to gain a foothold in deposit-rich Florida, all but three of the state's largest banks sold out to Georgia and North Carolina banks within the first several years. Barnett expanded into neighboring Georgia with the 1986 purchase of the First National Bank of Cobb County in the metropolitan Atlanta area. After several additional purchases of small banks, Barnett became the seventh-largest banking organization in Georgia. Barnett, however, never established a solid foundation in Georgia and, in 1993, sold its struggling Atlanta affiliate.

While non-banks began gathering deposits, making loans, and engaging in other traditional banking services, Barnett joined with other banking organizations to demand a "level playing field" to allow them to sell mutual funds, annuities, and other financial products. Under Rice's direction, the company formed a political action committee, Barnett People for Better Government (BPBG), to lobby state and national officials for the passage of legislation beneficial to the banking industry. BPBG grew to become the second-largest bank political action committee in the country. Barnett also sought legal remedies as it tried to expand its financial capabilities. When the state Insurance Department sought to block Barnett from selling insurance after it purchased a small insurance company in Belleview, Florida, Barnett successfully challenged the state ruling, winning a landmark decision before the U.S. Supreme Court in 1996.

The 1980s was a decade of tremendous growth and solid profitability for Barnett. The company became a favorite of both Wall Street bank analysts who recommended the purchase of its stock and senior citizens who valued the package of services that came with its "Senior Partners" program. By mid-1988, when Barnett had grown to more than 500 offices in Florida (with its closest competitor, Sun Banks, at 315), the *Miami Herald* printed an article, "Why Bankers Hate Barnett." It observed that Barnett "has become the undisputed powerhouse of Florida banking. It has accomplished that through a simple, straightforward strategy: build conveniently located branches, provide good basic service and never look back."

The 1980s saw a number of company reorganizations, as the size and complexity of the Barnett organization grew. Developed in conjunction with detailed management studies prepared by banking consultant Carter Golembe, the company adopted a "controlled autonomy" system of management, with increasingly focused areas of responsibility for BBFI functional support executives. Rice divided BBFI's activities among four vice chairman—Albert D. Ernest Jr., Earl B. Hadlow, Thomas H. Jacobsen, and Allen L. Lastinger Jr. This group, together with chief financial officer Stephen A. Hansel, led the company through the high-growth 1980s. In late 1988, after yet another Golembe study, Rice named Ernest as president and divided the banks into four regions, with the affiliate presidents reporting to regional bank executives who, in turn, reported to Lastinger as chief banking officer. Ernest chaired a new group, the Management Operating Committee (MOC), which was established to coordinate operational issues, improve line/staff communications, and resolve problems. This reorganization had several significant results. First, it set the company on a course of regional, and eventually statewide consolidations, beginning with backroom activities such as accounting and loan operations. Second, it resolved the issue of management succession, and when Ernest retired two years later, Lastinger became president and chief operating officer. Rice remained chairman and CEO, focusing on the large strategic issues at the Management Executive Committee (MEC) level.

The regional reorganization took place on the eve of the Florida real estate collapse. After 14 consecutive years of earnings increases, Barnett reported disappointing operating results in 1990. Over the next several years, Barnett struggled as non-performing assets rose to near $1 billion and regulatory scrutiny of its lending policies and loan quality controls intensified. Rice named Richard Jordan as "credit czar," and the company centralized its loan workout activities. The loan problems, and consequent high operating expenses associated with them, gave further impetus to management initiatives for consolidating operational functions and looking for more efficient, cost-effective ways to manage the company.

Recovering from the real estate crisis, Barnett began a broad range of initiatives in the 1990s—expense controls to lower the overhead ratio; consolidation of bank charters; development of a sales and service culture; and expansion into non-traditional financial areas, such as asset management and insurance. Barnett also developed an out-of-state expansion strategy to become a national consumer finance provider through the purchase of mortgage lenders (Loan America and BancPLUS), a consumer finance company (EquiCredit), and an automobile leasing company (Oxford Resources), while simultaneously expanding its automobile financing business into selected states.

As the company returned to profitability—it reported record earnings of $465 million in 1996—it frequently became the focus of acquisition speculation. Whether to employee groups or at investor presentations, Rice, Lastinger, and other senior officers reiterated Barnett's commitment to remain independent. Thus, it came as a shock when on August 29, 1997 it was announced that Barnett had been sold to NationsBank. After a brief four month transition period to organize the merger process and gain regulatory and shareholder approval, Barnett was gone. But it is not forgotten!

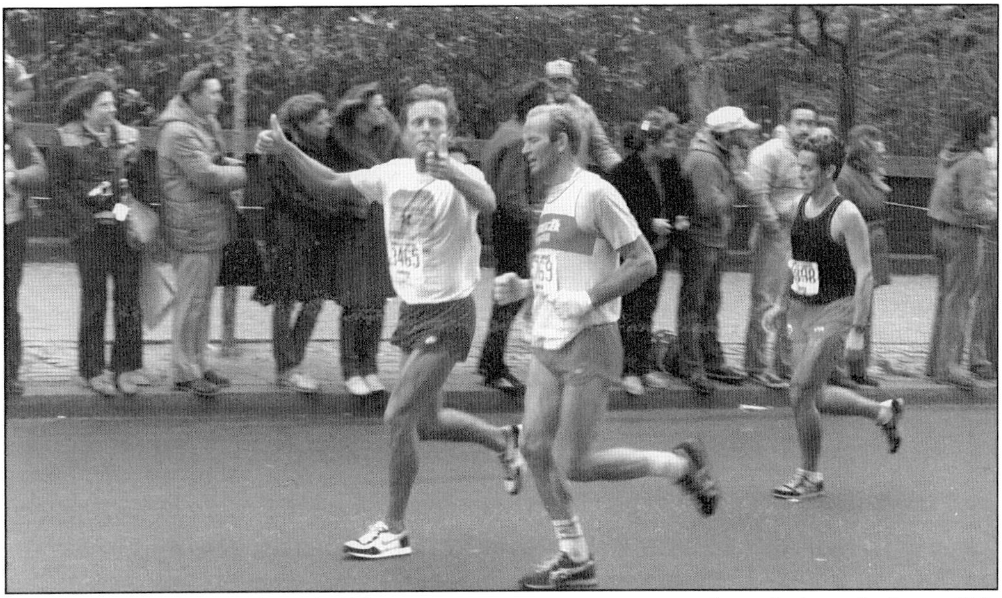

Charlie Rice, who ran for a half-hour every morning, participated regularly in Jacksonville's River Run. In October 1981, he competed in his first New York Marathon. He competed in several other New York Marathons, as well as the Boston Marathon.

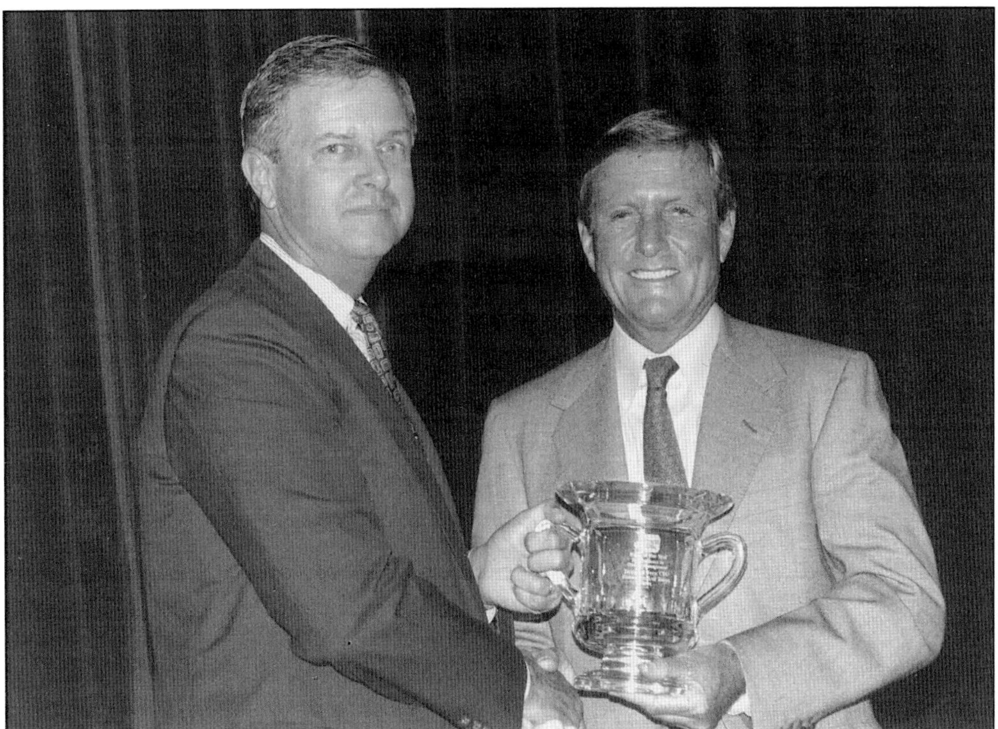

Each year at the Spring President's Meeting, Barnett presented awards to affiliates in various categories, such as earnings improvement, profitability, and sales. Above, Charlie Rice presents the 1994 Bank of the Year Award to Barnett Bank of Tampa president Jim Ivey. The Tampa affiliate also won this award for best overall performance in 1995.

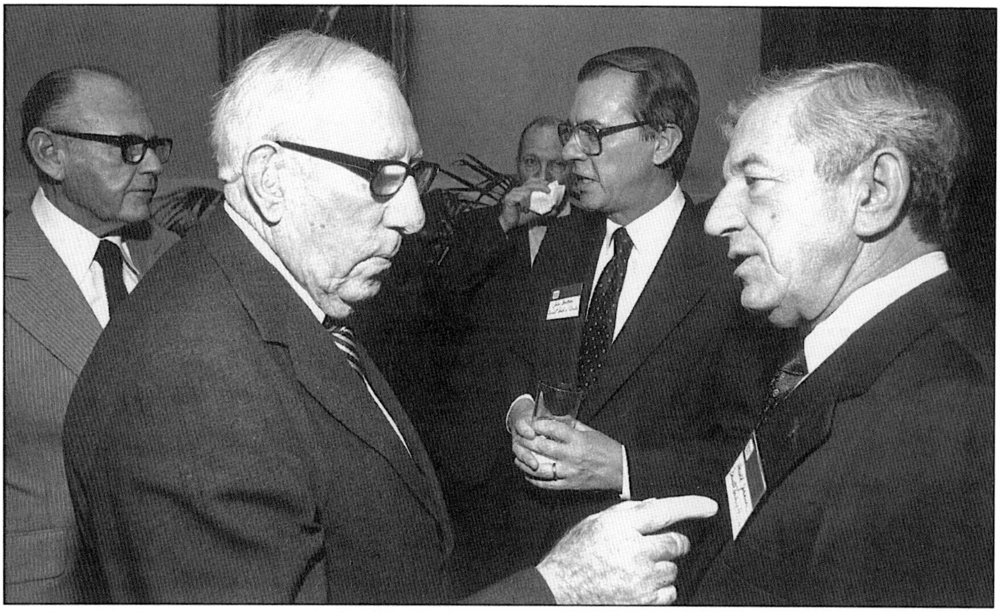

In March 1981, Barnett People for Better Government (BPBG) held its first legislative day in Washington. Bank presidents and BPBG captains had a special tour of the White House, held pre-arranged meetings with members of the Florida congressional delegation, and attended an informal reception for lawmakers and their staff. Above, Florida Congressman Claude Pepper talks with Barnett senior vice president for government affairs Harold C. Johnson. Behind Johnson, holding a drink, is John Benbow, BBFI executive vice president/corporate and international banking. (Photo by Ankers Capitol Photographer.)

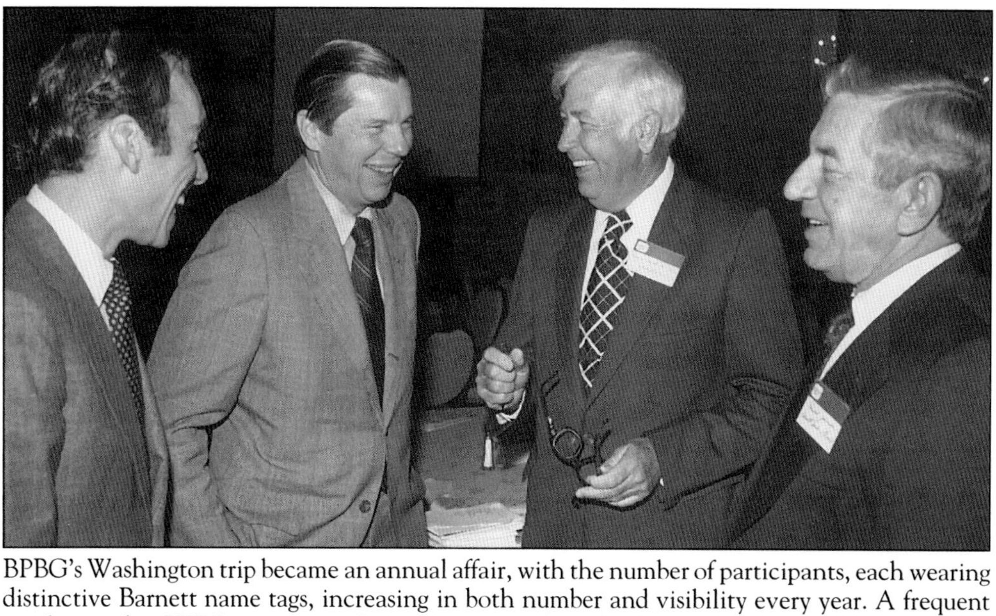

BPBG's Washington trip became an annual affair, with the number of participants, each wearing distinctive Barnett name tags, increasing in both number and visibility every year. A frequent speaker at this BPBG event was Congressman Andy Ireland, a former Barnett president and director. At the breakfast meeting above, from left to right, are BBFI executive vice president/corporate development Sam W. Cockrel, Ireland, Homestead president Vernon W. Turner, and Harold Johnson. (Photo by Ankers Capitol Photographer.)

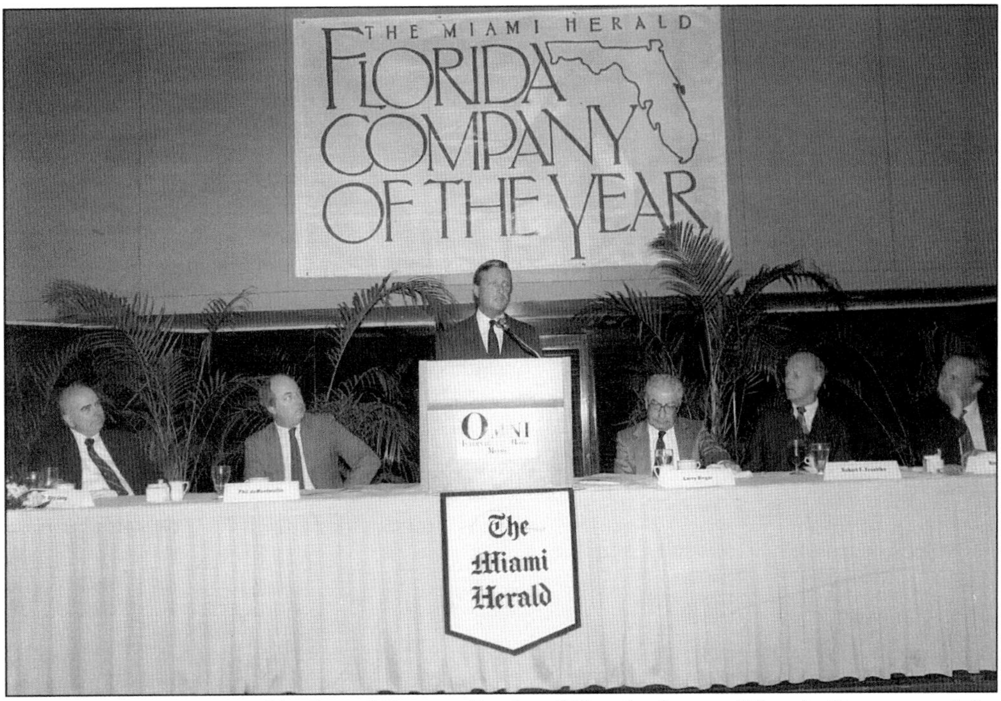

In 1986, the *Miami Herald* selected Barnett Banks of Florida, Inc. as "Florida Company of the Year." At a special banquet at the Miami Omni, Barnett chairman and CEO Charlie Rice accepted the award.

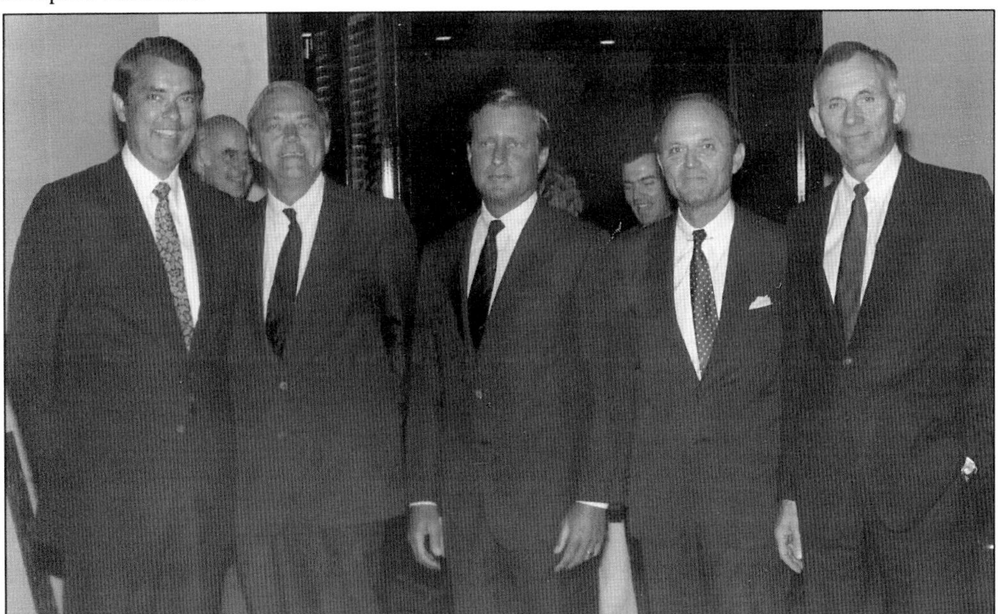

At the banquet honoring Barnett as "Florida Company of the Year" are, from left to right, BBFI vice chairman/administration Tom Jacobsen, BBSF chairman and CEO Hugh Gentry, Rice, BBFI vice chairman/banking-corporate Albert Ernest, and BBFI vice chairman and general counsel Earl Hadlow.

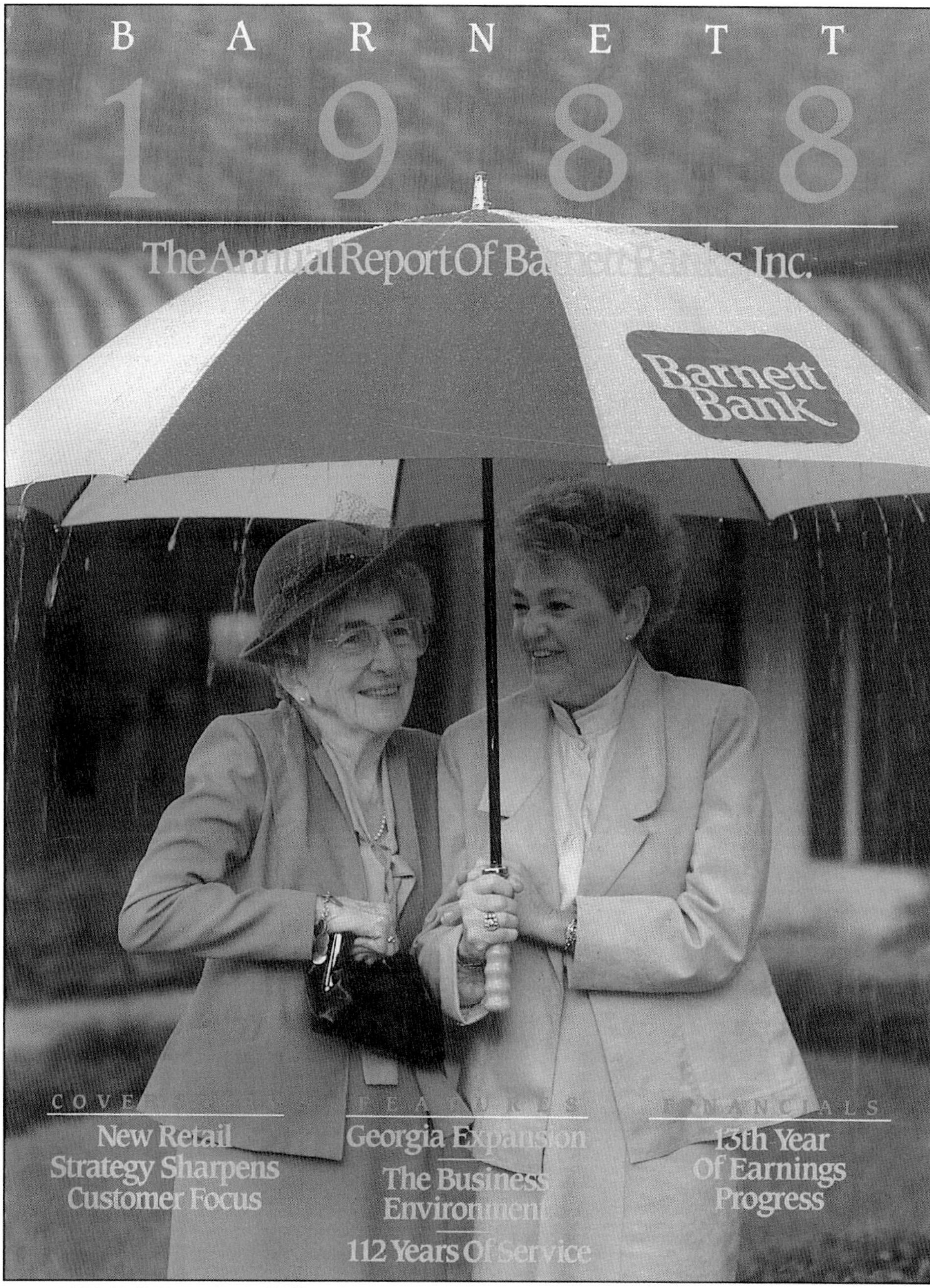

At its 1988 Fall Presidents/Office Managers Meeting, Barnett, for the first time, selected an office manager for its Overall Excellence Award, which in later years became popularly known as the Office Manager of the Year. The award was based on management skills in four areas: customer service, earnings performance, leadership and employee development, and community involvement. The first recipient was Belva Codding, manager of the downtown Mt. Dora office. Codding, featured on the cover of the company's 1988 Annual Report, explained her success as follows: "Treat your customers as you would like to be treated yourself . . . that's my motto."

Barnett's new Jacksonville headquarters opened in the summer of 1990, across Forsyth Street from the ten-story building that had housed the company's senior management since 1962. The 42-story office tower, with 600,000 square feet of space, was the tallest building in the city and occupied nearly the entire city block bounded by Forsyth, Laura, Bay, and Hogan Streets.

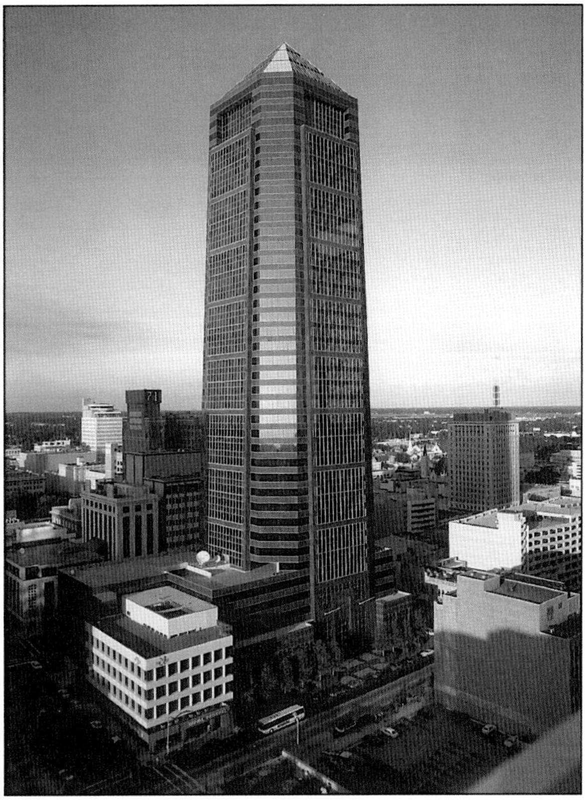

From the 42nd floor of the Barnett Tower, the view of downtown Jacksonville and south along the St. Johns River was spectacular.

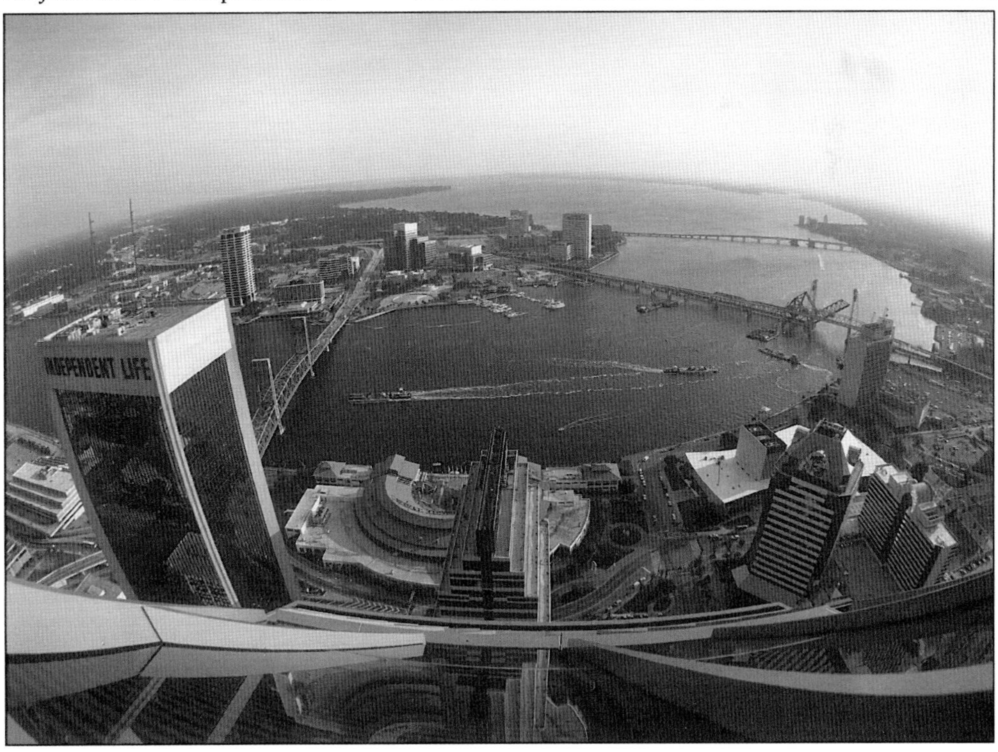

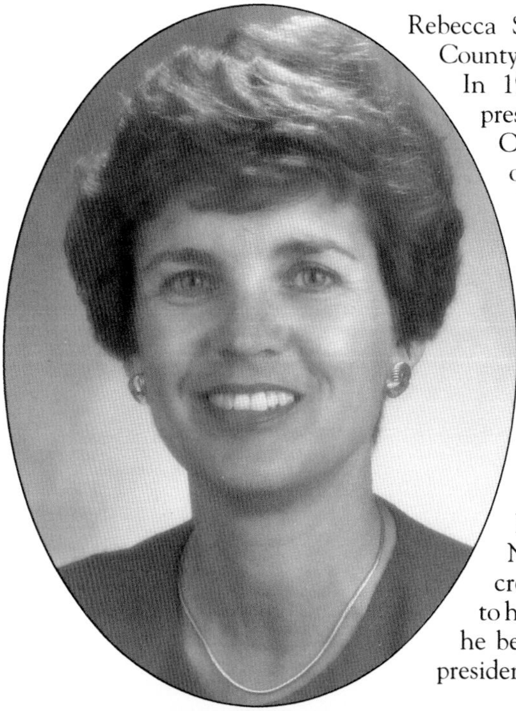

Rebecca S. Allen joined Barnett Bank of Alachua County, N.A. in 1984 as vice president/marketing. In 1987, she became Barnett's second woman president when named to head the Indian River County affiliate. She later served as president of Barnett Bank of Southwest Florida and Barnett Banks Trust Company, N.A., as well as on-site coordinator for managing the 1992 acquisition/merger of First Florida Banks.

Leo Hill joined Barnett Bank of Jacksonville, N.A. in 1991 as senior vice president and senior credit officer. In 1994, when Barnett named Hill to head the Barnett Bank of Martin County, N.A., he became the company's first African-American president. (Courtesy of *Florida Times-Union*.)

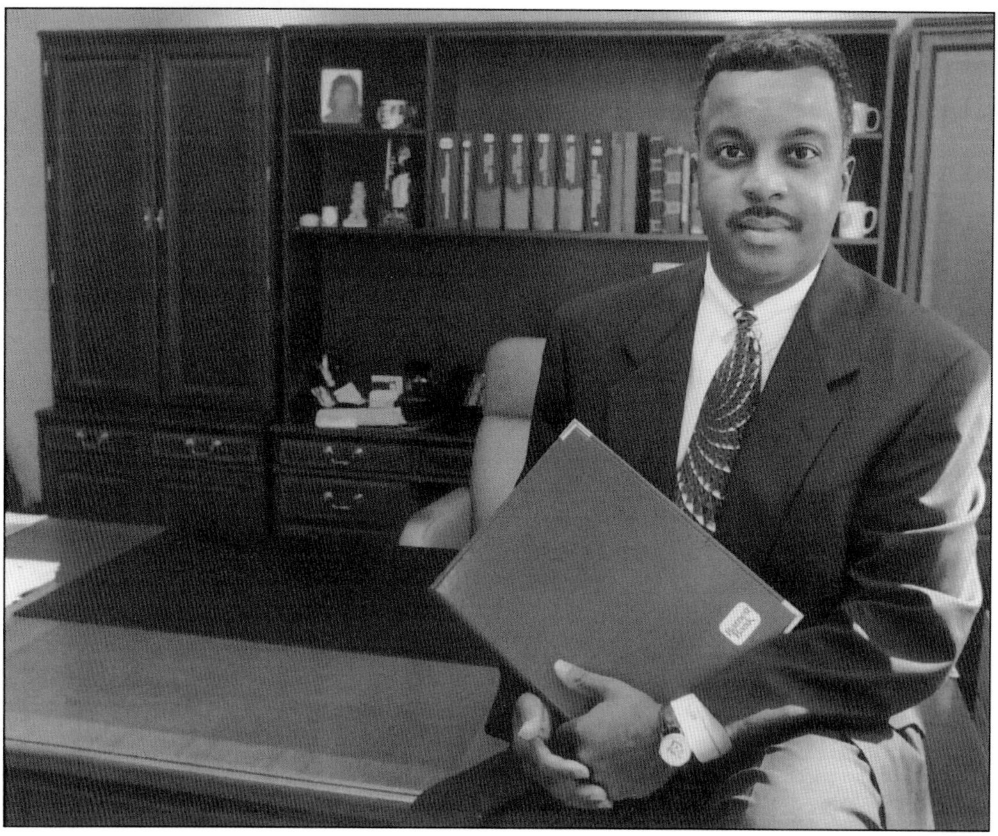

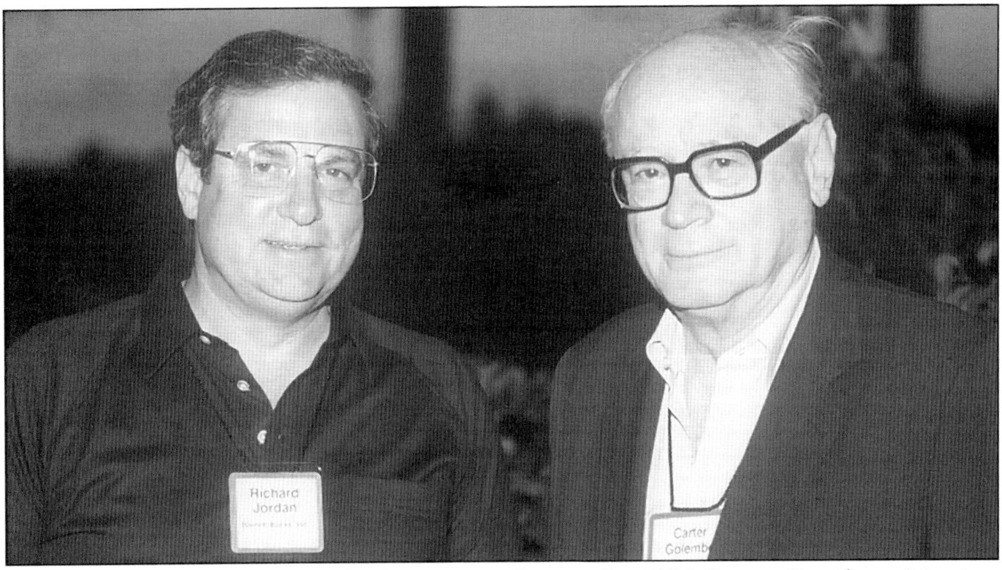

Richard Jordan and Carter Golembe get together at the 1994 Spring Presidents Meeting. Jordan, who had been president of the Pasco County and Pinellas County affiliates, became Barnett's first chief credit policy executive in 1991, establishing a centralized workout function to combat the company's increasing levels of problem loans. Golembe, a bank consultant, conducted several management studies in the 1980s, and his recommendations led to a series of reorganizations. Golembe served as a Barnett director from 1985 to 1994.

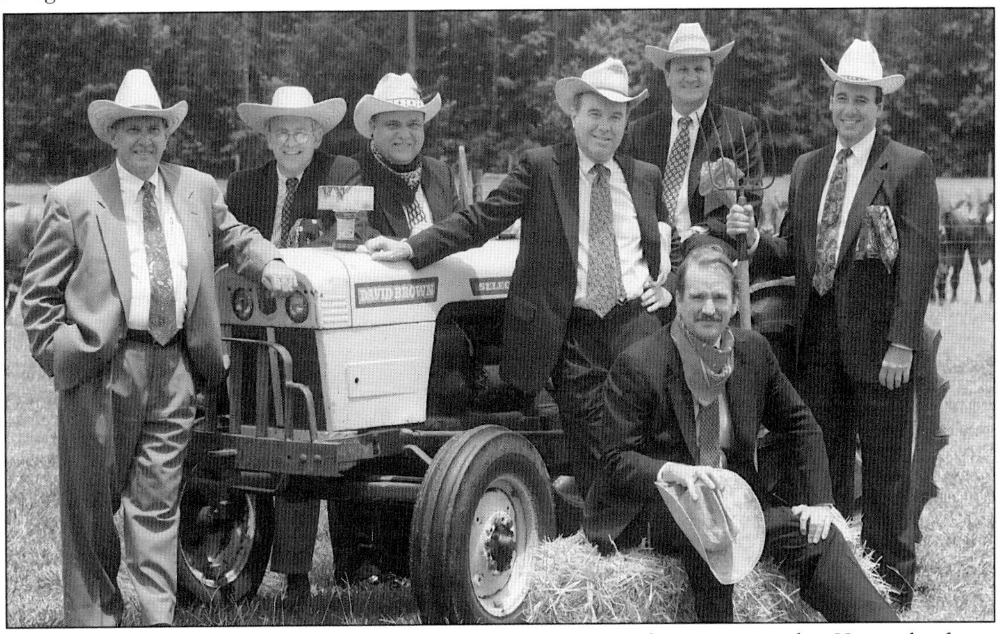

When Richard Jordan retired in 1994, with the intention of returning to his Kentucky farm, his staff posed for the above picture, which was presented to Jordan as a farewell gift to be hung in his barn. Standing, from left to right, are Burnis "Buck" Harnage (consumer credit policy), David Ginzl (commercial credit policy), Allen Jarboe (special assets), Ken Veniard (credit quality review), Rick Brewer (Jordan's replacement as chief credit policy executive), and Bob Miller (special assets). Seated is Rick Spencer (credit policy-special assets).

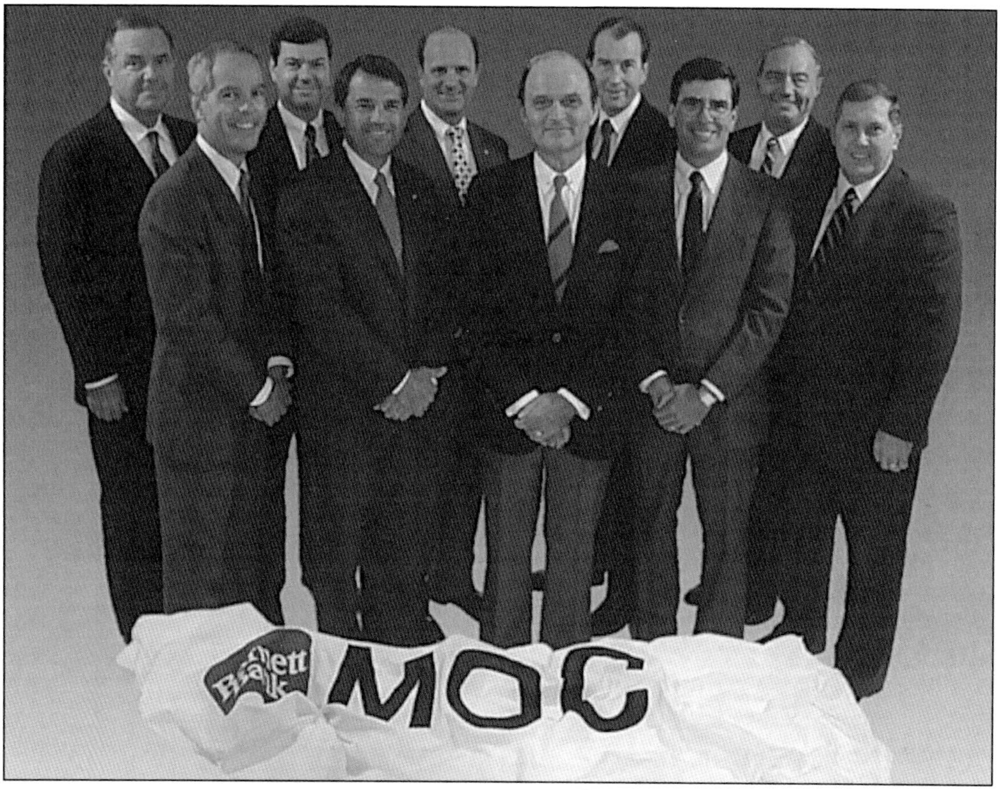

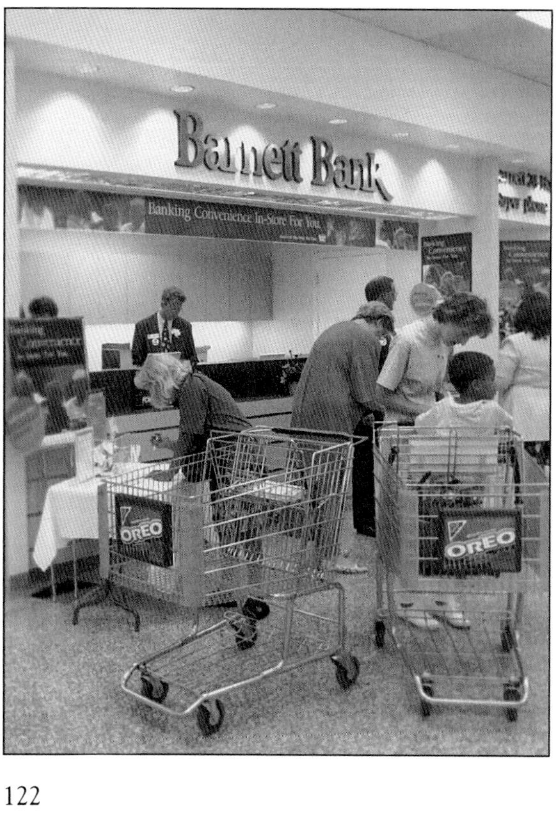

In a 1988 company reorganization, Barnett created a Management Operating Committee (MOC). The first MOC members were, from left to right, Roger Wiegmann (operations and computing), Lee Chaplin (South region executive), Tom Johnson (retail banking), Allen Lastinger (vice chairman and chief banking officer), Rick Brewer (Western region executive), Albert Ernest (president and chief operating officer), Paul Kerins (human resources), Jim Mondello (Eastern region executive), Hugh Gentry (corporate banking), and Buck Harnage (Northern region executive).

Barnett opened its first supermarket offices in Publix stores in Jacksonville in June 1996. In supermarket banking centers, customers could handle all of their banking needs through ATMs, Barnett Super Phone, or specially trained sales teams. (Courtesy of *Florida Times-Union*.)

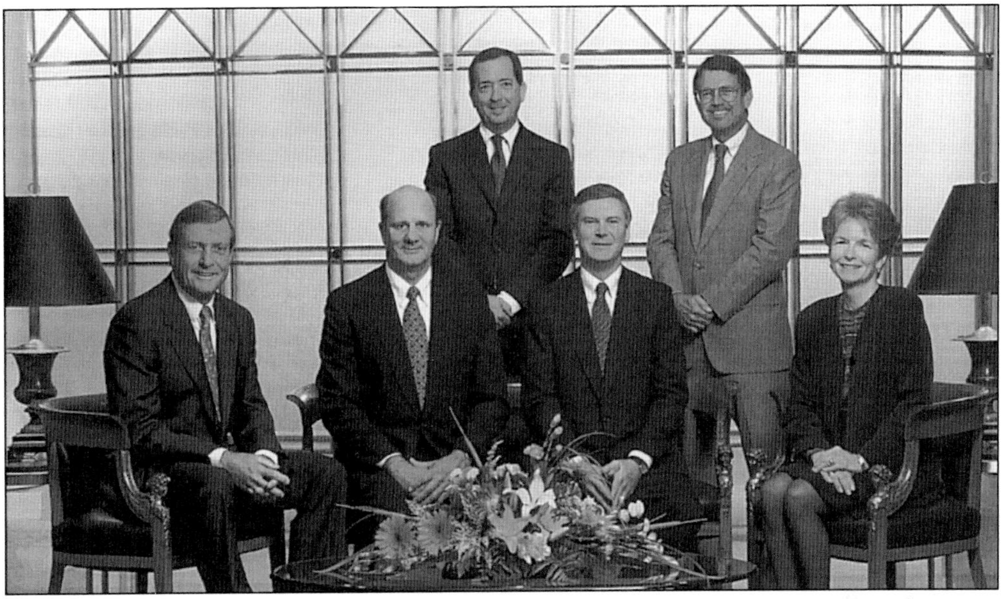

Barnett's Management Executive Committee (MEC) oversaw the company's strategic direction. In 1994, MEC members were, from left to right, (seated) chairman and CEO Charles E. Rice, chief credit policy executive Richard C. Brewer Jr., chief financial officer Charles W. Newman, and chief legal executive Judy S. Beaubouef; (standing) executive vice president Hinton F. Nobles Jr. and president and chief operating officer Allen L. Lastinger Jr.

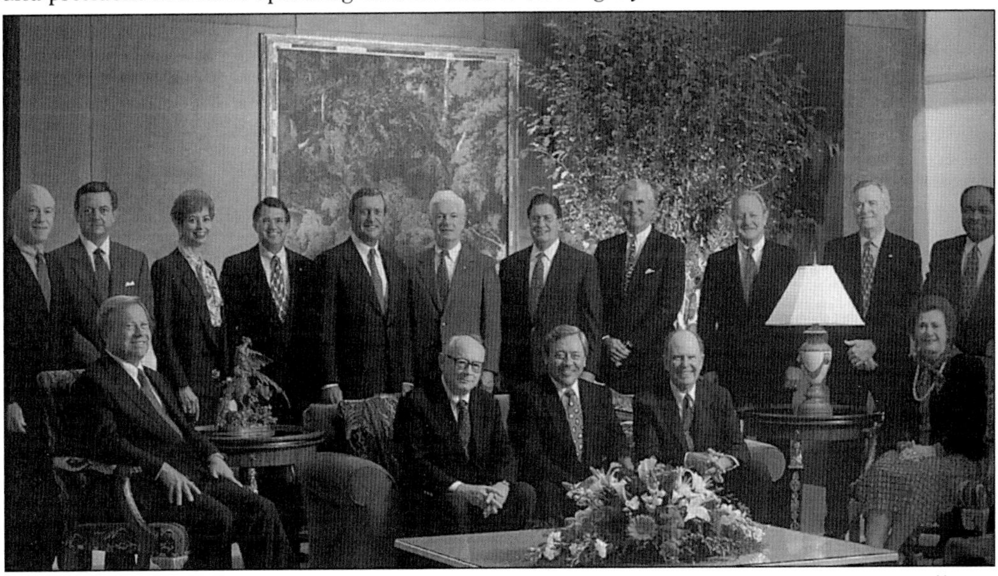

Barnett's Board of Directors in 1994 included, from left to right, (seated) John A. Williams (Post Properties), Carter H. Golembe (CHG Consulting), Jack B. Critchfield (Florida Progress Corporation), Frederick H. Schultz (Schultz Investments), and Jean McArthur Davis (McArthur Farms); (standing) James L. Broadhead (FPL Group), Armando M. Codina (Codina Group), Rita Bornstein (Rollins College), Lastinger, Rice, Tom L. Rankin (Lykes Bros.), Walter H. Alford (BellSouth Corporation), Alvin R. Carpenter (CSX Transportation), Marshall M. Criser (Mahoney Adams & Criser, P.A.), Stewart Turley (Eckerd Corporation), and Clarence V. McKee (McKee Communications).

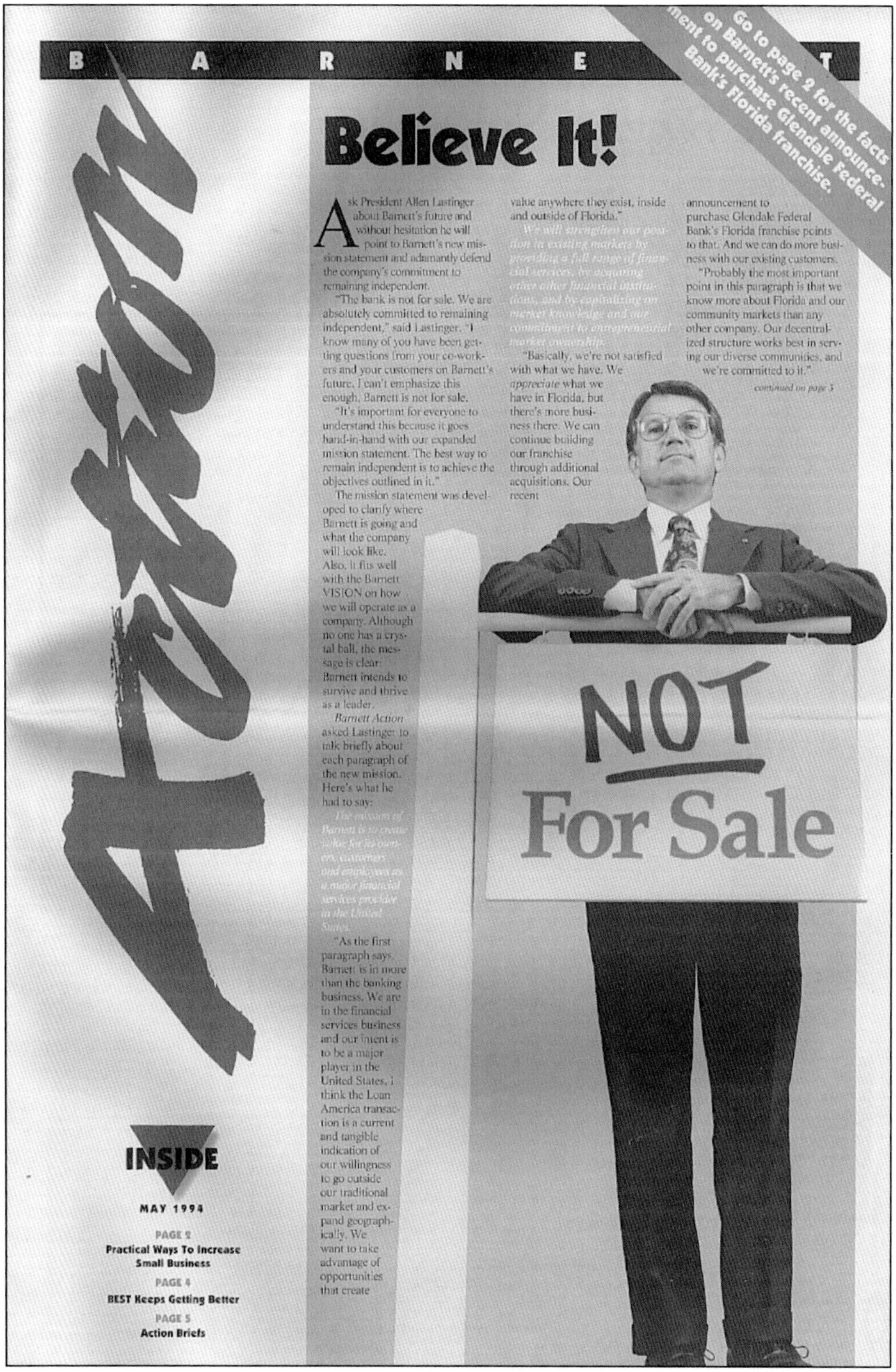

B A R N E T T

Action

Go to page 2 for the facts on Barnett's recent announcement to purchase Glendale Federal Bank's Florida franchise.

Believe It!

Ask President Allen Lastinger about Barnett's future and without hesitation he will point to Barnett's new mission statement and adamantly defend the company's commitment to remaining independent.

"The bank is not for sale. We are absolutely committed to remaining independent," said Lastinger. "I know many of you have been getting questions from your co-workers and your customers on Barnett's future. I can't emphasize this enough. Barnett is not for sale.

"It's important for everyone to understand this because it goes hand-in-hand with our expanded mission statement. The best way to remain independent is to achieve the objectives outlined in it."

The mission statement was developed to clarify where Barnett is going and what the company will look like. Also, it fits well with the Barnett VISION on how we will operate as a company. Although no one has a crystal ball, the message is clear: Barnett intends to survive and thrive as a leader.

Barnett Action asked Lastinger to talk briefly about each paragraph of the new mission. Here's what he had to say:

The mission of Barnett is to create value for its owners, customers and employees as a major financial services provider in the United States.

"As the first paragraph says, Barnett is in more than the banking business. We are in the financial services business and our intent is to be a major player in the United States. I think the Loan America transaction is a current and tangible indication of our willingness to go outside our traditional market and expand geographically. We want to take advantage of opportunities that create value anywhere they exist, inside and outside of Florida."

We will strengthen our position in existing markets by providing a full range of financial services, by acquiring other other financial institutions, and by capitalizing on market knowledge and our commitment to entrepreneurial market ownership.

"Basically, we're not satisfied with what we have. We *appreciate* what we have in Florida, but there's more business there. We can continue building our franchise through additional acquisitions. Our recent announcement to purchase Glendale Federal Bank's Florida franchise points to that. And we can do more business with our existing customers.

"Probably the most important point in this paragraph is that we know more about Florida and our community markets than any other company. Our decentralized structure works best in serving our diverse communities, and we're committed to it."

continued on page 5

INSIDE

MAY 1994

In 1994, Barnett Banks, Inc. adopted a company mission statement, which began, "The mission of Barnett is to create value for its owners, customers and employees as a major financial services provider in the United States." The company used this opportunity to reconfirm its commitment not to be sold with the advent of nationwide interstate banking. Allen Lastinger, pictured here on the front of the May 1994 issue of *Barnett Action*, stated, "The bank is not for sale. We are absolutely committed to remaining independent."

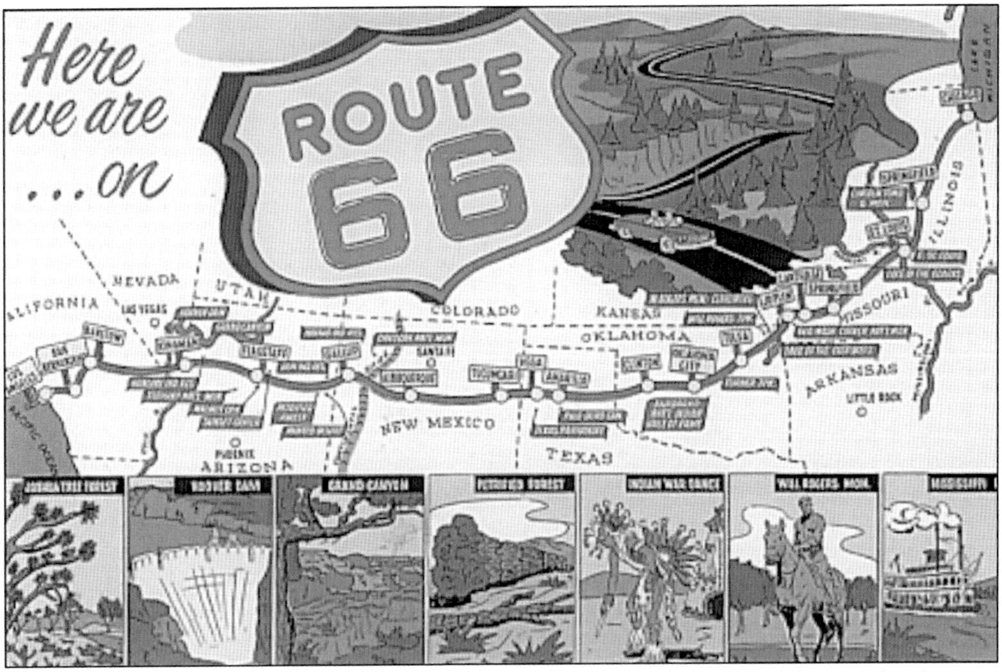

In 1997 Barnett initiated Goals 2000, with ambitious earnings targets to be met by the year 2000. To get everyone involved, the company introduced Options '97, granting stock options to all employees, exercisable when the stock reached $66 per share. Employees enthusiastically embarked on what was popularly called "Route 66." Allen Lastinger received numerous photographs, postcards, and other mementos from employees, including a postcard from Randy Gaffney and photograph (in her Barnett plastic rain poncho) from Dyann Fults.

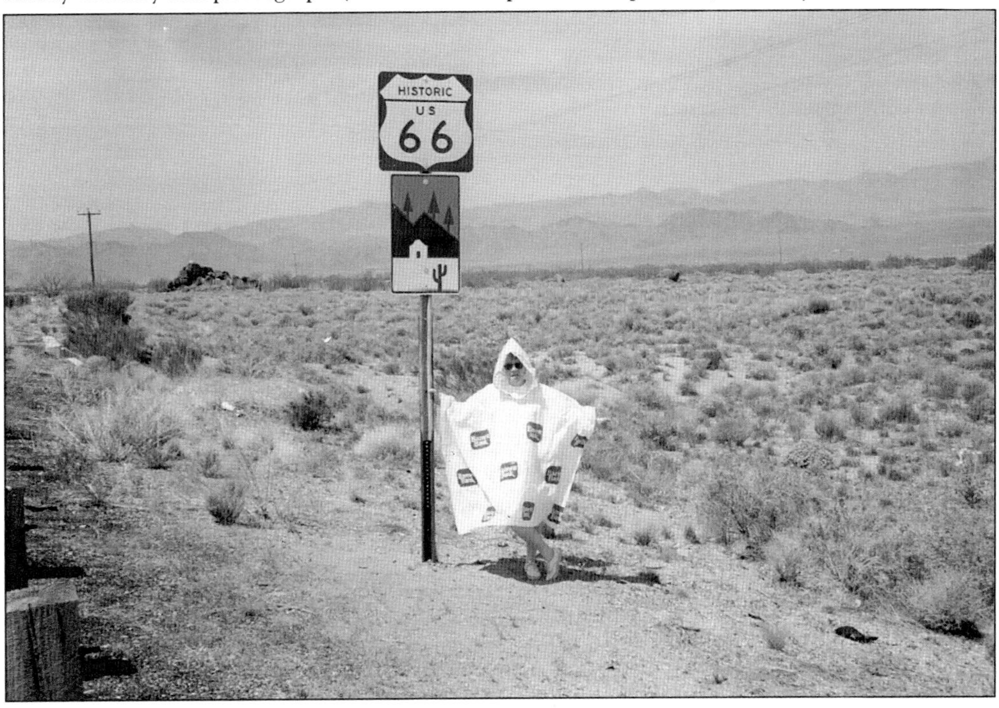

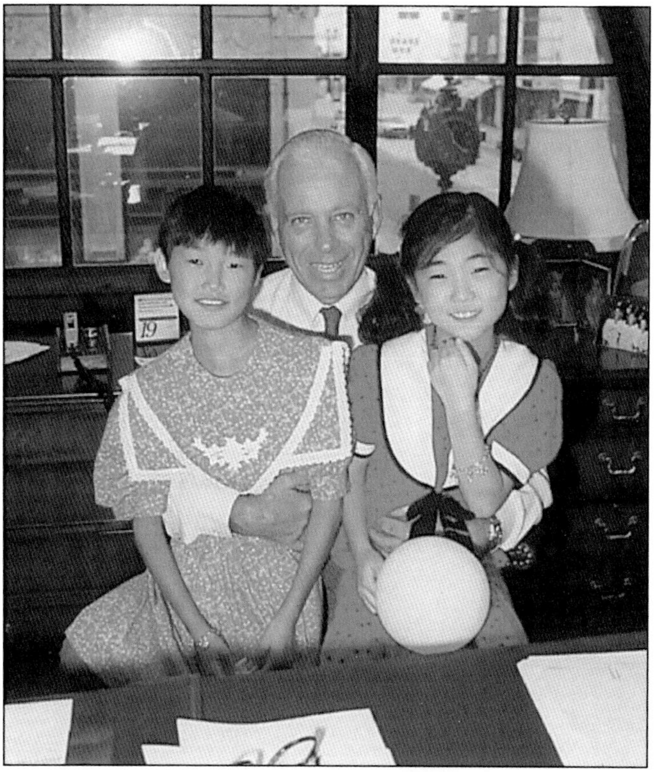

Barnett bankers throughout the state took leading roles in charitable and civic activities. One of the most active was Jacksonville chairman Hugh Jones. Jones established the Korean Heart Program in 1985 to provide financial support to bring indigent Korean children suffering from congenital heart disease to Jacksonville for life-saving surgery. This program, together with Jones's other volunteer activities, caused the Caring Institute to honor Jones in 1990 as one of the 20 most caring people in America. (Photo by Richard Turner.)

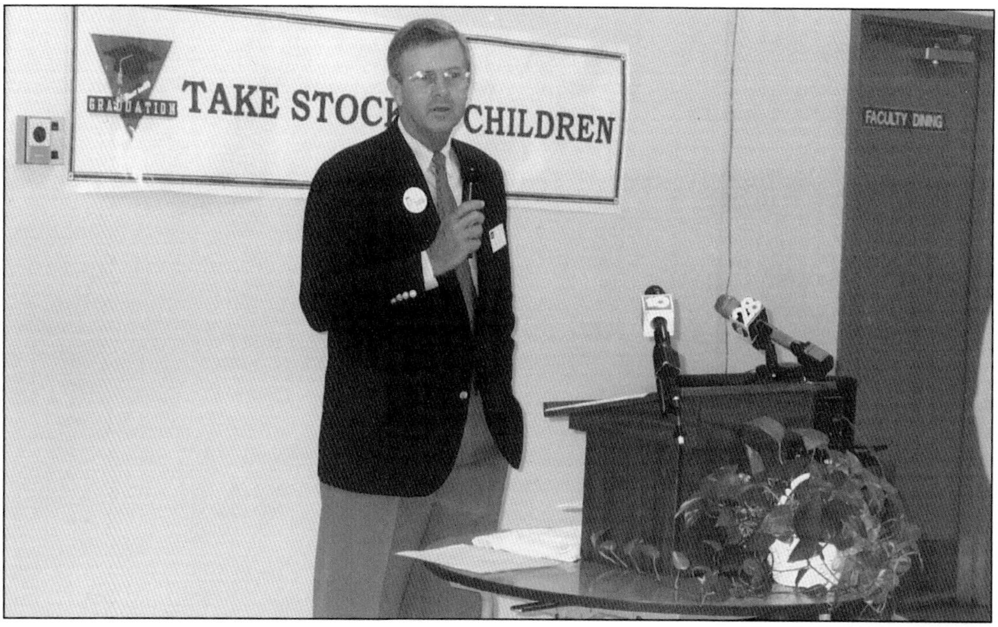

In 1996, Barnett affiliates throughout Florida launched kick-off campaigns for *Take Stock in Children*, a program designed to help at-risk students stay in school. Barnett provided $1 million in college scholarships to students who completed the program and an additional $1 million in operating funds and encouraged employees to volunteer as mentors. Barnett CEOs, including Jim Ivey of Tampa, pictured here, promoted the *Take Stock* program in their local communities.

In 1992, *Working Mother* named Barnett one of the top 100 companies in the United States. The magazine ranked companies for its annual award based upon the following criteria: support for child care; opportunities for women to advance; pay; and family-friendly benefits. The following year, Barnett made the top ten. From 1993 through 1996, four consecutive years, *Working Mother* rated Barnett one of the ten best companies in the country.

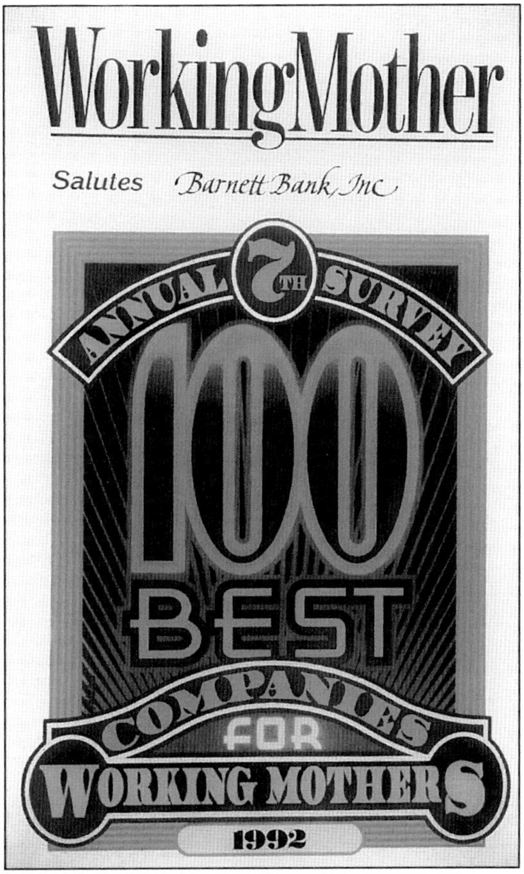

One reason why Barnett was considered a "Top 10" company for working mothers was its day care center at the Barnett Office Park campus in Jacksonville, which provided care for nearly 300 children of Barnett employees. In this photo, Sharon Blake feeds her seven-month-old daughter Jessica during her lunch break. (Courtesy of *Florida Times-Union*.)

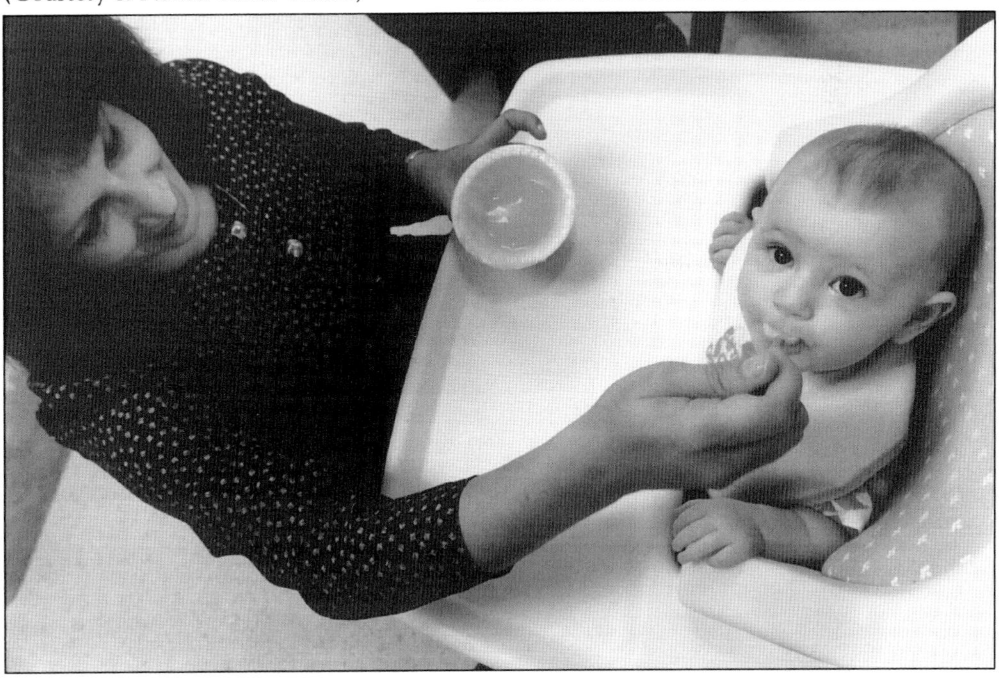

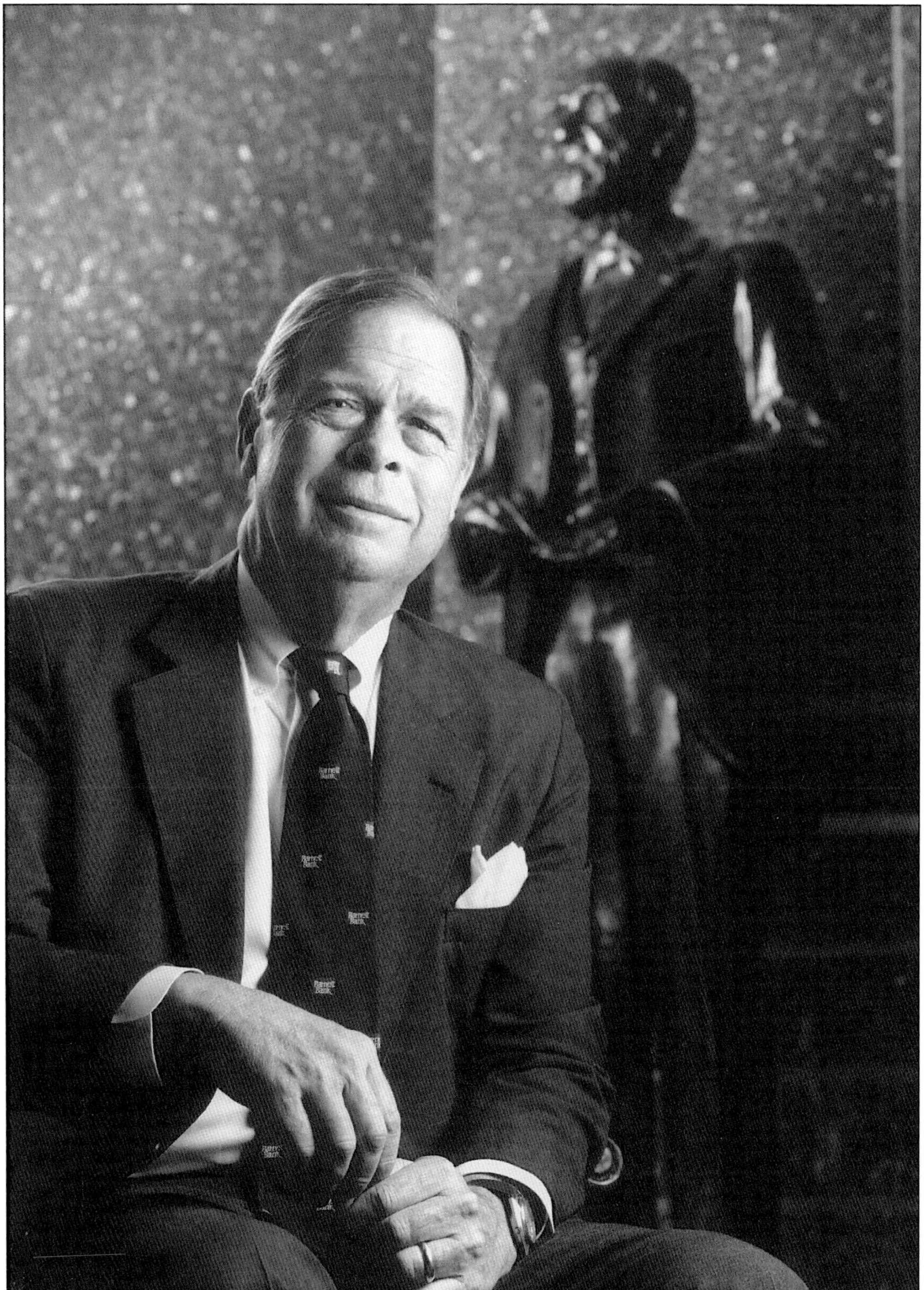

William Bion Barnett, the last of the founding family to work for the bank, sits in front of the statue of his great-great grandfather in the bank lobby in downtown Jacksonville several weeks before the sale of Barnett was finalized. This picture appeared on the cover of the last *Barnett Action* in January 1998. (Photo by McElwee & McElwee.)